James Joyce's Silences

Also published by Bloomsbury

James Joyce: Texts and Contexts, Len Platt
James Joyce and Absolute Music, Michelle Witen
James Joyce and Catholicism, Chrissie Van Mierlo
The Reception of James Joyce in Europe, edited by Geert Lernout

James Joyce's Silences

Edited by
Jolanta Wawrzycka and Serenella Zanotti

BLOOMSBURY ACADEMIC
LONDON • NEW YORK • OXFORD • NEW DELHI • SYDNEY

BLOOMSBURY ACADEMIC
Bloomsbury Publishing Plc
50 Bedford Square, London, WC1B 3DP, UK
1385 Broadway, New York, NY 10018, USA

BLOOMSBURY, BLOOMSBURY ACADEMIC and the Diana logo
are trademarks of Bloomsbury Publishing Plc

First published in Great Britain 2018
Paperback edition first published 2020

Copyright © Jolanta Wawrzycka, Serenella Zanotti and Contributors, 2018

Jolanta Wawrzycka and Serenella Zanotti has asserted their rights under the Copyright,
Designs and Patents Act, 1988, to be identified as Editors of this work.

For legal purposes the Acknowledgements on p. ix-x constitute
an extension of this copyright page.

Cover design: Toby Way
Cover image © Muzeum Narodowe w Warszawie

A catalogue record for this book is available from the British Library.

Library of Congress Cataloging-in-Publication Data
Names: Wawrzycka, Jolanta W., editor. | Zanotti, Serenella, editor.
Title: James Joyce's silences / edited by Jolanta Wawrzycka and Serenella Zanotti.
Description: London ; New York, NY : Bloomsbury Academic, 2018. |
Includes bibliographical references and index.
Identifiers: LCCN 2017056567 (print) | LCCN 2017056575 (ebook) |
ISBN 9781350036727 (ePDF) | ISBN 9781350036734 (ePUB) |
ISBN 9781350036710 (hardback : alk. paper)
Subjects: LCS H: Joyce, James, 1882-1941–Criticism and interpretation. | Silence in literature.
Classification: LCC PR6019.O9 (ebook) | LCC PR6019.O9 Z6454 2018 (print) |
DDC 823/.912–dc23
LC record available at https://lccn.loc.gov/2017056567

ISBN: HB: 978-1-3500-3671-0
PB: 978-1-3501-4005-9
ePDF: 978-1-3500-3672-7
eBook: 978-1-3500-3673-4

Typeset by RefineCatch Limited, Bungay, Suffolk

To find out more about our authors and books visit
www.bloomsbury.com and sign up for our newsletters.

In Memory of Rosa Maria Bollettieri Bosinelli

Contents

Acknowledgments

There are many people we wish to thank and acknowledge, but we owe a special debt to Rosa Maria Bollettieri Bosinelli who conceived the original plan for this book. It is only thanks to her uniquely creative mind, energy, and enthusiasm that the project was made possible. In her own academic work, she provided a model of interdisciplinary scholarship at its best and we consider ourselves lucky to be among the scholars who benefited from her support and friendship. Rosa Maria is no longer with us but her spirit lives on in these pages. We dedicate this book to her memory.

Rosa Maria came up with the idea for the Joyce's Silences panels at the 2013 Zurich Workshop. She then proceeded, in her all-inclusive fashion, to round up presenters and to co-organize, with Serenella Zanotti, a memorable three-session panel, *Silencing Joyce: Omission, Absence, Translation and Beyond*, at the 24th International James Joyce Symposium held at the University of Utrecht in 2014. We would like to thank the conference organizers, Onno Kosters, David Pascoe, Peter de Voogd, and Tim Conley, for the opportunity to set up the sessions and for their kind and friendly hospitality. Special thanks go to Alistair Stead, Richard Brown, and Murray Beja for acting as panel respondents.

We wish to thank Elizabeth Bonapfel, Luca Crispi, Tim Martin, Patrick O'Neill, Jean-Michel Rabaté, Paola Pugliatti, Sam Whitsitt, and Romana Zacchi for their comments on the initial submissions. They greatly contributed to the quality of the final essays.

Our sincere thanks are due to the editorial staff of Bloomsbury Publishing, especially to David Avital and Clara Herberg for their invaluable help and support, to the production team, Merv Honeywood and Lauren Crisp, and to our superb copy-editor, Ronnie Hanna.

We would like to thank the Mondadori Foundation, particularly archivist Annalisa Cavazzuti, and the RCS foundation for granting permission to Sara Sullam to quote from their materials. We also wish to acknowledge Franca Ruggieri, editor of Joyce's *Poesie e prose*, for permission to use three poems from *Musica da camera*, translated by Alfredo Guiliani. (Wydawnictwo Literackie, publisher of the Polish translation of *Chamber Music*, has not responded to our requests for permissions). Finally, we acknowledge Brill/Rodopi for permission to reuse a passage in Jolanta Wawrzycka's chapter that appeared in *Reading Joycean Temporalities* (2018).

Our deep gratitude goes to the authors whose original work has made this project possible, as well as to Jon Tso and Erika Mihálycsa for their help with indexing.

Jolanta Wawrzycka wishes to thank Radford University's Dean Katherine Hawkins and Chair Rosemary Guruswamy for grant and travel support to attend the 2014 James Joyce Symposium in Utrecht. And her family, Jon and Alexander Tso, for keeping it simple.

Contributors

Morris Beja is Honorary Trustee of the International James Joyce Foundation and recipient of the Foundation's Lifetime Achievement Award. He is the author of *Epiphany in the Modern Novel* (1971), *Film and Literature* (1971), *James Joyce: A Literary Life* (1992), and *Tell Us About ... A Memoir* (2011), in addition to numerous essays on Joyce, film, and Irish, British, and American fiction. He has edited or co-edited volumes on Joyce, Virginia Woolf, Samuel Beckett, Orson Welles, and on cinematic narrative. Beja has also directed or co-directed numerous international conferences: seven on Joyce and one on Beckett.

Rosa Maria Bollettieri Bosinelli was Professor Emeritus of English Language and Translation, University of Bologna, Italy, and directed the Advanced School of Modern Languages for Interpreters and Translators, University of Bologna-Forlì (1992–6). In 2000, she co-founded and directed the Department of Interdisciplinary Studies on Translation, Languages and Cultures for six years. She published widely on metaphor, screen translation, and the language of advertising and politics. As a Joycean, she published *Myriadmindedman: Jottings on Joyce* (1986), *The Languages of Joyce* (1992), *Anna Livia Plurabelle di James Joyce nella traduzione di Samuel Beckett e altri* (1996), *ReJoycing: New Readings of Dubliners* (1998), and *Joyce and/in Translation* (2007). She served as President of the International James Joyce Foundation from 2000 to 2004.

William S. Brockman is Paterno Family Librarian for Literature at Pennsylvania State University and bibliographer for the *James Joyce Quarterly*. He has lectured at the Joyce Schools in Trieste and Dublin, and is Trustee of the International James Joyce Foundation. Brockman has written for the *Journal of Modern Literature*, the *Joyce Studies Annual*, *Genetic Joyce Studies*, the *Papers of the Bibliographical Society of America*, and the *James Joyce Quarterly*, and contributed to *James Joyce in Context* (2009). He is co-editor of Joyce's correspondence (forthcoming) and edits the "James Joyce Checklist" website (http://norman.hrc.utexas.edu/jamesjoycechecklist).

Teresa Caneda Cabrera is Senior Lecturer at the University of Vigo, Spain. She has published extensively on Joyce, modernism, and translation. She is the author of *La estética modernista como práctica de resistencia en* A Portrait of the Artist as a Young Man (2002) and editor of *Vigorous Joyce: Atlantic Readings of James Joyce* (2010). Caneda Cabrera organized the 19th Conference of the Spanish James Joyce Society and currently sits on the editorial board of *European Joyce Studies*.

Tim Conley is Professor of English and Comparative Literature at Brock University, Canada. He is the author of *Joyce's Mistakes: Problems of Intention, Irony, and Interpretation* (2003) and *Useless Joyce: Textual Properties, Cultural Appropriations* (2017). Conley has edited *Joyce's Disciples Disciplined* (2010) and co-edited the anthology *Burning City: Poems of Metropolitan Modernity* (2012) and *Doubtful Points: Joyce and Punctuation* (2014). He serves as Trustee of the International James Joyce Foundation.

John McCourt is Professor of English at the University of Macerata, Italy, co-organizer of the Trieste Joyce School, and a Trustee of the International James Joyce Foundation. His books include *The Years of Bloom: Joyce in Trieste 1904– 1920* (2000) and *Writing the Frontier: Anthony Trollope between Britain and Ireland* (2015). McCourt has edited *James Joyce in Context* (2009), *Roll Away the Reel World: James Joyce and Cinema* (2010), and two recent *Joyce Studies in Italy* volumes: *Joyce, Yeats and the Revival* (2015) and *Shakespearian Joyce, Joycean Shakespeare* (2016).

Erika Mihálycsa is Lecturer in twentieth-century British and Irish literature at Babes-Bolyai University, Cluj, Romania. She has lectured at Joyce Schools in Dublin and Trieste and published on Joyce, Beckett, Flann O'Brien, modernism, theory, and Joyce in translation. Mihálycsa is editor of literary journal *HYPERION* and co-editor of *Scientia Traductionis* (2012) and *Portals of Recovery* (2017). Her translations into Hungarian include works by Flann O'Brien, Beckett, Patrick McCabe, William Carlos Williams, Anne Carson, Julian Barnes, and Jeanette Winterson.

Laurent Milesi is Professor of English Literature and Critical Theory at Shanghai Jiao Tong University and a member of the ITEM-CNRS Research Group on James Joyce's manuscripts in Paris. He has edited *James Joyce and the Difference of Language* (2003) and translated several works by Jacques Derrida—including *H. C. pour la vie, c'est à dire . . .* (with Stefan Herbrechter; 2006)—and by Hélène Cixous—including *Le Voisin de zéro. Sam Beckett* (2010), *Philippines* (2011), and *Tombe* (2014). Milesi is presently working on the monograph *Jacques Derrida and the Ethics of Writing*.

Laura Pelaschiar is Lecturer in English Literature at the University of Trieste, Italy, and Director of the Trieste Joyce School. She has written widely on Northern Irish Literature and James Joyce. Pelaschiar has written the monograph *Writing the North: The Contemporary Novel in Northern Ireland* (1998) and *Ulisse Gotico* (2009), and edited *Joyce/Shakespeare* for Syracuse University Press (2015). She is completing a monograph on the Gothic in all of Joyce's texts.

Franca Ruggieri is Professor Emeritus of Foreign Language, Literature and Culture at Roma Tre University, co-founder and President of the James Joyce Italian Foundation, and editor in chief of *Joyce Studies in Italy* and *Piccola Biblioteca Joyciana*. She is the author of *Le maschere dell'artista, il giovane Joyce* (1986), *Introduzione a Joyce* (1990), and *James Joyce, la vita, le lettere* (2012). Ruggieri has edited Joyce's *Poesie e prose* for Mondadori (1992) and contributed numerous articles and chapters to journals and books on Joyce and on the modernist novel.

Fritz Senn is Honorary Trustee of the International James Joyce Foundation and founder and Director of the Zurich James Joyce Foundation where he has led annual August Workshops since 1985. He has lectured at every Joyce School in Dublin and in Trieste and published criticism on Joyce, Homer, and translation. Senn's books include *Joyce's Dislocutions: Essays on Reading as Translation* (1984), *Nichts gegen Joyce* (1991), *Inductive Scrutinies: Focus on Joyce* (1995), *Ulyssean Close-ups* (2007), and *Portals of Recovery* (2017). His memoir, *Joycean Murmoirs*, was published in 2007.

Sam Slote is Associate Professor in the School of English at Trinity College Dublin and a Trustee of the International James Joyce Foundation. He is the author of *Joyce's Nietzschean Ethics* (2013) and editor of *Derrida and Joyce: Texts and Contexts* (2013) and *How Joyce Wrote* Finnegans Wake (2017). Slote directs the Trinity Centre for Beckett Studies and is the founding co-director of the Samuel Beckett Summer School. He has written on Joyce, Beckett, Virginia Woolf, Vladimir Nabokov, Raymond Queneau, Dante, Mallarmé, and Elvis.

Sara Sullam is Junior Lecturer in English Literature at Milan "Statale" University. She co-edited *Transits: The Nomadic Geographies of Anglo-American Modernism* (2010) and *Parallaxes: Virginia Woolf Meets James Joyce* (2014). Sullam has published the monograph *Tra i generi: Virginia Woolf e il romanzo* (2016) and translated Joyce's essays for the volume of *Lettere e saggi*, edited by Enrico Terrinoni (2016).

Ira Torresi is Associate Professor at the Department of Interpreting and Translation, University of Bologna-Forlì. With Rosa Maria Bollettieri Bosinelli, she has edited *Joyce and/in Translation* (2007), two dossiers on *Joycean Collective Memories?* (for the *mediAzioni* online journal), and has authored several papers on Joyce and translation.

Jolanta Wawrzycka is Professor of English at Radford University, Virginia, and Trustee of the International James Joyce Foundation. She has lectured at Dublin and Trieste Joyce Schools, edited *Reading Joycean Temporalities* (2018), co-edited *Gender in Joyce* (1997) and *Portals of Recovery* (2017), and guest-edited translation issues of *JJQ* (47, no. 4) and *Scientia Traductionis* (2010, 2012). Wawrzycka has contributed to *ReJoycing: New Readings of Dubliners* (1998), *The Reception of James Joyce in Europe* (2004), and *Joyce in Context* (2009), and translated Ingarden, Miłosz, Yeats, and Joyce's *Chamber Music*.

Serenella Zanotti is Associate Professor of English Language and Translation at Roma Tre University. She has published on James Joyce, Ezra Pound, and translingualism. Her interests include audiovisual translation, cross-cultural pragmatics, and translator manuscript genetics. Zanotti is author of *Italian Joyce: A Journey through Language and Translation* (2013) and co-editor of volumes related to translation, including *The Translator as Author* (2011), *Translation and Ethnicity* (*The European Journal of English Studies*, 2014), and *Linguistic and Cultural Representation in Audiovisual Translation* (forthcoming, 2018).

Bibliographical Note

In line with the conventions of Joycean scholarship, the following standard abbreviations for parenthetical textual references have been used throughout this volume. Also, the following editions of Joyce's works have been used unless where additional or alternative editions have been cited in the chapter concerned.

CP   Joyce, James, *Collected Poems*, New York: Viking Press, 1957.

CW   Joyce, James, *The Critical Writings of James Joyce*, ed. E. Mason and R. Ellmann, New York: Viking Press, 1959.

D   Joyce, James, *Dubliners*, ed. R. Scholes in consultation with R. Ellmann, New York: Viking Press, 1967.

E   Joyce, James, *Exiles*, New York: Penguin, 1973.

FW   Joyce, James, *Finnegans Wake*, New York: Viking Press, 1939; London: Faber and Faber, 1939.

GJ   Joyce, James, *Giacomo Joyce*, ed. R. Ellmann, New York: Viking Press, 1968.

JJI   Ellmann, Richard, *James Joyce*, New York: Oxford University Press, 1959.

JJII   Ellmann, Richard, *James Joyce*, New York: Oxford University Press, 1982.

JJA   *The James Joyce Archive*, ed. M. Groden et al., New York and London: Garland Publishing, 1977–9.

Letters I, Joyce, James, *Letters of James Joyce*, Vol. I, ed. S. Gilbert, New York:
  II, III   Viking Press, 1957; reissued with corrections 1966. Vols. II and III, ed. R. Ellmann, New York: Viking Press, 1966.

P   Joyce, James, *A Portrait of the Artist as a Young Man*, ed. R. Ellmann, New York: Viking Press, 1964.

SH   Joyce, James, *Stephen Hero*, ed. J. J. Slocum and H. Cahoon, New York: New Directions, 1944, 1963.

SL   Joyce, James, *Selected Letters of James Joyce*, ed. R. Ellmann, New York: Viking Press, 1975.

U   Joyce, James, *Ulysses*, ed. H. W. Gabler et al., New York and London: Garland Publishing, 1984, 1986. In paperback by Garland, Random House, Bodley Head, and Penguin between 1986 and 1992.

Introduction: "Listening to the unspoken speech behind the words" (*P* 242)

Jolanta Wawrzycka and Serenella Zanotti

The essays in this collection investigate how textual, rhetorical, and aesthetic silences function in the narrative landscape of Joyce's works. While this is the first collection where the concept of "silence" in Joyce receives a sustained and multi-angled critical attention, a number of critics have written about the crucial role that silence plays in Joyce's writing, including Hugh Kenner (1977) and Jean-Michel Rabaté (1982).[1] A closer examination of Joyce's deployment of textual gaps and ellipses reveals a larger rhetorical design embedded in his narrative strategies: it adds up to what Kenner calls "the rhetoric of silence" as he illuminates the instances of "hiatus[es] of perception," "narrative silences," and "skips" (385) as well as the "eloquent absence" (383) of crucial scenes that *must* have happened but that Joyce had not written down. Thus, Kenner's legacy includes a reminder that, when in "Sirens" Bloom reiterates "at four she said" (*U* 11.188, 309), Molly "didn't say it in our hearing any time in 'Calypso'" (385), and that, indeed, the marital exchanges in "Calypso" teach readers how *Ulysses* is "a book of silences despite all its din of specifying" and "how eloquent is not only the Blooms' rhetoric of avoidance but the author's" (Kenner 1977: 385). That author has, of course, tackled other kinds of silences in his oeuvre as well: early on, young Stephen Daedalus not only builds himself a "house of silence" but also "school[s] himself into silence" (*SH* 30) that will become one of the weapons in his triple armour of defense, "silence, exile and cunning" (*P* 274). But in a unique textual transaction of silencing, Joyce has also designed for Stephen a protracted exit from his work: Stephen's anticipated exile never materializes in *A Portrait* and, in *Ulysses*, Joyce's un-finalized hero fades eerily into the night. His disappearance recalls the exit of a different kind of an artist: Honoré de Balzac's Lucien Rubempré who, in following the axiom, "Fuge, Late, Tace"—reported by Richard Ellmann as a possible source of Stephen's "silence, exile, and cunning"

(*JJII* 354) – ends up imprisoned and commits suicide, the ultimate exit and silencing. Stephen's exit, his vanishing into the starlit night after con-micturation with Bloom marks, and is marked by, silence.[2]

Exit Stephen, master of the word, enter Bloom, master of the wor(L)d.

In contrast to Stephen's, the Blooms' narrative projects itself proleptically *beyond* June 16–17, plans for travel and various engagements having been sketched out by their creator. Bloom, a different kind of exile, proceeds by strategic silence and tactical cunning: "There is a touch of the artist about old Bloom" (*U* 10.582). And his nails are "well pared" (*U* 6.204). If Stephen's three-prong armour turns out to be just a palaver, grafted onto Bloom, it becomes a chainmail.

There are various ways to consider silence in Joyce's works. Jean-Michel Rabaté, like Kenner, reads Joyce (*Dubliners* in particular) for silence embedded in narrative gaps and textual blanks "that can be accounted for in terms of the characters who betray themselves by slips, lapses, omissions" (1982: 45), though he also considers silence that "can mean an inversion of speech, its mirror, that which structures its resonance, silence without silence"; or one that appears "as the end, the limit, the death of speech, its paralysis" (Rabaté 1982: 45). For Fritz Senn, the initial textual silences we encounter upon entering the Joycean text—at first, things are not readily understood or noted—are fruitfully illuminated through acts of "anagnosis" (Senn 1995: 57), one of the many concepts in Senn's Joycean critical-theoretical apparatus.[3] On the other hand, to consider the very frequency and textual permutations of the word "silence" and all manner of its cognates is to illuminate how the lexical stratum contributes to signifying narrativity. In *Stephen Hero*, the words "silence," "silent," and "silently" occur some thirty-six times; the occurrences multiply to ninety-six in *A Portrait* and to one hundred in *Ulysses*.[4] One could interpret these numbers: some words refer, simply enough, to an absence of sound; others are semantically inflected by qualifiers to articulate the signified with precision unmatched by its signifier: thus there are silences that are "scornful" (*U* 1.418) or "studious" (*U* 2.69), others concern the many *funeral* silences invoked in "Hades,"[5] and still others—"Shrieks of silence" (*U*. 14.1493)—explode signification all together. Many of Joyce's silences are quite eloquent in what they omit: we see this in the multifaceted narrative strategies that rely heavily on elliptical or "gnomonic language" (Herring 1987: 11). Indeed, as suggested by Susan Sontag in "The Aesthetics of Silence" (1967: 5), "[s]ilence remains, inescapably, a form of speech … and an element in a dialogue." The young protagonist of "The Sisters" reacts with indignation to Old Cotter's porous utterances that, to him, communicate *nothing*:

he "puzzle[s his] head to extract meaning from [Cotter's] unfinished sentences" (*D* 11), which is another way of saying that he tries to translate from the "foreign" language of the adults *that* which Cotter's usage never articulates. Cotter's meaning is shrouded in silence and presented to us, the readers, as "...". Thus we too engage in translating these textual *representations* of silence into some kind of meaning. But all we have is the name for the figure of omission: ellipses. We cannot know what they silence.

The essays in this book trace the complexities of Joyce's treatment of silence by considering rhetorical, linguistic, translatorial, aesthetic, and cultural dimensions of "silence" in his opus. Four essays in Part 1, "The Language of Silence," address the varying ways in which Joyce's works problematize language as a vehicle to convey silence. Fritz Senn's "Active Silences" explores Joyce's manner of enacting silences verbally: Senn studies silence as absence of noise ("He could hear nothing: night was perfectly silent," *D* 117) and absence of speech ("Nothing was said," *U* 6.21) while both are nevertheless articulated. A subspecies of these kinds of "silence" occurs when particular subjects are avoided in ongoing dialogues. For Senn, there is an inherent paradox in discussing silences since, by definition, they tend to be absences. Joyce's works are exceptional in conjuring up awkward, embarrassed silences and the actual techniques of implementing them are the main focus of Senn's chapter.

Laura Pelaschiar too focuses on the essential role of the unsaid that still manages to be conveyed in the language of narration. In "Joyce's Art of Silence in *Dubliners* and *A Portrait of the Artist as a Young Man*," she focuses on Joyce's deliberate and methodical construction of silence as a narrative device and suggests that Joyce came to recognize its power quite early, during the process of revising his 1904 version of "The Sisters." Pelaschiar offers insightful comparative reading of the two versions of the story, explores distinct articulation of female silences in all of *Dubliners*, and closes by considering the varied silences in *A Portrait*.

The chapter by Rosa Maria Bollettieri Bosinelli and Ira Torresi, "What Happens When 'The silence speaks the scene' (*FW* 13.3)?," explores silences as concealment and as silencing the "unspeakable." Silence here is read as a strategy of concealment of, and distancing from, the idea of death. It is also read as a weapon that can be used to erase the English language just as the English invaders had erased the Irish language when they colonized Ireland. Several examples are given from Joyce's text, including the *Epiphanies*, that illustrate these points: Bollettieri and Torresi discuss the examples of Joyce's textual treatment of death that, as one of the great unspeakables in most cultures, is concealed both by silence, that is, suppressed references to it, and by the use of words or details that distract attention from it.

Part 1 closes with Laurent Milesi's chapter, "In the Beginning was the Nil: The 'eloquence of silence' in *Finnegans Wake*." Milesi reads the Wakean dynamics of language and silence in terms of Joyce's awareness of the stereotyped gender constructions in language. He posits that, despite some studies of Joyce's thematic programming of silence evident in his earlier fiction, the dialectic of language and silence in *Finnegans Wake* remains underexamined, even as it intersects with several motifs that include the quest for the origin of the Nile (nil) and female sexuality, or the various instances of textual-historical "gaps," some in the form of a dramatic radio interruption (e.g. *FW* 500–1). Milesi's premise is that the Wakean dynamics of language and silence inform the text's narrative fabric. The chapter thus traces how textual motifs must be seen in conjunction with the problematic of (the origin of) language as inextricable from silence.

The common thread in Part 2, "The Aesthetics of Silence," is the critics' interest in the development of Joyce's stylistic prowess and of, what Sontag calls, "the aesthetics of silence." John McCourt traces these elements from their earliest manifestations in works that include *Giacomo Joyce, A Portrait* and culminate in *Ulysses*. His chapter, "'Fragments of shapes, hewn. In white silence: appealing': Silence and the Emergence of a Style from *Giacomo Joyce* to *Ulysses*," argues that for Joyce silence became not only a backdrop for words and gestures but also a form of communication that was nuanced in tone; it produced diverse textual results on the one hand and distinct readerly responses on the other. McCourt shows that *Giacomo Joyce* goes beyond conceiving silence in an aural sense; it conveys silence through the visual metaphor of the irregular white space. This focus on the visual leads back to Joyce's cinematic interests and understanding (from silent movies) that silence invariably communicates meaning.

Teresa Caneda Cabrera, in "Joyce and the Aesthetics of Silence: Absence and Loss in 'The Dead,'" reflects on Joyce's "aesthetics of silence" to argue that, by evading complete articulation and withholding voice, Joyce's story calls attention to the unsayable as the very essence of what the text attempts to communicate. Caneda Cabrera explores Joyce's story in terms of how much of what really matters remains unsaid: Joyce's narratives "articulate" inaudible stories of unspeakable losses and absences whose cultural, political and historical implications attentive readers, nevertheless, do hear.

In contrast, Sam Slote takes up the fluidity of style and of Molly's "yeses" in "Penelope" and contextualizes them further by including Samuel Beckett. In "'Affirmations and negations invalidated as uttered' in *Ulysses* and *How It Is*,"

Slote takes exception to a commonplace description of the "Penelope" episode as fluid in style. Instead, his chapter investigates Molly's "yeses" as indicative of Molly's multifarious and ever-changing perspective. It proposes that "yeses" function similarly to what the Unnamable in Beckett's *How It Is* refers to as "affirmations and negations invalidated as uttered," whereby every step taken is also a step retracted. The chapter concludes that Molly's "yes," with all its ambivalences and equivocations, is not unlike Nietzsche's "great Yes to life," and Beckett's (Bom's) great Yes to death, all of them affirming the indeterminate modalities of life.

In the final chapter of this section, Morris Beja, like Slote, expands his reading to include Beckett, but also Pinter. Beja's chapter, "'Shut up he explained': Joyce and 'scornful silence,'" analyses the connection between Stephen's "scornful silence" at the beginning of *Ulysses* and separation, distance, aloneness, alienation, and exile. Particularly intriguing are such connections between silence and alienation within Joyce's epiphanies, especially the manuscript epiphanies he wrote and collected; arguably, they provide the ultimate examples of the revelatory power of what is "unsaid"—the Wake's "aristmystic unsaid."

Three very different takes on silence are tackled in Part 3, "Writing Silence," in that they cover selected aspects of Joycean meta-text: the archives, the issues of publication, and the looming Homeric presence in *Ulysses*. William Brockman's original reading of Joyce's dictated letters touches on the issue of the authorial voice (prone to alterations while recorded by his amanuenses) and argues that the ambivalence about the authorial voice is reflected in the narrative voice. Brockman's chapter, "The Silent Author of James Joyce's Dictated Letters," explores Joyce's authorial silence by examining the identity of the voice in Joyce's dictated letters. Brockman posits that intermediaries helped Joyce maintain privacy and elude direct dealings on "sensitive topics that might have been offensive if communicated directly." Dictated letters afforded Joyce some "authorial silence" and Brockman sees them as potentially illuminating for interpreting corresponding situations in his published works.

Sara Sullam's archival research investigates the silence that surrounded the publication of the first Italian translation of *Ulysses* in the mid-twentieth century. Her chapter, "'Secrets, silent ... sit' in the Archives of Our Publishers: Untold Episodes from Joyce's Italian Odyssey," explores the translation history of Joyce's essays and letters. Their publishing history—spanning from 1946 to the 1970s—is intriguing when studied in relation to the silence that surrounded *Ulysses*, belatedly published in translation only in 1960. To answer some of the questions that such a silence raises, Sullam studied the unpublished papers at the

Mondadori Foundation in Milan and at the Apice Archive, which also holds the papers of the publisher Cederna, a key player in the reception of Joyce in Italy. Sullam's archival investigation reveals crucial information that advances a fuller understanding of the "Joyce factor" within Italian culture.

Finally, Tim Conley offers an original reading of Joyce's engagement with Homeric meta-text as a peculiar kind of translation. Conley's "The Silence of the Looms" starts with a close reading of Homer's epithet for Queen Penelope: "periphron" (thoughtful/cautious). Conley observes that, among all Homeric translators, Fitzgerald is the only translator who opted to render the epithet as "quiet queen." And while the readers of *Ulysses* do not necessarily imagine Molly as "quiet," Conley explores "how the reader 'hears' (or does not 'hear') the women" in *Ulysses*. One of Conley's arguments is that translations almost always amplify what the original text leaves silent. His discussion provides a fortuitous transition to the next section that centres on the issues of translation.

Thus, Part 4, "Translating Silence," presents an innovative approach to silence by addressing complex issues of silence and/in translation. The critics tackle these issues in three different ways. First, Serenella Zanotti, in "Silent Translation in Joyce," develops an important notion of "silent translation," which she defines as the unacknowledged incorporation of translated texts into one's writing. Postulating that this deeply intertextual writing methodology contributed to Joyce's artistic development, Zanotti also calls attention to the inherently translatorial nature of Joyce's writing. By investigating the silent operations carried out by Joyce in dealing with other writers' words in translation, such as Dante's, Zanotti proposes that "silent translation" should be viewed as one of the key components of Joyce's radically intertextual writing method, a strategy he made use of to question the traditional notions of originality and derivation.

Jolanta Wawrzycka, in "'Mute chime and mute peal': Notes on Translating Silences in *Chamber Music*," explores a translatorial toolbox: her process of translating *Chamber Music* revealed silences embedded in the phonetic values of lexes, and her chapter studies the poems' syntactic and rhetorical gestures of muteness and silence that, she proposes, form the "poetics of the ineffable" that contributes to translatorial obstacles. Her chapter postulates that the poetic tonality of *Chamber Music* is driven as much by the abstract and non-representational sound-sense of language as it is by its referentiality, and focuses on the instances where silences in the poems are denoted through the formations of vowels, in addition to the infrequent lexes that connote silences. Wawrzycka notes the peculiar linguistic silence of the nonce words that pepper Joyce's youthful poems: largely absent from dictionaries and from everyday speech, they pose particular challenges to translators. In broader translatorial terms, Joyce's nonce words play into the importance of the "inventive singularity" of translation evoked by Erika Mihálycsa in the chapter that follows Wawrzycka's.

Indeed, in terms of "inventive singularity," Mihálycsa's interests are in those elements of language that elicit the sensation of music and of immersion in the sound-world that extends into silence. Her answers to the question of how such a sensation can be carried over into another language are tackled in her chapter, "'Music hath jaws': Translating Music and Silence in *Ulysses*," which discusses recent retranslations of *Ulysses* into Italian and Hungarian. Proposing to map the linguistic sound effects in translation, Mihálycsa addresses such issues as normative vs. non-normative language use and the different stylistic conventions that are observed and/or broken in target languages, to mention just a few of her preoccupations. Recent retranslations of *Ulysses* into Italian and Hungarian come in the wake of the "canonical" translations with an agenda of revising the former translations' fallacies and addressing translation issues left unsolved, or downright silenced.

The volume's coda, "Modernism/Silence," features Franca Ruggieri's erudite and widely cast discussion that contextualizes Joyce's silences by considering how silence functions in modernist literature beyond Joyce. In "Forms of Silence in Literary Writing: James Joyce and Modernism," Ruggieri situates Joyce's deployment of silence within the framework of artistic and philosophical modernist experiments with language, narratology, and representation. She proposes that modernist silence often indicates cultural fragmentation and social unease made manifest, for example, in the technique of stream of consciousness that expresses silence—in silence. Her chapter compares the functions that silence performs in Joyce's writings with those found in other modernist writers such as Kafka, Eliot, Nietzsche, Hofmannsthal, Broch, and Conrad, and analyses silence as an indicator of the unsayable and the mystery of the "not-said" in the writings of Joyce. The silence of interruption and return joins "riverrun" to the final word "the" of *Finnegans Wake*: the final materialization of what Giorgio Melchiori called the great "epiphany of language."

One could argue that the sheer range of scholarly approaches gathered in this book makes it a challenge to present "silence" as a unifying concept through which to read Joyce. But such a challenge is not necessarily a shortcoming. Rhetorical, linguistic, aesthetic, translatorial, and cultural silences that permeate Joyce's opus have been in dire need of sustained critical attention that, we hope, will meet with ample scholarly follow-up.

Notes

1   In addition, a number of more recent critics, including Nels Pearson ("Death
    Sentences: Silence, Colonial Memory and the Voice of the Dead in *Dubliners*,"
    2005), contextualize Joyce's silences through political and post-colonial lenses;
    such readings approach Joyce's works as encoding (but also uncovering) Ireland's
    sense of colonial dislocation and loss. Cf. also work by Anne Fogarty (2014) or
    Andrew Gibson (2001). While Sam Slote's monograph, *The Silence in Progress of
    Dante, Mallarmé, and Joyce* (1999), fronts "silence" in its title, the stated thesis of
    Slote's volume is to trace the language of "enunciation" in the three titular authors
    that "aims towards some achievement" (4) but one that also "aims towards the very
    destruction of itself-as-enunciation" (4), whereby the "works of Dante, Mallarmé
    and Joyce are—by simple virtue of being works—subject to a force: they can be
    called obscure ... these works effect a negative interval upon discourse. This is
    what we call their silence" (5).
2   "*Fuge, late, tace*" translates roughly as "flight, subterfuge, silence" or "escape, deceit,
    silence," as rendered by Franca Ruggieri who evokes this phrase in the closing
    chapter of this volume. Ellmann writes that, "in bringing [*A Portrait*] together Joyce
    found unexpected help in Balzac" (*JJII* 354) and grafted "the Carthusian motto" onto
    Stephen. He acknowledges Stuart Gilbert for pointing him to Honoré de Balzac's *Le
    Médecin de campagne* as the source of the motto. However, Lucien Rubempré does
    not appear in that novel. But Ellmann got it right in the first biography, where he lists
    Balzac's *Splendeurs et misères des courtisanes* as a possible source (*JJI* 365) and also
    acknowledges Gilbert. Citing *JJI*, Don Gifford (1982: 280) confirms the source to be
    Splendeurs.
3   See Senn's "Anagnostic Probes" (1989), esp. 47–9.
4   The results come from the online concordances to *A Portrait* and *Ulysses* and from
    the transcribed text of *Stephen Hero*.
5   Marc McGahon (2017) discusses silence in the funeral carriage in "Hades"; see esp.
    103–4. See also Fritz Senn in this volume.

References

Attridge, D. (2004), *The Singularity of Literature*, London and New York: Routledge.
Fogarty, A. (2014), "'I Think He Died for Me': Memory and Ethics in 'The Dead,'" in
    O. Frawley and K. O'Callaghan (eds), *Memory Ireland: James Joyce and Cultural
    Memory*, 46–61, Syracuse: Syracuse University Press.
Gibson, A. (2001), "'And the Wind Wheezing Through That Organ Once in a While':
    Voice, Narrative, Film," *New Literary History* 32, no. 3: 639–57.

Gifford, D. (1982), *Joyce Annotated; Notes for* Dubliners *and* A Portrait of the Artist as a Young Man, Berkeley: University of California Press.

Herring, Phillip (1987), *Joyce's Uncertainty Principle*, Princeton, NJ: Princeton University Press.

Kenner, H. (1977), "The Rhetoric of Silence," *James Joyce Quarterly* 14, no. 4: 382–94.

McGahon, M. (2017), "Silence, Justice, and the *Différend* in Joyce's *Ulysses*," in M. McAteer (ed.), *Silence in Modern Irish Literature*, 98–109, Leiden: Brill/Rodopi.

Pearson, N. (2005), "Death Sentences: Silence, Colonial Memory and the Voice of the Dead in *Dubliners*," in C. Jaurretche (ed.), *Beckett, Joyce and the Art of the Negative*, 141–70, Amsterdam: Rodopi.

Rabaté, J.-M. (1982), "Silence in *Dubliners*," in C. MacCabe (ed.), *James Joyce: New Perspectives*, 45–72, Bloomington: Indiana University Press.

Senn, F. (1989), "Anagnostic Probes," in C. van Boheemen, *Modernity and Its Mediation* 37–61, Amsterdam: Rodopi.

Senn, F. (1995), *Inductive Scrutinies. Focus on Joyce*, ed. C. O'Neill, Dublin: Lilliput Press.

Slote, S. (1999), *The Silence in Progress of Dante, Mallarmé and Joyce*, New York: Peter Lang.

Sontag, S. (1967), "The Aesthetics of Silence," in *Styles of Radical Will* (1994), 3–34, London: Vintage.

Part One

The Language of Silence

1

Active Silences

Fritz Senn

The focus of this probe is, unassumingly, on the kinds of silences in Joyce's works, on some distinctions, and above all on how Joyce verbally acts them out. For the present purpose, "silence" is used in two main meanings or aspects: 1) the absence of noise, as for example the end of "A Painful Case" ("He could hear nothing: night was perfectly silent," *D* 117); or, more narrowly, 2) the absence of speech when speech is expected, or as a lull in conversation ("Nothing was said," *U* 6.21). A non-acoustic subsection is when particular subjects are avoided in an ongoing dialogue.

There is an inherent paradox in discussing silences since by definition they tend to be absences. In fiction, silences generally are worth mentioning when they are framed, that is to say, atmospherically felt or experienced, often in socially awkward situations. Conceivably the various stories in *Dubliners* or the parts of *A Portrait* and *Ulysses* could be categorized according to their noise and speech levels. How "loud" are the stories? On the one hand "Counterparts," "Ivy Day," or "Grace" are full of conversations while "Eveline" or "A Painful Case," with only one single spoken sentence (*D* 109), are relatively silent. In *Ulysses*, the wide-angle episodes like "Aeolus" or "Wandering Rocks" are naturally full of noise and talk. There is music in "Sirens" and vivid, even violent talk in "Cyclops," while "Circe," both in its realistic setting and its imaginative expansion, is full of clamor and tumult. At the other end of the spectrum the monologue chapters like "Proteus" and "Penelope" are quiet by their nature.

But distinctions are precarious and partly artificial. An episode like "Oxen of the Sun" is full of agitated conversation, with "there nighed them a mickle noise," "tumultuary discussions," "the noise of voices" (*U* 14.124, 848, 1126). Yet the indirect presentation in parodic reports tends to mute the sound, even a volley of deprecations at one point—"whiles they all chode with him, a murrain seize the dolt ... thou chuff, thou puny, thou got in peasestraw, thou losel ..." (*U* 14.326)—because of their historical refraction are not felt to be loud, all the less so since readers know the words quoted are not those actually spoken. An onomatopoeic imitation, "A black crack of noise in the street ere, alack, bawled back" with an echoing impact (*U* 14.408), looks like an exception. The end, the so-called Coda, changes from basically written reports to an apparent rendering of partly loud and unassigned utterances as though a device not yet invented like a tape recorder had registered them. It ends in the resonant vituperations of an American evangelist, Alexander Dowie, caused by the sight of a poster that announces his appearance. It indicates a sonorous voice from a pulpit: "Come on, you winefizzling, ginsizzling, beetle-browed … fourflushers … Just you try it on" (*U* 14.1580). But it is not clear whether this is actually voiced in joking imitation by someone present on the spur of an original moment, or else only textually imagined in a chapter of literary phantasms. Is, in other words, the "Oxen" episode silent or loud? The "voices" do indeed "blend in clouded silence" (*U* 14.1078). Blurred distinction between reality and imagination also characterize the chapter immediately following, "Circe."

The distant, emotionless style of "Ithaca" practically stifles whatever discussions take place in Bloom's kitchen and even more so later in bed. Whatever is spoken is transposed into an indirect distant report and if it is recited aloud a low-level voice with minimal emphases will be most appropriate. Fittingly the night of *Ulysses* ends in a protracted silence, which is interrupted merely by "the chime of the bells of Saint George," footsteps, "the double vibration of a jew's harp in the resonant lane" (*U* 17.1226, 1239), or the "brief sharp unforeseen heard loud lone crack" of a timber table (*U* 17.2061). In "Penelope" few sounds intrude, as of a distant train or the noise of Molly on the chamber pot: "O Lord how noisy … Lord what a row youre making like the jersey lily easy O how the waters come down at Lahore" (*U* 18.1142–8). Paradoxically, the most silent part of the whole book is the one that is most often turned into audible speech on a stage.

Charting *Ulysses* according to its presumed decibels would be a tricky but not necessarily futile endeavor.

Circean amplitudes

Seen in very rough outlines, *Ulysses* begins in relative quiet in the early single-track episodes, while the collective ones, "Aeolus" and "Wandering Rocks," considerably increase the noises and the speech levels. "Circe" is a climax—realistically with shouts and whistles and songs, a blaring gramophone, the gong of a fire engine, and on the imaginary plane with cannon shots, a "choir of six hundred voices" singing "Allelujah ..." (*U* 15.1953), and so on—but such external noises as well as speech diminishes towards the end. The last two episodes, as already indicated, are practically silent.

The overall pattern is echoed on a smaller scale in "Circe." After all the bustle and excitement with a multitude of persons the cast is finally reduced to just Bloom and Stephen along with Cornelius Kelleher, who manages to appease the guards. The abatement of noise sets in with Kelleher's departure, when mute but precisely meaningful gestures take over in parodic dumb show (and in practical implausibility):

(The car and horse back slowly, awkwardly, and turn. Corny Kelleher on the sideseat sways his head to and fro in sign of mirth at Bloom's plight. The jarvey joins in the mute pantomimic merriment nodding from the farther seat. Bloom shakes his head in mute mirthful reply. With thumb and palm Corny Kelleher reassures that the two bobbies will allow the sleep to continue for what else is to be done. With a slow nod Bloom conveys his gratitude as that is exactly what Stephen needs.)

U 15.4909

After meaningful gestures replace the sound of words the stage direction is infiltrated by a melody, the refrain of a song. The lingering echo may be something actually heard or else a textual carry-over, referring back to "Corny Kelleher ... Singing with his eyes shut ... With my tooraloom, tooraloom, tooraloom, tooraloom," Bloom's first association of him (*U* 5.12).

The car jingles tooraloom round the corner of the tooraloom lane. Corny Kelleher again reassuralooms with his hand. Bloom with his hand assuralooms Corny Kelleher that he is reassuraloomtay. The tinkling hoofs and jingling harness grow fainter with their tooralooloo looloo lay.

After the final light tingling and jingling an unstated silence takes over:

Bloom, holding in his hand Stephen's hat, festooned with shavings, and ashplant, stands irresolute. Then he bends to him and shakes him by the shoulder.

The rest of the episode is silence or muffled, softened speech. Bloom begins timidly in what must be a low voice: "Eh! Ho! ... Mr Dedalus" and then, bringing his mouth nearer, probably somewhat louder, "Stephen!" Stephen then wakes up with Yeats's poem from the early morning on his lips:

... (*frowns*) Who? Black panther. Vampire. (*He sighs and stretches himself, then murmurs thickly with prolonged vowels*)
> Who ... drive ... Fergus now
> And pierce ... wood's woven shade ...?

U 15.4930

He speaks so low and indistinctly that Bloom hardly understands; he notably misinterprets "*Fergus*" as the name of a romantic companion, such as would spring to the lips of a young man waking up: "Ferguson ... a girl ... Best thing could happen him" (*U* 15.4950). Almost complete absence of sound is not stated, but affectingly implied:

> He stretches out his arms, sighs again and curls his body. Bloom, holding the hat and ashplant, stands erect. A dog barks in the distance ...

A dog heard in the distance emphasizes the quietness just as a donkey braying far away does in "Hades" (*U* 6.837; see below). The same effect is conveyed when Bloom "*communes with the night*"[1] and then "murmurs" an oath, while he stands "Silent, thoughtful, alert, his fingers at his lips," until a figure, a dark fairy boy of eleven, appears and Bloom, "*wonderstruck*," has one more word to utter: "Rudy!"—but "*inaudibly*" it would not be heard by anyone. ("Inaudible speech" would be one definition of the interior monologue.) No further sound is heard at the vision of Bloom's dead son. The last scene is enveloped in silence.

In *Dubliners* "The Dead" has an analogous sound curve, After the bustle, the music, dancing, and the speech of a crowded party, the number of guests decreases before departure, at the end only Gabriel and Gretta in the Gresham hotel late at night are left. There is little light and almost less noise impinging.

> ... their feet falling in soft thuds on the thickly carpeted stairs ... In the silence Gabriel could hear the falling of the molten wax into the tray and the thumping of his own heart against his ribs.

D 19

The conversation in the room takes a different turn from what Gabriel expected and turns towards the past, a memory called up by a few bars of a song heard offstage. In the end, Gabriel is all alone with his thoughts; even the snow on the window pane emits, or is imagined to do so, "a few light taps," and in the end the snow in widening perspective enfolds all of Ireland in a profound silence.

"The [Silent] Sisters"

In Joyce's very first short story silences are most prominent and so have deservedly attracted a lot of critical attention. Lacunae set in right at the beginning, the first spoken words in Joyce's prose canon:

> —No, I wouldn't say he was exactly ... but there was something queer ... there was something uncanny about him. I'll tell you my opinion ...
>
> *D* 9

It would be hard to squeeze less information and more suggestion into an utterance full of halts, hesitancy, groping for words, and internal censorship. The note is struck right away: things that are not said, and certainly not "exactly," are associated with being queer and uncanny, something outside a respectable order of things. The opinion also will never be told, nor the "theory" in the next non-statement. Joyce begins with something he was extremely adroit at, a constrained atmosphere. In such a predicament, smoking may bridge an uneasy gap: "He began to puff at his pipe." The story fittingly ends with something unsaid: "...that made them think that there was something gone wrong with him ..." (*D* 18), so that it is bracketed with gaps that range from "queer" to "something wrong." Joyce incidentally offers a technique of interpretation—to "extract meaning from ... unfinished sentences" (*D* 11).

Silences can be explicitly named, even emphasized. The presence of the dead priest in a room imposes customary constraints:

> A silence took possession of the little room and, under cover of it, I approached the table and tasted my sherry and then returned quietly to my chair in the corner. Eliza seemed to have fallen into a deep revery. We waited respectfully for her to break the silence: and after a long pause she said slowly ...
>
> *D* 17

Silences do in fact "take possession" of most of the story, and so do pauses. The tension becomes oppressive and affects people's behavior. The somewhat formal diction, that the boy "*approached* the table," indicates self-consciousness. The silence has to be "broken," and the purely figurative breaking is immediately followed by the incident of a broken chalice (most likely an inaccurate sense of "breaking" in a colloquial meaning of a mere dropping):

> —It was that chalice he broke ... That was the beginning of it. Of course, they say it was all right, that it contained nothing, I mean. But still ... They say it was the boy's fault.
>
> *D* 17

Silences, indicated by ellipses or not, "contain nothing," they are gaps in speech or actions—empty parts. Emptiness is a motif in the story, as it emerges in "vacation time"; an "idle chalice" on the priest's breast contains nothing. Even words can be "idle," in contrast to those that are "true." Emptiness is paired with "filling": "The word *paralysis* . . . filled me with fear" (*D* 9).

When nothing is spoken, the resulting protracted discomfort is conveyed in minute focusing on insignificant details and acts in what appears like slow motion. But something, after all, has to be said, and any commonplace will serve:

> Nannie went to the sideboard and brought out a decanter of sherry and some wineglasses. She set these on the table and invited us to take a little glass of wine. Then, at her sister's bidding, she filled out the sherry into the glasses and passed them to us. She pressed me to take some cream crackers also, but I declined because I thought I would make too much noise eating them. She seemed to be somewhat disappointed at my refusal and went over quietly to the sofa, where she sat down behind her sister. No one spoke: we all gazed at the empty[2] fireplace.
>
> My aunt waited until Eliza sighed and then said:
> — Ah, well, he's gone to a better world.
>
> *D* 15

Perhaps the most poignant silence in the story occurs towards the end when the almost expected ghost of Father Flynn does not turn up and yet, unnamed, seems to haunt the scene:

> She stopped suddenly as if to listen. I too listened; but there was no sound in the house: and I knew that[3] the old priest was lying still in his coffin as we had seen him, solemn and truculent in death, an idle chalice on his breast.
>
> *D* 17

The odd word is "idle," echoing the "idle" words of the opening paragraph. The biblical adjective renders Greek "*argos*," contracted from "*a-ergos*,"[4] the negation of something active, as in "idle," not "working."[5] In fact English "work" is a cognate of Greek "*ergos*." At the end of the first paragraph the boy longs "to be nearer to it [the word "*paralysis*"] and to look upon its deadly work" (*D* 9). It may be Joyce's subtle hint that words have the potential of being active, energetic. Silences, seemingly empty, have dynamics of their own.

Funereal

Silence is appropriate for death, which is one reason for its predominance in "The Sisters" as well as in the "Hades" episode of *Ulysses*. The first impression of the cemetery contains "white shapes . . . white forms and fragments streaming by mutely, sustaining vain gestures on the air" (*U* 6.487). Many statues are passed; by their nature they are silent and reduced to gestures.[6] Voices in the chapter are lowered, whispering is dominant ("Whispering round you," *U* 6.846), Haines speaks "below his breath" (*U* 6.880). The men carrying the coffin are called "mutes" (*U* 6.52, 1.579).

The "Hades" episode shows silences of both major kinds: the absence of noise and the temporary suspension of speech. They do not have to be spelled out, in particular at the quiet graveside scene before the actual burial:

> The coffin dived out of sight, eased down by the men straddled on the gravetrestles. They struggled up and out: and all uncovered. Twenty.
>
> *U* 6.833

Pauses are filled by close observation ("gravetrestles") and reflection. "Twenty" may indicate Bloom's counting the attendant persons, but it almost seems as though he or the readers were measuring the silent moments of the pause. It finds expression as a single word that again makes up a whole paragraph,

> Pause.

Standing alone, "Pause" is surrounded by pauses. The device is continued in Bloom's reflection, which also fills a ponderous paragraph of its own.[7]

> If we were all suddenly somebody else.

The silence needs no mention:

> Far away a donkey brayed. Rain. No such ass. Never see a dead one. Shame of death. They hide. Also poor papa went away.
>
> *U* 6.837

A noise heard from a distance marks the prevailing quietude. During a long passage of silent monologue nothing is spoken or heard until the journalist Hynes approaches Bloom, speaking "below his breath" (*U* 6.839–80).

"Hades" also foregrounds silence in the form of the disruption of speech in company, especially when gaps in conversation cause a feeling of uneasiness, as when a group of four men have just entered a narrow funeral carriage and the decorum of the occasion excludes habitual levity, at least initially, before the constraint will be relaxed.

> All waited. Nothing was said.
>
> U 6.21

One of the paradoxes in narrative is that "Nothing was said" has to be stated and cannot be conveyed by stating nothing.[8] Social silences often induce uncomfortable awareness. Bloom generally withdraws into his thoughts: "Stowing in the wreaths probably . . . ," or, in this case, attends to the soap in his hip pocket.

The next paragraph again begins with "All waited." When the carriage begins to move the pattern is repeated: "They waited still, their knees jogging" (U 6.29). In the absence of speech, physical contact can be felt all the more. The first words finally uttered, "—Which way is he taking us?" are caused less by topographical curiosity than the need to break the constrained silence. The conversation then gets haltingly under way.

Silence of course is a normal occurrence and deserves mention only when it is consciously experienced. A lull in conversation can also be caused by (what is considered) a wrong move. After some jocular remarks in the funeral carriage the occupants are reminded of the seriousness of the occasion. The subject is then changed to commonplaces on the subject of Dignam's death: "As decent a little man as ever wore a hat." The cause for the death is brought up both in the public version, "Breakdown . . . heart," and in Bloom's internal "Too much John Barleycorn." A known fact is naturally excluded by tacit agreement. The trite lament "He had a sudden death, poor fellow" leads Bloom to what looks like a spontaneous remark: "—The best death" (U 6.310). His companions' reaction, the sudden hiatus in conversation, is presented visibly: "Their wideopen eyes looked at him." In his discernible embarrassment Bloom explains what for him is self-evident: "—No suffering, he said. A moment and all is over. Like dying in sleep." The justification only increases the tension; a short but weighty sentence, again comprising a whole paragraph, is all the more effective:

> No-one spoke.
>
> U 6.315

Bloom's humane view of the best death, without suffering pain, has clashed with the religious notion of a good death, one accompanied by the proper ecclesiastical rites. For a few extended moments, the conversation has stopped. In this instance silence is the temporary death of speech. Bloom, probably by now aware of his social gaffe, is thrown back on his own thoughts. They appropriately set in with "Dead side of the street ..." (*U* 6.316).

Rhetorical

After "Hades," with its generally muted utterances, the newspapers episode "Aeolus" is full of street noises and an abundance of talk. Complementarily it also emphasizes writing and print. Language is first a matter of air shaped by vocal organs, transient vibrations that can be heard, often against concomitant noises, and are understood or not, remembered or forgotten. Against realistic plausibility complex speeches are remembered verbatim. But visually language consists of culturally determined graphic symbols in a certain alignment. In the composing room movable letters are arranged and again distributed, to be read from left to right or, as in Hebrew, in reverse. The special case of palindromes ("Madam, I'm Adam," *U* 7.683) allows for both directions. Spelling is a tricky issue since identical sounds can be differently presented ("am*u*sing" and "vi*ew*" both contain a long *u* of changed appearance), which makes spelling bees possible ("ORTHOGRAPHICAL," *U* 7.165). Hearing and Seeing[9] (reading) are in agreement or at variance.

Letter combinations can be pronounced differently, but other typographical signs defy articulation: how is "HOUSE OF KEY(E)S" spoken aloud? The voice cannot articulate a parenthesis, and even less three question marks: "???" (*U* 7.512). These question marks announce Lenehan's riddle, for which he expressively commands "Silence! What opera resembles a railway line?" (*U* 7.514). His earlier stab—"Silence for my brandnew riddle!"—has fallen on deaf ears (*U* 7.477). Because of his compulsive jocularity, he is generally disregarded and needs to call for attention. He is the one to enjoin silence emphatically.

"Aeolus" highlights rhetorical exploits. Skilled orators not only handle words but also use strategic pauses for emphasis. J. J. O'Molloy is about to recite one "of the most polished periods," but by stalling first creates suspense. It is again Lenehan, true to type, who steps in gratuitously and intrusively:

—A few wellchosen words, Lenehan prefaced. Silence!
Pause. J.J. O'Molloy took out his cigarettecase.
False lull. Something quite ordinary.

U 7.759

The speaker's tactical silence is filled with, first, Lenehan's gratuitous intervention, then a weighty pause, similar to the one at the gravesite in the cemetery, and an act, and finally with Stephen's internal thoughts in which he translates the event into what looks like an imagined passage in a novel or biography:

> Messenger took out his matchbox thoughtfully and lit his cigar.
>
> I have often thought since on looking back over that strange time that it was that small act, trivial in itself, that striking of that match, that determined the whole aftercourse of both our lives.[10]
>
> U 7.762

In literature, and conspicuously in films, lighting a cigarette is one of the time-honored standard devices for creating suspense or else to detract from a tense situation. This happens in "Telemachus" when Haines, probably put off by one of Stephen's brusque responses, "stopped and took out a smooth silver case," offered it to Stephen and in elaborate slow motion lit the cigarettes before he resumes the conversation (U 1.615–21).

The second speech held up as a model in the chapter also turns around Moses.[11] It too is carefully staged by J. J. O'Molloy, obviously an ear witness, who reports how

> ... John F. Taylor rose to reply. Briefly, as well as I can bring them to mind, his words were these.
>
> U 7.824

But the words have to wait, and so do the listeners. For a few moments attention is focused on the not-yet speaker. "He raised his head firmly. His eyes bethought themselves once more." The pause leads to a close-up in Stephen's imagination: "Witless shellfish swam in the gross lenses to and fro, seeking outlet" (U 7.826). Only then are the words resumed.

"He began: ..."

Halts during the speech itself are again filled with attention to cigarette smoke and Stephen's reflections, a "dumb belch of hunger," prepares for the peroration (U 7.860). Silence precedes the prominent speech, interrupts and then also ends it. "He ceased and looked at them, enjoying a silence" (U 7.870). Aeolian speeches are carefully framed.

Silentium! (*U* 14.1457)

The first silence in *Ulysses* is part of Buck Mulligan's parody, a mock silence, and a purely imaginary one since he is the only one who so far has said, or declaimed, anything in an otherwise quiet morning scene. He of all people, who vocally dominates the episode, commands, "Silence, all!" (*U* 1.23). The scene he calls up is of a transubstantiation debased into a music hall performance. His mouth, open for a whistle, reveals gold points as though to indicate that silence is proverbially golden. The view is then translated, internally, probably by Stephen, into a Greek epithet, "Chrysostomos," golden-mouthed, a classical epithet that was attributed to excellent speakers.

Mulligan's histrionics contrast with Stephen, who has said nothing so far until he asks, "quietly," "Tell me, Mulligan" (no exclamation mark), and changes the subject to a noise made by the visitor Haines, "raving about a black panther" in the stillness of the night (*U* 1.47–58). It is probably also Buck Mulligan who at the end of "Oxen of the Sun," when the group of men make a precipitate rush to a nearby pub, enjoins "*Silentium!*" (*U* 14.1457). He and Lenehan, the obstinate talkers and jokers, have a monopoly of imposing silences on others.

Silences can be commanded or stopped, or "broken," with equal chances of success. It happens by tacit consent as in "The Dead," when Mr. Browne has tactlessly taken over the conversation:

> As the subject had grown lugubrious it was buried in a silence of the table during which Mrs Malins could be heard saying to her neighbour in an indistinct undertone:
> —They are very good men, the monks, very pious men.
>
> D 201

In a story called "The Dead," where the dispute turns about monks sleeping in their coffins, it is in tune that a subject can be "buried" (*D* 201) in silence.

Orchestrated silence

Gaps in conversation also occur when there is nothing to communicate, as it does in desultory talk between Simon Dedalus and the barmaids of the Ormond hotel in "Sirens." To keep the talk going he expands on a place, Rostrevor, where Miss Douce spent a holiday, and he is neither informative nor entertaining. Pure talk:

—By Jove, he mused, I often wanted to see the Mourne mountains. Must be a great tonic in the air down there. But a long threatening comes at last, they say. Yes. Yes.

U 11.219

A trailing "Yes. Yes" often fills a gap, almost a reflex, a muted exclamation, coming close to a sigh. (As such, it contrasts drastically with other, significant powerful "Yeses" in the book.) It is immediately taken up in a typical tonal link:

> Yes. He fingered shreds of hair, her maidenhair, her mermaid's, into the bowl. Chips. Shreds. Musing. Mute.

U 11.222

This "Yes" may simply carry on the preceding ones, but it also looks like a narrative stocktaking of a moment when nothing is said and attention focuses on trivia like, again, the preparation for a smoke. The one-word series "Chips. Shreds. Musing. Mute" may express groping for something to say, but it equally serves as a narrative repetition, a common meta-feature in "Sirens." The sequence "hair, her maidenhair, her mermaid's,"[12] possibly representing associations among those present, also has the air of a musical embroidery. One of the themes of the episode is that awkward or painful gaps are filled with the distractions of conversation and, dominantly, with music.

Whatever the exact nature of the paragraph (probably impossible to determine with certainty), it does mark a lull emphasized by a triple negation in the next line:

> None nought said nothing. Yes.

U 11.224

Silence is framed by nothing. At that point, it is audibly broken by music:

> Gaily Miss Douce polished a tumbler, trilling:
> —*O, Idolores, queen of the eastern seas!*

U 11.225–6

Silence reigns supreme

An analogous situation occurs in the cabman's shelter in "Eumaeus," where a random group of nocturnal creatures are sitting in relative proximity and where, apart from adventures recounted by a loquacious sailor, casual talk is kept going in the face of general boredom, fatigue, and the discomfort setting in when nothing is spoken. Any pointless remark may serve to dispel it and at times even Bloom steps into the breach with a brave but futile effort:

> A silence ensued till Mr Bloom for agreeableness' sake just felt like asking him whether it was for a marksmanship competition like the Bisley.
>
> *U* 16.406

The sailor's subsequent blunt "Beg pardon?" shows that the atmosphere has not been relieved. Even less successful is the contribution of a cabman, no doubt well intended yet devoid of any interest:

> The cabby read out of the paper he had got hold of that the former viceroy, earl Cadogan, had presided at the cabdrivers' association dinner in London somewhere.
>
> *U* 16.1661

The remark unsurprisingly falls flat and actually leads to increased awkwardness:

> Silence with a yawn or two accompanied this thrilling announcement.
>
> *U* 16.1664

Such social silences lend themselves to strained or lumbering Eumaean articulation:

> Silence all round marked the termination of his finale
>
> *U* 16.1010

> There ensued a somewhat lengthy pause.
>
> *U* 16.601

The awkwardness of the situation affects the heavy-handed expression of a silence or a pause "ensuing." But then it is in the nature of intrusive silences to just "follow" or "take place." It is fitting that in Eumaean parlance, silences or pauses ponderously "ensue," or they "mark" a "termination." Some marked silences thereby become active grammatical subjects (which is not normal usage);[13] they cause at least a sense of being ill at ease. In "The Sisters" already "[a] silence [actively] took possession of the little room" (*D* 17, see above). Silence really comes into its own when in the general prevailing boredom even a minor event is pedantically observed with seemingly full attention to pointless details:

> Some person or persons invisible directed him to the male urinal erected by the cleansing committee all over the place for the purpose but after a brief space of time during which silence reigned supreme[14] the sailor ... eased himself closer at hand ...
>
> *U* 16.937

The "brief space of time" lends particular glamor to the supreme moment, but after a short pause it is bathetically ended by "the noise of his bilgewater ... splashing on the ground."

Tactics of evasion

Certain topics or issues may not be spoken of, either by internal strategy or by tacit collusion. When Bloom is asked about his wife's impending concert tour he is, for understandable reasons, at visible, though often futile, pains not to give away any details in conversation. On two occasions he replies to a very specific question about the tour—"Who's getting it up?"—by evasion. To M'Coy he explains, "It's a kind of tour, don't you see? There's a committee formed ..." (*U* 5.153–63), and in the same vein to Nosey Flynn, "Getting it up? ... Well, it's like a company idea, you see. Part shares and part profits" (*U* 8.773–85). In each case Bloom answers after a short pause and he elides his rival by vague pluralities. As it happens there will be no other mention of either a company or a committee.

The second bedroom scene in "Calypso" is vibrant with issues unstated and tacit agreement while some conversation has to be kept going. When Bloom brings the tea and toast to Molly's bed, he pretends not to know the sender of the letter that has noticeably troubled him when he picked it up: "His quickened heart slowed at once. Bold hand. Mrs Marion" (*U* 4.244). The letter is now conspicuously half hidden, peeping from "under the dimpled pillow." Collusion by definition is something partly concealed. Homerically, the episode is under the aegis of Kalypso, the goddess of hiding. Not to refer to the letter might be more embarrassing for both than an offhand question: "—Who was the letter from?, he asked," while remembering "Bold hand. Marion." The answer is a quick and dismissive, almost overly casual, "O,[15] Boylan, she said. He's bringing the programme" (*U* 4.508). Bloom's next question, "—What are you singing?," poses some problems. How could he not know about Molly's repertoire? Given that she has been long without singing engagements, that moreover the Ulster Hall in Belfast is a highly renowned venue, it seems unlikely that the couple did not discuss the upcoming event before. As we will read later, he knows that "all the topnobbers" will take part, "J. C. Doyle and John MacCormack," so the topic must have come up before (*U* 6.222). If Bloom's question makes sense at all it could only refer to which particular arias the duo might be rehearsing during the visit. Otherwise it appears to be a vacuous attempt to feign normal curiosity.

The programme consists of "*La ci darem . . .*" and "Love's Old Sweet Song" and must be familiar to Bloom, as he instantly associates "*Voglio e non vorrei,*" which he may well have heard his wife singing before. It is intriguing that he knows enough of the aria in Italian to insert a wrong indicative which significantly occurs elsewhere in *Don Giovanni*, "*voglio*" (for an actual "*vorrei*"). The potential mispronunciation of a foreign word is clearly not Bloom's uppermost worry, but it concerns itself with his wife's *will* or want, and as it happens the plain English translation closes the book, "yes I *will* Yes," where it is framed between two Yesses.

After a pause, Molly abruptly changes the subject that is hovering over the whole scene and diverts attention by enquiring about the funeral. Her next move brings up the book she has been reading, where her remark "There's a word I wanted to ask you" may be less due to semantic curiosity than her knowledge of how much her husband likes to hold forth and to instruct, with hardly anyone ever ready to listen. She baits Bloom with a difficult word, "Metempsychosis," and, true to form, he rises to the occasion with didactic persistence though there is little indication of her evincing any interest in his elaborate explication.[16] The trick is so successful that even readers may be deceived. The passage, at any rate, vibrates with what is left out and what, moreover, is a main plot of the novel.

The story "The Boarding House" hinges on a similar collusion, this time between mother and daughter against a trapped victim, but, in contrast to *Ulysses*, the situation is overtly stated: "Polly knew that she was being watched, but still her mother's persistent silence could not be misunderstood" (*D* 63). An elaborate scene of a thematic silence is acted out in perhaps the most contorted passage of all *Dubliners* stories:

> Both had been somewhat awkward, of course. She had been made awkward by her not wishing to receive the news in too cavalier a fashion or to seem to have connived, and Polly had been made awkward not merely because allusions of that kind always made her awkward, but also because she did not wish it to be thought that in her wise innocence she had divined the intention behind her mother's tolerance.
>
> *D* 64

The awkwardness, also of its articulation, is much more conspicuous than the alleged frankness.

Lacunae

A special case of textual silence occurs when something is said but not clearly heard or attended to, or not understood, and therefore not recorded *verbatim*, but results in a blank. In "Telemachus" Stephen, resentful that the milkwoman speaks to Mulligan and not to him, listens "in scornful silence" and hears "the loud voice that now bids her be silent with wondering unsteady eyes" (*U* 1.418). Readers are not told what the loud voice says and what makes Stephen interrupt his otherwise aloof reticence in order to put her to a test:

—Do you understand what he says? Stephen asked her.

U 1.424

Did Haines really want to "bid her be silent" at a moment when he wants to practice his no doubt somewhat elementary Gaelic on the presumed native speaker? Whatever is not spelled out becomes all the more intriguing. But the conversation instantly diverts into the question of what language the statement we did not hear is spoken in and the conversation turns on the complicated historical relationship between Ireland, England, and France and their respective languages. Ironically the English usurper is the only one in the group who speaks some Irish and it is mistaken for French by an Irishwoman.

Stephen appears to have some notion of what Haines has been articulating. In contrast, Bloom talking to Molly in a vaguely similar situation does not accurately hear what word his wife is actually pronouncing, as his question about "the word" indicates, "—Met him what? he said" (*U* 4.335), referring back to sounds made that are not part of the text, another blank. Once the word is seen in print, "Metempsychosis," it becomes clear that Bloom apprehended a garbled phonetic version, or *Wake*-like approximation, which is later rendered as "Met him pike hoses" of multiple suggestiveness (*U* 8.112). The point here is that something voiced that is not correctly absorbed is presented not as it was intended and spoken, but as a lacuna, and therefore only inspected in the sequel. The momentary absence and then garbled reproduction gives the word all the more weight. "Metempsychosis" becomes a companion to the renowned "word known to all men"[17] that haunts the book.

Servile letters

Silences could extend to such trivia as written letters doing duty for phonetic absences, written letters that are not pronounced, or wherever the visual sign does not harmonize with its sound. They occur in both Hebrew and Irish, as "epenthetic and servile letters" (*U* 17.747). Such letters may lead to misspellings: "I have a special nack of putting the noose" (*U* 12.427), "acute neumonia" (*U* 18.727). Inversely they can be inserted by jocular analogy: "Do ptake some ptarmigan" (*U* 8.887).

Epiphanic

The most efficient and incisive silences are where the word itself does not occur, nor any references to the absence of sound or speech. A prime instance is the Christmas dinner scene in *A Portrait* which sets out quietly, though full of tension all along, in a dispute gradually gaining force and acerbity and, no doubt, in volume. It reaches its climax in a furious and loud outbreak: "—God and religion before anything! Dante cried. God and religion before the world!" It is noisily countered by her opponent:

> Mr Casey raised his clenched fist and brought it down on the table with a crash.
> —Very well then, he shouted hoarsely, if it comes to that, no God for Ireland.
> . . .
> Uncle Charles and Mr Dedalus pulled Mr Casey back into his chair again, talking to him from both sides reasonably. He stared before him out of his dark flaming eyes, repeating:
> —Away with God, I say!
>
> *P* 39

It is then that a tense, almost vibrant silence is evoked by mere implication:

> Dante shoved her chair violently aside and left the table, upsetting her napkinring which rolled slowly across the carpet and came to rest against the foot of an easychair.
>
> *P* 39

In tense situations, or "upsetting" ones (the base import of the word is mechanical, and only secondarily emotional), attention focuses on a tangential detail of perception, often a visual one. A wholly insignificant napkinring is watched, breathlessly, in its slow noiseless move across a soft carpet until it comes to a standstill. The seconds seem drawn out, the slow motion (it is here maintained) affecting the speed of reading. That the motion ends with an "*easy*" chair contrasts oddly with the overall markedly uneasy tension, just as "upsetting" clashes with "rest." The hovering silence is experienced, not told. It is abruptly broken by violence and shouting: "Dante turned round violently and shouted down the room, her cheek flushed and quivering with rage" (*P* 39).

The silence is immediate and effective and needs no explicit telling.

Notes

1 There may be a faint echo of "commune with your own heart" (of Psalm 4.4), which at any rate suggests wordless communication.

2 Note again that sherry glasses are "filled out" and that a fireplace is "empty."

3 "I knew that the old priest was lying still in his coffin" circularly corresponds to "I knew that two candles must be set at the head of a corpse" in the opening paragraph (*D* 9).

4 Translations do not easily cope with the "idle chalice": it becomes "*vide*," "*vain*," "*insignificant*" in French, "*vuoto*," "*inutile*," "*inerte*," "*abbandonato*" in Italian, "*inútil*, "*vacio*" or "*desmayado*" in Spanish, and "*leer*" or "*nutzlos*" in German. There is similar doubt about "lying still in his coffin." Is "still" an adjective for not moving or speaking, or else, less likely, a temporal adverb? Translators go both ways and use "*immobile*" in French or Italian, "*still*" in German, but others settle for the adverbial meaning, "*toujours*," "*ancora*," or "*noch*."

5 "But I say unto you, That every idle word [*rhema argon, verbum otiosum*] that men shall speak, they shall give account thereof in the day of judgement" (Mt.12.36). Conceivably Joyce conceals an early hint that words are active and significant.

6 The one of Moses is a "stony effigy in frozen music" (*U* 7.768).

7 The device of turning one or two words into a separate paragraph is typical for "Sirens" where it effectively punctuates the musical arrangement and underlines its elaborate rhythm. One- or two-word paragraphs, abundant in "Sirens," are particularly weighty by stressing intervals.

8 Stage directions can take over this function, as in "Circe": "*Immediate silence*" (*U* 15.1500).

9 The question "Is the editor to be seen?" is answered "Very much so . . . To be seen and heard" (*U* 7.298).

10 In a chapter devoted to rhetoric it might be interesting to count the number of "that's" in the sentence—no fewer than six out of thirty-five words.

11 Moses by his own admission was not a good speaker: "I am not eloquent . . . I am slow of speech, and of a slow tongue" (Exod. 4.10).

12 Bloom later on, eying "a poster, a swaying mermaid smoking mid nice waves" and reading, "Smoke mermaids coolest whiff of all," will also remark on "Hair streaming: lovelorn" (*U* 11.300), another "Sirens" motif.

13 In general usage and in *Ulysses* "silences" occur mainly with prepositions (often "in") or as grammatical objects, but in "Eumaeus" some of them emerge to be the subjects of active verbs.

14 "Supreme reign" is rarely granted except in parodic use, as in the execution scene of "Cyclops" where "general harmony reigned supreme" (*U* 12.1291).

15 The register and pitch of the various O's or Ah's in *Ulysses* might be worth a separate study.

16 The word "metempsychosis" in Molly's ignorant adaptation, "Met him pike hoses" (*U* 4.336, 8.112), has overtones of suggestive female clothing, "hoses," while "Met him" may well anticipate the imminent meeting. Surprisingly Bloom is familiar with the theosophical term, while an astronomical one, "Parallax," gives him pause (*U* 8.110). Bloom's correct definition, "That means the transmigration of souls," could have been taken straight out of Walker's *Pronouncing Dictionary*, which Gerty MacDowell once consulted (*U* 13.342): "The transmigration of the soul into the bodies of other animals as taught by Pythagoras ... and still believed in some parts of the East'; see B. H. Smart (1860: 379). Bloom goes on to explain, "Some people believe ... that we go on living in another body ... They used to believe you could be changed into an animal or a tree, for instance," at which point he unwittingly diverts into metamorphosis, a similar Greek word (*U* 4.362–77).

17 Most scholars, but not the present writer, know what "that word known to all men" (*U* 3.435, 9.429, 15.4192) is. Not known, it would be all the more tantalizingly powerful.

References

Smart, B. H. (1860), Walker's *Pronouncing Dictionary of the English Language*, 6th edn, London: Longman & Co (first published 1846).

2

Joyce's Art of Silence in *Dubliners* and *A Portrait of the Artist as a Young Man*

Laura Pelaschiar

> OTHELLO   I do believe it, and I ask your pardon.
>   Will you, I pray, demand that demi-devil
>   Why he hath thus ensnared my soul and body?
> IAGO   Demand me nothing: what you know, you know:
>   From this time forth I never will speak word.
>
> *Othello*, V, 2, 344–9

Iago's famous refusal to explain why he has "thus ensnared" Othello's body and soul and Shakespeare's contextual choice of eternal silence are possibly *Othello*'s most legendary features and the source of much critical commentary. They are also the icing on the cake of Iago's perfect trap and one of Shakespeare's many strokes of genius. More to the point, they are one of the most famous literary examples of the principle that silence, when properly managed, is as effective and powerful a means of communication (and seduction) as words are. In literature, a masterful control of the challenging rhetoric of silence is an undisputable sign of greatness.

Beginning with Hugh Kenner's "The Rhetoric of Silence" (1977), silence has long been an object of critical attention in Joyce studies, and understandably so, since in Joyce's works it plays, not surprisingly, a major role. Especially in a post-structuralist era, silence has been more often *culturally* considered than *textually* investigated and it has profitably been intercepted by sophisticated philosophical lenses and transformed into a vastly complicated topic. A remarkable example of this treatment of silence is Sam Slote's *The Silence in Progress of Dante, Mallarmé and Joyce* (1999), where silence is conceptualized within a dense net of theoretical references, including Blanchot, Hegel, Wittgenstein, Derrida, Nancy, Agamben, and others.

In readings inspired by deconstructive perspectives, silence is seen as the inevitable choice in a world which has become painfully aware of the insufficiencies of language and of the unreliability of human communication. From this perspective, with the crisis of shared normative values and the loss of long-standing traditions, and in times of profound communicational disorientation, enigmatic languages, fragmented structures, and textual silences are the only inevitable (if perhaps temporary) option. This is why the central claim of Slote's book is that writing silence—the expression of the artist's apophatic condition and experience—is the very project which Dante, Mallarmé, and Joyce, through all their difficulty and obscurity, try to achieve. Similarly, Jean-Michel Rabaté's conclusion in his study of silence in *Dubliners* is that "*Dubliners* and *Ulysses* manifest the mutism of a world condemned to silence by the destruction of centered values" (Rabaté 1982: 46–7).

Silence has also been inspirational for critics—such as Anne Fogarty, Kevin Whelan, and Nels Pearson—who focus on political readings of the Joyce canon and who, working within the critical frameworks of gender studies and post-colonial studies, envisage in the multifarious rhetorics of silence the signs and traces of diverse forms of subalternity, loss, and displacement.

Yet silence can mean several things in a text. It can refer to textual or poetic silence, in other words to those caesuras, metaphors, and ellipses by which the text intentionally omits and skips scenes or details in the narration or in the plot; it can indicate human silence, in the form of unuttered and semi-uttered sentences or even refusal or impossibility to speak on the part of the characters; it can entail overt or covert acoustic absence or lack of noise and sounds in specific narrative moments or sections of the narration. In Joyce, all of these forms and figures of silence are present and meaningful.

I would like to begin by suggesting that Joyce became aware of the power of silence as a narrative device in a specific moment very early on in his career, and that this moment is the revision of the short story "The Sisters."[1] "The Sisters" is an interesting case in terms of genetic studies because it is the only story of *Dubliners* that Joyce reworked extensively and over a significant amount of time[2] (Walzl 1973). Several critics have analysed the transformations from the 1904 *Irish Homestead* version to the 1914 *Dubliners* format: Hugh Kenner (1956), Therese Fischer (1971), Florence Walzl (1973), and William Johnsen (1997), to name a few. Other scholars have written on the changes from different angles and perspectives, though L. J. Morrissey's detailed 1986 analysis is perhaps the most extensive scrutiny of the narrative effects of Joyce's alterations.

Indeed, a comparison between the 1904 edition and the 1914 published version shows how remarkable and radical the stylistic transformation is. My claim is that it is in the course of this revision that Joyce discovers and expands the potential of the rhetoric of silence, while also contextually beginning a representational custom by which it is mainly the feminine sphere which "speaks" through silence and which is characterized, both passively and actively, by wordlessness or by its predictable and negative opposite, excess of speech, inopportune lack of silence.

"The Sisters" is a powerful story because what lies at its heart is an enigma. The sense of mystery which haunts the text is mainly achieved by the rhetorical stratagem which Joyce adopts in the later version, loading the story with multiple instances of aposiopesis. Most of the overt examples of this linguistic device appear at the beginning and at the end, in Old Cotter's and Eliza's truncated sentences. It is not silence proper, nor is it a passage from "reliable to unreliable narrator," as these changes have been interpreted to mean in, for instance, Therese Fischer's essay (1971). Joyce's rhetoric in "The Sisters" is in fact an intentional and ad infinitum suspension of meaning, with some of the speakers in the text refusing to deliver the closing words of their sentences, and their listeners—both intratextual, that is, the other characters, and extratextual, that is, us readers—struggling to find them.

In the 1914 version, Old Cotter's cryptic language sets the atmosphere and turns the story into a mystery text. Joyce's rhetorical choice provokes a reaction in the reader, activating a tense hermeneutic frustration, a readerly restlessness, and a Lacanian symptom: a need to find *the* answer to a question which (at least at the beginning) is just as unidentifiable as the answer itself, a desire to detect or imagine or at least supply the missing words, to complete Old Cotter's unfinished sentences and find the solution for that exasperating suspension of meaning. But this answer will never come in a proper, or in *its* proper final and *authorized* form because neither Old Cotter, nor Joyce, nor the text itself in any of its many elaborations, will ever yield it to us. Not unlike what happens with Iago's perennial silence, the non-stop interrogation of "The Sisters" and the proliferation of plausible and possible answers to its impossible, implausible questions constitutes the text's main force. So the pathological discourse identified by Doherty (1998: 660) as one of the two split narratives of the story does not concern our Joycean "imperfect speaker" (to borrow a Shakespearean term), but rather it infiltrates the reader's mind, just as the patient's symptom "infiltrates" the analyst. From this point of view, it becomes clear how "The Sisters" works like no other Joycean text as the perfect entry into, if not a prefiguration of (in the biblical sense of the word), what is still to come: *Finnegans Wake*, a text made of words with multiple meanings but no stable and final significance, functions according to the same principle.

This powerful hermeneutical effect was not even remotely present in the 1904 version, where the kitchen scene, with the three adults talking and the boy listening to their conversation, is much shorter and there is no sign of that disjointed narrative relating strange events. Old Cotter speaks very clearly, leaves not one single sentence unfinished and makes no reference to the relationship between the boy and the priest, the nature of which does not seem to bother him in the slightest. What's more, Old Cotter's good-mannered reference to the priest's insanity does not communicate any sense of doubt or ambiguity:

> "Without a doubt. Upper storey (he tapped an unnecessary hand at his forehead)—gone".
> "So they said. I never could see much of it. I thought he was sane enough".
> "So he was, at times", said Old Cotter.
>
>   9

The conversation follows without interruptions and no silence at all, which means that the "reader's ethical dilemma," as Margot Norris calls the push that we feel to decide whether the relationship is guilty or innocent (2003: 22), was not part of the earlier text.

In the second version, Cotter is transformed into a totally different character whose reticence originates one of the greatest mysteries of Joyce's texts.

> —No I wouldn't say he was exactly ... but there was something queer ... there was something uncanny about him. I'll tell you my opinion ...—
>
>   9

And later on:

> "I have my own theory about it", he said. "I think it was one of those ... peculiar cases ... But it's hard to say ...".
>
>   10

And again:

> "It's bad for children", said old Cotter, "because their minds are so impressionable. When children see things like that, you know, it has an effect ...".
>
>   11

While it is impossible not to experience in the reading of this short story the endurable impact of unknowable utterances, it is also difficult not to fall prey to the suspicion that what is unuttered—a content which is known to the speaking character but not to the listeners or the reader—is too unacceptable from a moral, cultural, and religious point of view to be fully verbalized.

"The Sisters" deals with these forbidden, unspeakable areas of the human. The "grammar" of silence returns in the final part of the story when the boy narrator is taken to the house of mourning by his aunt to pay his respects to the Flynn sisters. The house is inhabited by two shadowy, silent, enigmatic female figures and invaded by an unsettling silence which Joyce intensified in the later versions. In the 1904 version, Nannie prays "noisily"; in the 1914 version, the boy refuses to eat the crackers because he thought he "would make too much noise eating them" (15). In the 1904 version, the boy's aunt is much more talkative: "my aunt spoke a great deal, for she is a bit of a gossip-harmless," while in the final version she is silent like all the others ("No one spoke: we all gazed at the empty fireplace," 15). Originally, the conversation between Eliza and the aunt took place without any interruption in between the verbal exchanges; in the later version, many pauses are inserted, and Eliza becomes a much more enigmatic talker, a sphinx-like figure who speaks and pauses at random, entering trance-like states of silence during which she communes with the past (17) and falls into deep reverie (17). Of course, one must never forget that what Eliza is talking about, and what the story revolves around, is death, yet this is not the most unsettling element of the scene; it is the narration of the chalice episode—the breaking of which, according to Eliza's reading of things, precipitated James's decline—which brings the story to its climax. The night scene of the three men entering the dark chapel with a light and their discovery of the mad priest laughing to himself in the gloom of his confession box is so disquieting that even Eliza stops again, this time "suddenly" "as if to listen" (18)—another creepy detail which was added in the later edition—expecting to hear the dead brother come to life in his coffin, while silence is once again all that there is to listen to.

As Cheryl Glenn writes in her study of the rhetoricity of silence, "[l]ike the zero in mathematics, silence is an absence with a function" (2002: 263). Fritz Senn expresses a very similar concept when he comments on Joyce's choice of leaving the three first-person narrators of "The Sisters," "An Encounter," and "Araby" nameless: "[t]he technique of gnomic elision or silence" he writes, "extends to names: one that is pointedly withheld seems to assume even more power than those known" (Senn 1995: 11). Indeed, after the in-depth exploration of this "absence with a function" in the revision of "The Sisters," silence will take multifarious forms and shapes in Joyce's texts.

I would like to suggest that, after the "The Sisters," *Dubliners* displays an enticing diversity in its rhetoric of silence and that, when connected to female characters and female texts, this rhetoric acquires a distinctly sophisticated and articulated meaning which I propose here to explore.

There are only four stories in *Dubliners* which feature a female protagonist—"Eveline," "The Boarding House," "Clay," and "A Mother"—but they are not the only textual spaces where silence and the feminine amalgamate to create meaning. By suggesting that female characters' muted words and soundless moments are particularly meaningful, I do not mean to say that silence is gendered, but rather the opposite: through the different forms of silence which can be found in Joyce's work, female characters acquire *more textual power*: a paramount example of this could be the "Penelope" episode in *Ulysses*, where no single word is uttered by anybody and which takes place in complete acoustic isolation, except for the two trains which Molly hears whistling in the distance: "frseeeeeeeefronnnng train somewhere" (*U* 18.596) and "Frseeeeeeeeeeeeeeeeeeeeeefrong theres that train far away" (*U* 18.874).

Like "Penelope," "Eveline" takes place in almost complete human silence. Words are almost entirely absent, except for the three that Frank pronounces at the end of the story ("Come!" and "Eveline! Evvy!," 41) and those which the protagonist remembers from the past: her father's comments on the nameless priest of the yellowing photograph ("—He is in Melbourne now," 37), his sarcastic remark about Frank ("—I know these sailors chaps, he said," 39), Miss Gavin's acidic rebukes, and her mother's meaningless words the "last night of her illness" ("Derevaun Seraun! Derevaun Seraun!," 40). Eveline says nothing in the story and silence is what defines her from beginning to end. Yet, as with Molly's monologue, the narrative is totally dominated by her psyche, and her silence at the North Wall might as well be an instrument to exercise an *active* choice in an apparently *passive* act, rather than a *passive* mode of performing paralysis, since, consciously or not, Eveline manages to avoid the deadly risk of falling victim to potentially dangerous and exploitative Frank, if critics who cast him as a liar and a seducer are to be believed.

"The Boarding House" is another female-centered story in which silence turns out to be textually and narratively relevant. Like the two Flynn sisters in "The Sisters," mother and daughter in "The Boarding House" communicate in an intentionally silenced form, and it is this muted understanding which sits at the core of the sinister web of seduction arranged by the two women to trap Bob Doran.

> Things went on so for a long time and Mrs. Mooney began to think of sending Polly back to typewriting when she noticed that something was going on between Polly and one of the young men. She watched the pair and kept her own counsel.

Polly knew that she was being watched, but still her mother's persistent silence could not be misunderstood. There had been no open complicity between mother and daughter, no open understanding but, though people in the house began to talk of the affair, still Mrs. Mooney did not intervene.

63

"Persistent silence," "no open complicity," "no open understanding": the syntax of the phrases underscores the covert, non-verbal, clandestine collaboration between Polly Mooney, the "little perverse Madonna" (63), and her mother, the "butcher's daughter" (61), and heightens the semantic effects of the text. As with the mysterious and possibly perverse relationship between the boy and the priest in the "The Sisters," the silence with which the text "un-represents" the wicked nature of the mother-and-daughter muted deal makes the text more powerful, the two female characters more sinister and therefore more narratively enticing. Like in "The Sisters," it is the reader's job to recognize the nature of the silent arrangement and to morally classify it, since the text itself, thanks to the very wordlessness of the transaction, is utterly covert and therefore neutral.

In "Clay," too, Joyce employs yet another form of meaningful silence: omission. Maria, the old and unattractive protagonist of the story, famously mis-sings Arline's aria *I Dreamt that I Dwelt in Marble Halls*, and instead of singing the second stanza, she proceeds to sing the first stanza twice. This is a cunningly covert form of silence which the text somehow disguises, or hides, as the reader's attention is diverted away from the omission and directed towards its rhetorical opposite, that is, repetition: "She sang I Dreamt that I Dwelt, and when she came to the second verse she sang again ... But no one tried to show her mistake" (*D* 109). Maria's mistake is thus presented not with a direct reference to what she *does not* sing, which is *the* relevant absence, but with a direct mentioning of what she sings *twice*. So it is once again up to the alert reader to understand that repetition here *also*—and possibly even *in the first place*—means omission, to fill the gap and finally explain why what has been silenced has indeed been silenced. As many critics have suggested,[3] since she does not sing the lines which make clear reference to happiness and marriage, Maria's "mistake" is very likely an attempt, conscious or unconscious, to avoid explicit references to what her own existence has never had and therefore to the emptiness, futility, and disappointment of her sad and lonely life. As in "Eveline," in "The Boarding House," and, as we shall see, in "The Dead," female silence is contiguous to the motif of romance (whether aborted or fulfilled) and, as in the other stories, it functions as a very efficient intensifier of the hermeneutical power of the text, as the mass of critical attention given to Maria's mistake clearly shows.

In "A Mother," the fourth female-centered story of the collection, Joyce turns his female rhetoric of silence upside down. It is here that his least likable female creation, Mrs. Kearney, is introduced, and her most evident defining feature is *lack* of silence and *excess* of words. In Jane E. Miller's positivizing feminist reading, Mrs. Kearney's wordiness is labelled in affirmative terms as "outspokeness" (Miller defines her as a "strong, outspoken woman," 350). There is little doubt that in "A Mother" Mrs. Kearney does most of the talking and that the vast majority of the verbs connected to her belong to the semantic field of verbal communication, even when she manages to *restrain* from speaking and keeps quiet ("However, she said nothing and waited to see how it would end," 140; "she had all she could do to keep from asking," 141; "But she knew it would not be ladylike to do that: so she was silent," 141). Her aggressive verbal energy explodes with the climaxing of her rage, and the text becomes completely colonized by her words, reported, reproduced by direct speech, or simply described. Interestingly, Miller reads Mrs. Kearney as the only character in the collection who is actively "attempting to avoid the paralysis that the other characters succumb to" (355); she is a powerful female who dares to trespass the boundaries of a male-dominated public world of business and economics. However, she is defeated because of her gender, and consequently her vocal determination must be seen as positive: "[M]rs Kearney's insistence upon speaking about payments breaks social codes of silence" (358). Miller also sees the protagonist silenced at the end by Mr. Holohan "in that her words are no longer transcribed in the text" (364), yet in reality the text does transcribe more words spoken by her; and if it is true that the story leaves the last disparaging word to her male antagonists, Mr. Holohan and O'Madden Burke, it is equally undeniable that if there is one form of discrimination which Mrs. Kearney is not subjected to by characters and text alike, this is speechlessness.

Perhaps the most famous silence in *Dubliners* is that which comes at the end of "The Dead," and more than one critical investigation has been devoted to this topic, especially by scholars who interpret the text politically and investigate it as a representation of memory and of its disturbing processes. The Irish past with its unspoken secrets of colonial traumas, deprivation, and dispossession—linguistic as well as cultural and territorial—finds a voice through silence and emerges to affect and haunt the present.

From this perspective, the most important silence, in the sense of an unrevealed past, is of course Gretta's tragic Connemara love story. Once again, therefore, silence is connected to the main female character and to the theme of (terminated in this case) romance. Gretta is, indeed, the main agent of the stylistics of silence firstly because it is her revelation about her past which creates the main event of the story and secondly because silence slowly begins to take over when Gretta begins to slide into it, after hearing Bartell D'Arcy's *The Lass of Aughrim*. Anne Fogarty reads Gretta's story as disrupted by ellipsis and reluctance to speak, but I would like to problematize this reading by suggesting that Gretta is not a reluctant speaker at all. The text's silent space comes in the final section, with its moving focus on death, the dead, and the dying. Gretta is asleep, Gabriel is meditating on what has just happened between them, and, not unlike Mr. Duffy and his epiphany, he is acquiring through the solitary emotional apprehension of someone else's death a new sense of the choral and the communal, national and otherwise. Outside, snow famously begins to fall. It is on this specific part of the text that post-colonial readings of "The Dead" usually focus. Yet the story, which certainly does move towards this highly symbolic snowy quietness, is the fullest of noises and sounds of the entire collection, with its pages buzzing with human voices, laughter, music, singing, dancing, the clatter of dishes and glasses, and festive conversation: "There was a great deal of confusion, and laughter and noise, the noise of orders and counter-orders, of knives and forks, of corks and glass-stoppers" (197).

In his analysis of sound and satire in "The Dead," Bruce Avery writes that, "[f] or all their paralysis, the characters in the final story of *Dubliners* make plenty of noise" (1996: 409). From a sonic point of view, it is this very abundance of noise which makes the silence of the ending also so meaningful. Yet silence does not really belong to Gretta anymore. She does indeed enter a trance-like state immediately after hearing D'Arcy's song and during the trip to the Gresham; but, as soon as she arrives in her hotel room and Gabriel asks her what she is thinking about, she returns slowly to being vocal and the sad story of Michael Furey is actually told by her in great detail and with no interruptions, apart from those compelled by tears and emotion ("she paused for a moment to get her voice under control and then went on," 221), neither is the telling itself forced upon her by Gabriel ("He did not question her again for he felt that she would tell him of herself," 220). Gretta is articulate in her anamnesis and, once she has overcome her initial shock, she is willing to voice—not to silence—her memories and her past. Silence is not therefore her cipher, nor is it the stylistic code of "The Dead," even though the text ends on a silent note.

Though my contention is that Joyce's most powerful silences are those constructed around the feminine, in *Dubliners* silence is also very significant when articulated around male-centered stories, where it takes on a much darker hue and is mainly connected to motifs of failure, punishment, guilt, sin, and the darker hidden side of the human psyche; a procedure that will also be adopted in *A Portrait of the Artist as a Young Man*, the most intensely male of all of Joyce's texts.

Already in "The Sisters" silence was *also* a defining feature of the young nameless protagonist, who utters only four words in the story—"Who?" and "Is he dead?" (10)—all of them spurious, as he knows perfectly well the answers to the questions he is asking. Nameless male narrators turn out to be *also* reticent talkers, as the boy of "An Encounter" comes across as reluctant a speaker as his predecessor in "The Sisters." The speaking frugality of the boy is in sharp contrast to the unrelenting, sinister, and soliloquizing loquaciousness of the old josser.

Verbal impotence, rather than intentional absence of words, is also a feature of the third and last nameless protagonist of the collection, the boy in "Araby," a story in which silence is mainly acoustic, rather than textual and human; it is all-pervasive and it operates as a powerful objective-correlative for disappointment, failure, belatedness, and emptiness. Strangely positivized in more than one occasion by the young narrator, who finds it congenial to his delusional outpouring of naïve emotions, silence as absence of sound opens the text as a feature belonging to spaces and places: North Richmond Street is a "quiet street except at the hour when the Christian Brothers' School set the boys free" (29) and again "silent" in the following paragraph (30); the house where the boy lives is also utterly soundless ("One night I went into the back drawing room in which the priest had died. It was a dark rainy evening and there was no sound in the house," 31), and this absence of noise is particularly relished by the protagonist during his Oriental reveries ("The syllables of the word Araby were called to me through the silence in which my soul luxuriated and cast an Eastern enchantment over me," 32).

At the end of the story, acoustic silence takes on a negative connotation when the bazaar, instead of buzzing with noises, voices, and music, is eerily noiseless, which the boy associates with the stillness of churches at the end of Mass ("Nearly all the stalls were closed and the greater part of the hall was in darkness. I recognised a silence like that which pervades a church after service," 34). Silence, as verbal and emotional fiasco, also defines the protagonist's relationship with the object of his romantic desire, Mangan's sister: "I had never spoken to her except for a few casual words" (30); "I did not know whether I would ever speak to her or not or, if I spoke to her, how I could tell her of my confused adoration" (31); and "At last she spoke to me. When she addressed the first words to me I was so confused that I did not know what to answer" (31). Absence of sounds in the bazaar and absence of words in the narrator's encounters with the girl are symbols of inadequacy, frustration, and failure.

Little Chandler's "silent" dark side is hinted at from the very beginning in the reiterated revulsion he feels for children.[4] This revulsion is all the more significant in the picture of self-pity, self-delusion, and self-contempt which the story offers through the image of the protagonist's own mouth being crowned—we are told—by a "row of childish white teeth"; it is also a prefiguration of that repressed and aggressive impulse which Little Chandler will not be able to control in the final scene and which he will direct towards his own baby.

His dark side also manifests itself in the strange excitement he feels walking through secondary alleyways, when silence becomes part of a psychological experiment he carries out on himself in order to test his courage and his resistance to fear:

> He had always passed without turning his head to look. It was his habit to walk swiftly in the street even by day and whenever he found himself in the city late at night he hurried on his way apprehensively and excitedly. Sometimes, however, he courted the causes of his fear. He chose the darkest and narrowest streets and, as he walked boldly forward, the silence that was spread about his footsteps troubled him, the wandering, silent figures troubled him; and at times a sound of low fugitive laughter made him tremble like a leaf.
>
> 72

Silence as functional to Chandler's dark side becomes relevant in the closing of the story: it is what the protagonist yearns for when he is left to mind the baby and attempts to read Byron's poems, but is disturbed by the baby's cries. At this point, silence has become part of a sophisticated intertextual architecture which connects Byron's elegy to Joyce's short story. In the poem, the poet imagines himself visiting the grave of a very young girl, Margaret, who died tragically after a fall at the age of fifteen. The elegy, sinisterly entitled "On the Death of a Young Lady," thematizes silence by connecting it to death in the very first lines of the first stanza (*"Hushed are winds and still the evening gloom"*) which, with the first two lines of the second stanza, is all that Tommy manages to read before being interrupted. When the baby wakes up and starts crying, the word "hush" slides directly from Byron's death poem into the pages of "A Little Cloud," a contamination which is not accidental: "He turned from the page and tried to hush it: but it would not be hushed. He began to rock it to and fro in his arms but its wailing cry grew keener" (84). Chandler's frustration turns into anger and then into aggression. The various forms of silence which have coalesced in the final part of the text—the interruption of acoustic silence, the literary connection between silence and the death in Byron's elegy, and Little Chandler's attempt at violently silencing the child—all seem to lead to the disquieting *textual* silence of the suspended sentence which ends the paragraph with triple dots: "He counted seven sobs without a break between them and caught the child to his breast in fright. If it died! … (84). The dots mark the misgiving that the aposiopesis in the narration is once again—as in "The Sisters"—the space for forbidden and unspeakable desires; in other words it is that moment in which Little Chandler wishes, just for the duration of a triple-dot punctuation, for the child to die and to be silenced forever. A thought which is reinforced by the fact that the much more overtly violent ending of "Counterparts" will in fact re-enact the paternal violence which "A Little Cloud" manages to elide.

Absence of sound also seals "A Painful Case," another male-centered text which connects silence to a female death, that of the ghostly deuteragonist, Mrs. Sinico. Like "Eveline," "A Painful Case" is a silent story with no dialogue and very few uttered words, unsurprisingly since Mr. Duffy lives in isolation from his fellow humans. But if James Duffy's life is silent by choice, it contaminates the text and returns with vengeance in the latter part of the story as a sonic, internal condition whereby the protagonist is forced to approach and face his dismal final epiphany. As is well known, Duffy comes very gradually to comprehend the reality of Emily Sinico's (and of his own) mortality and his moral and human implication in it. It is in the total silence of death, symbolically present in the *cold* and *gloom* of the Park, in the *gaunt* trees and in *bleak* alleys, and in the *darkness* of the night, that the dead female character becomes more powerful and the living male protagonist more insignificant:

> He turned back the way he had come, the rhythm of the engine pounding in his ears. He began to doubt the reality of what memory told him. He halted under a tree and allowed the rhythm to die away. He could not feel her near him in the darkness nor her voice touch his ear. He waited for some minutes listening. He could hear nothing: the night was perfectly silent. He listened again: perfectly silent. He felt that he was alone.
>
> 117

Duffy's sin and guilt, and his responsibility in the death of Emily Sinico, are both symbolized and amplified by the "perfectly silent" night to which the text consigns its male protagonist at the end of the story, so that the reader's inevitable repulsion from the main character and the acoustic stillness of the scene reach their climax contemporaneously.

The connection between silence and some form of moral guilt, which was so central in the opening story "The Sisters" and which is clearly revisited in "A Painful Case," will be also developed in *A Portrait of the Artist as a Young Man*. After all, "silence, exile and cunning" is without doubt the most famous syntagm of the novel. Yet, though it is one of the devices which Stephen claims and declares he is going to use as the only "arms of defence" he will allow himself in his future life as an artist, by and large silence is less weighty in *A Portrait* than it is in *Dubliners*, mainly because the voice of the third-person narrator is completely invaded by Stephen's own psyche, and the style follows the protagonist's linguistic development. This also means that in *A Portrait* the external world—other characters, objects, and all that *physically* happens outside Stephen's mind— becomes less pertinent. And since silence, as well as noises and sounds, are external factors, it is not surprising that they do not play a meaningful role in this text. Yet a scrutiny of the rhetoricity of silence in *A Portrait* reveals how consistent and coherent this is with the stylistic choices of *Dubliners*.

Following a practice which he had discovered, explored, and developed in the rewriting of "The Sisters," in *A Portrait of the Artist as a Young Man* Joyce connects once again diverse forms of silence to motifs of sin, guilt, fear, and punishment and to objects and figures representing the Catholic Church and its ideology. Narratively speaking, Dante and Father Arnall are the most important of these figures and, as such, they are also clearly coupled, in the first place by being the most terrifying characters in the novel but also in the power they exercise over Stephen's psyche. Both are associated by the text with fear and with forms of silence.

Interestingly, Dante is the only female character that is allowed some verbal space in what is a coldly minimalistic text when it comes to female characters and voices, even though the noise that she is allowed to make is that of an angry and aggressive Catholic fanaticism, the ideology of which she has thoroughly come to internalize. In line with Joyce's inclination to use silence in connection with the feminine, Dante is the character which introduces the power of silence in the novel. She is initially portrayed as a (powerful) silent character, stubbornly hostile to conversation, prone to antisocial negativity and intentionally and disagreeably short in her responses: when Mr. Dedalus tries to include her in polite conversation during the Christmas dinner scene, she refuses to join in, and it is, indeed, her refusal to chat, in other words her aggressive social silence, that makes her presence so disturbingly strong. Yet she moves from wordlessness to its negative counterpart, that is, surfeit of speech, and becomes pugnaciously fluent (and indeed very similar to Mrs. Kearney in her excessive vocalism) as soon as the conversation veers towards politics, religion, and Parnell's guilt. Thus, intentional silence and antagonistic noise combine in this scene as female discourse markers which intensify the tension, the violence, and the fear of an occasion—the Christmas dinner—which Stephen had looked forward to with great expectations which would be tragically disappointed.

Silence plays a very important role in the following section, when sin, guilt, religion, and deserved or underserved punishment become thematically central. Back in Clongowes Wood College, a "crime" committed by the older boys is discussed by Wells, Athy, and other students in a *muted* conversation which Stephen listens to and tries to make sense of. Silence also defines the atmosphere of the imagined location of the crime, since it is in the "dark silent sacristy" where "you had to speak under your breath" because it is a "holy place" (40) that the older boys have apparently committed their mysterious "deed with no name" (to borrow from *Macbeth*). It is also the form of collective punishment which the boys have to endure for a sin which the text keeps intentionally secret ("Three days' silence in the refectory and sending us up for six and eight every minute," 43). Fear, silence, guilt, punishment return in the Latin lesson episode, during which Stephen is unjustly reprimanded by Father Dolan for not writing his Latin exercises. Again, the text, through the figure of Father Arnall, carefully orchestrates the development of tension through a gradual suspension of noise. Decrease in speech—"Father Arnall became very quiet as each boy tried to answer and could not" (47)—becomes silence proper—"A silence filled the classroom and Stephen, glancing timidly at Father Arnall's dark face, saw that it was a little red from the wax he was in" (47)—and turns finally into the "dead silence" which announces Father Dolan's arrival in the classroom.

Chapters 3 and 4 are "silent chapters" in that the prose obsessively adheres to Stephen's consciousness and little else. Yet in Chapter 3 it is important to notice that this silence serves the purpose of heightening the effect of the only noise/ voice we hear: that of Father Arnall, delivering his lengthy and powerful sermons about hell. Other human voices are muted, every other noise is silenced, and all the textual space available is left to the priest's powerful rhetorical tour de force. Some human communication comes back at the very end of the chapter in the form of confession, and even then Joyce is careful to make silence recede reluctantly from the pages, with noise (human voices) coming back tentatively, as "faint murmur," "murmuring," "soft whispering noise," "whispering cloudlets" in the chapel where Stephen decides to confess.

It is only in Chapter 5, *after Stephen has found his own voice* and has realized that his destiny is to create "proudly out of the freedom and power of his soul, as the great artificer whose name he bore, a living thing, new and soaring and beautiful, impalpable, imperishable" (170), that the text becomes vocal again and leaves its silent, monotonous, and at times heavy mode. The discovery of Stephen's artistic vocation also means that the *voice* of the race whose uncreated conscience he is going to forge is allowed to come back. Noise *as* voices is reintroduced in the cacophonic sounds of the Dedalus household ("His father's whistle, his mother's muttering and the screeches of an unseen maniac were to him now so many voices offending and threatening to humble the pride of his youth. He drove the echoes even out of his heart with an execration," 175), in the voices of Stephen's fellow students, and in the long conversations between Stephen and Davin, Stephen and the Dean of studies, Stephen and Cranly, and Stephen and Lynch, which do turn the final chapter of *A Portrait* into a long Platonic dialogue (*Symposium*, perhaps?), with Stephen in the guise of a young and very vocal Socrates. The way is open to the polyphonic symphony of the hundreds of voices of *Ulysses*.

It is impossible to know whether the fictional artist Stephen Dedalus kept faith with his commitment to silence, as he so boldly announces at the end of *A Portrait*, but there is no doubt that his creator James Joyce honored the immensely expressive potential aesthetics of what might be called eloquent silence, to borrow a fascinating oxymoron used by linguists. After all, it is thanks to the *absolute silence* of "Penelope"—the most noiseless episode in the whole book— that Molly gets to sing her unrestrained, unforgettable, and universally celebrated speechless song.

Notes

1 The 1904 version of "The Sisters" is easily accessible online. In this chapter, I will make reference to the version which appears in the illustrated edition with annotations of *Dubliners* edited by John Wyse Jackson and Bernard McGinley.

2 See discussion by Walzl (1973), especially 375–91.

3 See, for example, Brooks (1964: 60–5), Walzl (1962), Smith (1965), Staley (1966), and Tindall (1971: 29–31).

4 "A horde of grimy children populated the street. They stood or ran in the roadway or crawled up the steps before the gaping doors or squatted like mice upon the thresholds. Little Chandler gave them no thought. He picked his way deftly through all that minute vermin-like life and under the shadow of the gaunt spectral mansions in which the old nobility of Dublin had roistered" (*D* 71–2).

References

Avery, B. (1996), "Distant Music: Sound and the Dialogics of Satire in 'The Dead'," in J. R. Scholes and A. Walton Litz (eds), James Joyce, *Dubliners*, 408–20, London: Penguin.

Brooks, C. et al. (1964), *An Approach to Literature*, 4th edn, New York: Appleton-Century-Crofts.

Doherty, G. (1998), "The Art of Confessing: Silence and Secrecy in James Joyce's 'The Sisters'," *James Joyce Quarterly* 36, no. 1: 657–64.

Fischer-Seidel, T. (1971), "From Reliable to Unreliable Narrator: Rhetorical Changes in Joyce's 'The Sisters'," *James Joyce Quarterly* 9, no. 1: 85–92.

Fogarty, A. (2014), "'I Think He Died for Me': Memory and Ethics in 'The Dead'," in O. Frawley and K. O'Callaghan (eds), *Memory Ireland: James Joyce and Cultural Memory*, 46–61, Syracuse, NY: Syracuse University Press.

Glenn, C. (2002), "A Rhetorical Art for Resisting Discipline(s)," *JAC: A Journal of Composition Theory* 22, no. 2: 261–91.

Johnsen, W. A. (1997), "Joyce's Many Sisters and the Demodernization of Dubliners," in M. Power and U. Schneider (eds), *New Perspectives on Dubliners*, 69–90, Amsterdam: Rodopi.

Joyce, J. (1995), *Dubliners. An Illustrated Edition with Annotations*, ed. J. Wyse Jackson and B. McGinley, London: Sinclair-Stevenson.

Kenner, H. (1977), "The Rhetoric of Silence," *James Joyce Quarterly* 14, no. 4: 382–94.

Miller, J. E. "'O. she's A Nice Lady!': A Reading of 'A Mother'," in James Joyce, *Dubliners*, ed. J. R. Scholes and A. Walton Litz, 348–72, London: Penguin.

Morrissey, L. (1986), "Joyce's Revision of 'The Sisters': From Epicleti to Modern Fiction," *James Joyce Quarterly* 24, no. 1: 33–54.

Norris, M. (2003), *Suspicious Readings of Joyce's* Dubliners, Philadelphia: University of Pennsylvania Press.

Pearson, N. (2005), "Death Sentences: Silence, Colonial Memory and the Voice of the Dead in *Dubliners*," in C. Jaurretche (ed.), *Beckett, Joyce and the Art of the Negative*, 141–70, Amsterdam: Rodopi.

Rabaté, J.-M. (1982), "Silence in *Dubliners*," in C. MacCabe (ed.), *James Joyce: New Perspectives*, 45–72, Bloomington: Indiana University Press.

Romero, J. S. (2012), "Voice and Voices for the Boy in Joyce's 'The Sisters'," http://www.siff.us.es/iberjoyce/wp-content/uploads/2013/11/POJ-121.pdf (accessed January 17, 2017).

Senn, F. (1995), *Inductive Scrutinies: Focus on Joyce*, ed. C. O'Neill, Dublin: Lilliput Press.

Slote, S. (1999), *The Silence in Progress of Dante, Mallarmé, and Joyce*, New York: Peter Lang.

Smith, G. R. (1965), "A Superstition in Joyce's 'Clay'," *James Joyce Quarterly* 2, no. 2: 133–4.

Staley, T. F. (1966), "Moral Responsibility in Joyce's 'Clay'," *Renascence* 18, no. 3: 124–8.

Tindall, W. Y. (1971), *A Reader's Guide to James Joyce*, New York: Noonday Press.

Walzl, F. L. (1962), "Joyce's 'Clay'," *The Explicator* 20, no. 6: 87–91.

Walzl, F. L. (1973), "Joyce's 'The Sisters': A Development," *James Joyce Quarterly* 10, no. 4: 375–421.

Whelan, K. (2002), "The Memories of 'The Dead'," *Yale Journal of Criticism* 15, no. 1: 59–97.

3

What Happens When "The silence speaks the scene" (*FW* 13.3)?

Rosa Maria Bollettieri Bosinelli and Ira Torresi

In "The Aesthetics of Silence," Susan Sontag suggest that "silence remains, inescapably, a form of speech" (1967: 11). That silence is a necessary and meaningful component of language is a fact in Joyce's writings as well as in human communication at large. Without silence (and its graphic counterpart, the blank space), language would only be a sort of continuous white noise, ultimately devoid of any meaning. It is not too far-fetched, therefore, to maintain that silence helps create sound, and language. Silence, however, is also usually unperceived even as it performs its logopoietic function, providing the neutral background against which the spoken or written word—the signifier—comes across in its full and seemingly solid meaning.

But in Joyce, silence often refuses to provide a mere backdrop for the signifier, and claims the scene for itself. One way Joyce makes silence visible is through explicit invitations to hush, as if just before a theatrical play:

Silence, all. (*U* 1.23)

—Silence for my brandnew riddle! (*U* 7.477)

—Silence! What opera resembles a railwayline? (*U* 7.514)

The silence speaks the scene. (*FW* 13.3) List! (*FW* 13.16)

    SILENCE.

Act drop. Stand by! Blinders! Curtain up. (*FW* 501.6–7)

Unlike the written page, theatrical action requires silence to be properly received. If the audience does not oblige, hushing them before a play is therefore necessary for the actors to be heard or understood properly, and for the silences in the script to emerge in all their significance. At the theater, the silence of the audience is a gesture of total attention and absorption in what happens on the stage—the very first condition for the suspension of disbelief. It is perhaps in this sense that the great Italian actor and director, Giorgio Albertazzi, has stated that "the aim of theatre is to reach *audible silence*."[1]

What Joyce appears to do in the previous examples, then, is to change readers into the spectators of a play. He synesthetically evokes an altogether different mode of expression (the spoken and performed, rather than written, word) and a setting that would make it impossible to read from a book (a dark theater audience) only to draw attention to the silence that normally accompanies the experience of reading, which would otherwise go unnoticed. In this way, silence as the absence of speech becomes as solid as words themselves, highlighting that something is missing without describing what it is. In this function, silence works as an epiphany: it brings attention to something that is "wrong," that is not in order or complete. What does remain around that kind of silence is like the figure of the Euclidean *gnomon* mentioned on the first page of "The Sisters." A gnomon, well covered in Joycean criticism,[2] appears to be *missing* one of its parts; but if it did have that part, it would be a parallelogram. Like a human body after paralysis, and not unlike the simony-ridden Catholic Church of the Middle Ages, a gnomon is a figure that *used to be* whole.

What makes the irregular shape of the gnomon relevant—the missing piece, the solid silence embedded in its mass—has a distracting effect: we are drawn to the non-standard shape of what *is* there and so we tend to lose sight of the whole parallelogram that the gnomon used to be; that is, since we are never quite sure of *what* is missing, we notice its absence even more. Similarly, what we are drawn to in Old Cotter's figure is the irritating incompleteness of his speech, made all the more visible and solid by the punctuation that marks his ellipses:

> No, I wouldn't say he was exactly . . . but there was something queer . . . there was something uncanny about him. I'll tell you my opinion . . . (*D* 1)[3]

> I think it was one of those . . . peculiar cases . . . But it's hard to say . . . (*D* 2)

> My idea is: let a young lad run about and play with young lads of his own age and not be . . . Am I right, Jack? (ibid.)

The fragmentation of Father Flynn's speech is explicitly noted by the narrating boy: "I puzzled my head to extract meaning from his unfinished sentences" (*D* 3). Significantly, while the events surrounding Father Flynn's death are recounted by the narrator matter-of-factly and with full detail, the boy's own feelings about his death are silenced, as is the word *die* itself in the aunt's question: "– Did he . . . peacefully? She asked" (*D* 7).

By the end of "The Sisters," "the boy has already learned the use to which language is put—to *conceal*" (French 1978: 448; our emphasis). To conceal what? Of course, to conceal what is inappropriate, socially unacceptable, or taboos such as—recurrently in *Dubliners*—the reasons why life is worth living in full. One such reason is that life ultimately comes to an end, therefore we do not have all the time in the world to do things or experience emotions and feelings. Death is one of the great unspeakables in most human cultures, and it is concealed both by the suppression of direct references to it and by the use of words or details that distract attention from it. The imperative to elide the very mention of death, the desire to keep it (and the anxiety it carries) under the threshold of acknowledgement, can, in itself, be potentially deadly as it happens in the seventeenth scene of the *Epiphanies*:

> [Dublin: in the house in Glengariff Parade: evening]
> Mrs. Joyce—(*crimson, trembling, appears at the parlour door*) . . . Jim!
> Joyce—(*at the piano*) . . . Yes?
> Mrs. Joyce—Do you know anything about the body? . . . What ought I do? . . .
> There's some matter coming away from the hole in Georgie's stomach . . . Did you
> ever hear of that happening?
> Joyce—(*surprised*) . . . I don't know . . .
> Mrs. Joyce—Ought I send for the doctor, do you think?
> Joyce—I don't know . . . what hole?
> Mrs. Joyce (*impatient*) . . . The hole we all have . . . here (points)
> Joyce—(*stands up*)
>
> E XVII[4]

That Joyce's little brother, Georgie, eventually died of peritonitis after a period of fever and sickness, during which his brother—like the rest of the family—had the time to become well aware of what was happening, is a biographical fact (*JJII* 93–4). Regardless of what happened in reality, however, this Epiphany conveys a sense of powerless paralysis and stupor at the onset of an apparently unexpected symptom (pus oozing from Georgie's navel). In this scene, Joyce seems to ignore or negate the medical issue altogether—he is found playing the piano in the parlor and is surprised by his mother's request for indications. Rather than taking responsibility and calling the doctor straight away, a very distressed ("crimson, trembling") Mrs. Joyce talks the matter over with him. In her distress ("what ought I do? . . . Ought I send for the doctor?"), Mrs. Joyce silences the

direct reference to the navel, the omphalos, euphemistically calling it "the hole
we all have" and thus removing the seriousness and medical nature of the
situation even further. Her inability or fear at uttering the words that would
describe the matter in a clear, starker light is mirrored by her failure to act
immediately and, ultimately, by the impossibility of saving the child. Deadly
inaction and the silencing of what is actually happening is masked by a flurry of
words and activities (James's playing the piano, Mrs. Joyce's questions about the
body) that distract from the real issue at stake.

The silencing becomes even more evident in the reuse of the same epiphany
in *Stephen Hero*, where it is accompanied by a more explicit visual counterpart.
The characters are described as faceless, blurred "forms," like presences on a stage
rather than real people with names and distinct individual identities:

> A form which he knew for his mother's appeared far down in the room, standing
> in the doorway. In the gloom her excited face was crimson. A voice which he
> remembered as his mother's, a voice of a terrified human being, called his name.
> The form at the piano answered:
> —Yes?
> —Do you know anything about the body? . . .
> He heard his mother's voice addressing him excitedly like the voice of a
> messenger in a play:
> —What ought I do? There's some matter coming away from the hole in
> Isabel's . . . stomach . . . Did you ever hear of that happening?
> —I don't know, he answered trying to make sense of her words, trying to say
> them again to himself.
> —Ought I send for the doctor . . . Did you ever hear of that? . . . What ought
> I do?
> —I don't know . . . What hole?
> —The hole . . . the hole we all have . . . here.

SH 147

In both transpositions of the same autobiographical event, the mother "appears"
as a ghost or dream. In *Stephen Hero*, she becomes so disembodied, so remote
from the narrator's conscious awareness of the perceivable material world, that
both her form and her voice are not immediately recognized but have to be
retrieved from what the narrator (a mere "form" himself) knows to be his mother,
like a distant, blurred recollection. In this respect, this ineffably evanescent
motherly figure brings to mind another version of Stephen's mother that appears
in the first episode of *Ulysses* as a ghost proper, thoroughly silent. Here, too,
silence as an attribute of being dead is reinforced by a different sensory stimulus

that, this time, is both visual and olfactory, and refers to death through typical metonymies (ashes, and the candles and wooden coffin of the funeral):

> *Silently*, in a dream she had come to him after her death, her wasted body within its loose brown graveclothes giving off an odour of wax and rosewood, her breath, that had bent upon him, *mute*, reproachful, a faint odour of wetted ashes.
>
> U 1.102–5; our emphasis

Like the two Stephens' mothers we have just discussed, the images that intersemiotically translate "The Dead" in the staging by the Italian research theater ensemble, Città di Ebla, are also dreamlike, silent, and blurred, detached from the mundane reality of life.

In this theatrical piece, which is entirely silent, the narrative representation of the story is replaced by a series of photographs taken in real time, a sequence of frozen moments that appear on a milky screen that is interposed between the stage and the audience. Some action, therefore, does take place with the precise, clear lines and three-dimensional, solid shapes of real life. Yet, that action cannot be accessed directly by the spectator, who is left to interpret it through the discontinuous language of two-dimensional photographs that are weightless, yet larger than life.

The milky screen therefore seems an apt embodiment of the snow "falling faintly . . . faintly falling" at the end of Joyce's story, and also of the "white silence" mentioned in the "Hades" episode of *Ulysses* (U 6.461). It is against that white silence backdrop that Gretta appears as a giant blurred figure at the beginning of the play (Città di Ebla 2013, minute 3:48 on). The equally blurred figures of the dead appear at the end (from minute 7:37 on), in a powerful visual echo of Thomas Dennany's funeral monuments in *Ulysses*:

> Crowded on the spit of land silent shapes appeared, white, sorrowful, holding out calm hands, knelt in grief, pointing. Fragments of shape, hewn. In white silence: appealing.
>
> U 6.459–61

Once again, then, silence and its synesthetic counterparts, here visual (whiteness) and tactile/proxemic (immobility, gestures of pitiful appeal), have the precise role of marking a divide between the real life and the realms of death. With all their "appealing" poses, the funeral statues are confined to their enclosed "spit of land," and Stephen's mother in *Ulysses* can only visit him "in a dream." By contrast, in the Epiphany XVII, *Stephen Hero*, "The Sisters," and "The Dead" (in both Joyce's and Città di Ebla's version), silence and its visual accompaniment of indistinct shapes contribute to the sense of paralytic inaction by hiding or confusing events that invariably have to do with death. Readers and viewers are left to observe the (in)action as if behind a frosted glass pane, led to wonder about what would fill the three dots on the page, pushed to try and bring those blurry images into sharper focus. In so doing, they, like the characters in the stories, miss the "real" point—that someone is dying or had died and that something may be done, or might have been done. In the Epiphany XVII and *Stephen Hero*, a doctor might still be called for Georgie/Isabella; in *Ulysses*, Stephen might have mediated between his mother's religiousness and his principles; and in "The Sisters" and "The Dead," so much more might be brought to open discussion so as to remove the cumbersome veil of paralysis and incompleteness that weighs on all the characters' lives (such as the role of the Catholic Church, priests in general, and Father Flynn; the importance of the body vs. the spirit; and the sense of guilt at having unwittingly caused death).

What happens when "silence speaks the scene," then, can be unspeakable. Silence is a cover for what must stay off-scene, a membrane separating what can be shown in the scene (part of public life) and what must be left behind the scene. After all, silence and, in general, suppression of everything loud (from voices and laughter to colors) is part of the unwritten funeral rituals in most parts of the world and certainly in most Western cultures. In the Zoroastrian tradition of sky burials, corpses were actually taken to the top of tall buildings (dakhmas) to be eaten by birds and thus be physically removed from the world, far from the perception of the living. Dakhmas were accordingly, and euphemistically, called "towers of silence"—and it appears that their mention in "Hades" is no coincidence:

> Where is that Parsee tower of silence? Eaten by birds. Earth, fire, water. Drowning they say is the pleasantest.

U 6.987

The parallel that immediately comes to mind is, of course, the Tower of Babel, as pointed out by Katharina Hagena (2005)—the noisiest and liveliest of towers, but also one where so many languages are spoken at the same time that mutual understanding becomes impossible, and therefore functional silence ensues: "voices blend and fuse in clouded silence: silence that is the infinite of space" (*U* 14.1078).

The intentional use of silence as a precise narrative device implies that Joyce was perfectly aware of the deadly potential of silence. Silence, as we have seen, can be the death of speech as carrier of action (silence is paralysis), as Joyce repeats across his prose. This, however, leads us to look critically at another way in which he actively used silencing strategies in his own life as well as in his writing. Let us consider Joyce's well documented attitude to language spoken in his own country:

> I have been at the theatre with my father and sister—a wretched play, a disgusting audience . . . I felt proud to think that my son—mine and yours, that handsome little boy that you gave me, Nora—will always be a foreigner in Ireland, a man *speaking another language* and bred in a different tradition.
>
> *Letters II* 255; our emphasis

As we know, during the years he spent in Trieste, Joyce chose the Triestine dialect as his home and everyday language (McCourt 2004: 112)—so much so, that in this letter, dated October 27, 1909, he predicts that his son will grow up speaking a language other than English. From the letter to Nora, above, we can deduce that he did so to silence and remove from his own private and family life a specific cultural identity: his own Irishness ("my soul is in Trieste . . . I loathe Ireland and the Irish," *SL* 255). We now know that this endeavor was not successful, since his son did come to participate both in the English language and Irish culture. Ironically, today James Joyce himself is regarded as one of the most central figures of Irish literature and identity.[5] The content of the letter thus remains largely wishful thinking, but its author's intention of sentencing the English language to death by silence is all too clear. Joyce's dismay at the direction of the Irish theater and cultural scene, coupled with his conscious effort at excluding English from his Triestine family life, seems a mirror reflection of the deletion of the Irish language that was perpetrated by the English colonizers of the Emerald Isle, one of the ways in which the invaders crippled—paralyzed—the identity and culture of the colonized (Bollettieri Bosinelli 2008).[6] As is well known, what Joyce "loathed" about Ireland and the Irish was their sense of helplessness and resignation at not having a voice of their own, using the language of the oppressor ("so familiar and so foreign," "an acquired speech," as Stephen famously puts it; *P* 189), and living inauthentic lives, incomplete like a *gnomon*, as deadly as unspoken words.

In Joyce's life as well as across his works, then, silence "appear[s] as the end, the limit, the death of speech, its paralysis," as notes Rabaté (1982: 45). As a narrative device, we have argued that making silence audible and visible, through dots that mark ellipses or through images of immobility or fading into white, is also a way to bring to the fore the process of removing death from the threshold of one's conscious thoughts and public life. Thus, restoring silence, the unsaid, to its rightful semiotic importance, Joyce imbues it with an existential and political significance and teaches us that silence or emptiness are never quite silent or empty, and that, as linguistic beings, we humans are forever condemned to meaning-making. In the words of John Cage, "There is no such thing as an empty space or an empty time. There is always something to see, something to hear. In fact, try as we may to make a silence, we cannot" (Cage 1939: 8).[7]

Notes

1 "Che tempo che fa," Rai 3, May 11, 2014 (our translation and emphasis).
2 See for example Albert (1990), Herring (1987: 3–4), Benstock (1988), and Eide (2002: 34–5).
3 References in this chapter are to *Dubliners*, with an introduction and notes by T. Brown, London: Penguin (1992).
4 References in this chapter are to *Epiphanies*, with introduction and notes by O. A. Silverman, Buffalo (NY): University of Buffalo (1956). We are grateful to Carlo Avolio for bringing to our attention this *Epiphany* by including it in his book of translations (Joyce 2014: 50).
5 See Torresi (2013) for a discussion of the transition of James Joyce from the outskirts to the very center of the Irish literary and cultural polysystems.
6 This process was so successful that even during the Celtic Revival the English translations of Celtic Irish sagas forced the Irish epics into English and classical frameworks (Tymoczko 1999: 90–121).
7 We are grateful to Morris Beja for mentioning this quote in replying to our paper at the 2014 James Joyce Symposium in Utrecht.

References

Albert, L. (1990), "Gnomology: Joyce's 'The Sisters,'" *James Joyce Quarterly* 27, no. 2: 353–64.

Benstock, B. (1988), "The Gnomonics of *Dubliners*," *Modern Fiction Studies* 34, no. 4: 519–39.

Bollettieri Bosinelli, R. M. (2008), "James Joyce and the Trans-Creation of the Word," in M. B. Papi, A. Bertacca, and S. Bruti (eds), *Threads in the Complex Fabric of Language: Linguistic and Literary Studies in Honour of Lavinia Merlini Barbaresi*, 59–68, Pisa: Felici.

Cage, J. (1939), "Experimental Music," in *Silence: Lectures and Writings by John Cage* (1961), 7–12, Middleton, CT: Wesleyan University Press.

Città di Ebla (2013), *The Dead*. Video on the making of the theatrical play, http://vimeo.com/59218656 (accessed January 13, 2017).

Eide, M. (2002), *Ethical Joyce*, Cambridge: Cambridge University Press.

French, M. (1978), "Missing Pieces in Joyce's *Dubliners*," *Twentieth Century Literature* 24, no. 4: 443–78.

Hagena, K. (2005), "Towers of Babble and of Silence," in A. Fogarty and T. Martin (eds), *Joyce on the Threshold*, 187–99, Gainesville: University of Florida Press.

Herring, P. F. (1987), *Joyce's Uncertainty Principle*, Princeton, NJ: Princeton University Press.

Joyce, J. (1956), *Epiphanies*, with introduction and notes by O. A. Silverman, Buffalo, NY: Lockwood Memorial Library, University of Buffalo.

Joyce, J. (1992), *Dubliners*, with introduction and notes by T. Brown, London: Penguin.

Joyce, J. (2014), *Epiphanies/Epifanie*, trans. C. Avolio, Florence: Clinamen.

McCourt, J. (2004), *James Joyce: Gli anni di Bloom*, trans. V. Olivastri, Milan: Mondadori. Trans. of J. McCourt (2000), *The Years of Bloom: James Joyce in Trieste 1904–1920*, Dublin: Lilliput Press.

Rabaté, J.-M. (1982), "Silence in *Dubliners*," in C. MacCabe (ed.), *James Joyce: New Perspectives*, 45–72, Bloomington: Indiana University Press.

Sontag, S. (1967), "The Aesthetics of Silence," in *Styles of Radical Will* (2002), 3–34, New York: Picador.

Torresi, I. (2013), "The Polysystem and the Postcolonial: The Wondrous Adventures of James Joyce and his *Ulysses* Across Book Markets," *Translation Studies* 6, no. 2: 217–31.

Tymoczko, M. (1999), *Translation in a Postcolonial Context: Early Irish Literature in English Translation*, Manchester: St. Jerome.

4

In the Beginning Was the Nil: The "eloquence of silence" in *Finnegans Wake*

Laurent Milesi

Speech is of Time, Silence is of Eternity
Carlyle, *Sartor Resartus*

Decades of diligent textual and genetic exegesis have established that Joyce's last work is a compendium of at least seventy-odd idioms that dramatize the origins of language, between Adamic "prefall paradise peace" (*FW* 30.15)—the infancy (from Latin *infari*: not to speak) of language or the language of infancy (see Wolff 1979)—and postlapsarian glossolalia, as well as between post-Babelian linguistic fall (xenolalia) and the ceaselessly deferred promise of a Pentecostal atonement (xenoglossia).[1] However, less at the forefront of critics' attention, despite some significant studies of Joyce's thematic programming of a performative silence in his earlier fiction,[2] is the more surprising dialectic of language and silence, that other of language, in such a verbose, polyglottal text as *Finnegans Wake*, where it intersects with several conspicuous motifs, such as the quest for the origin of the Nile (nil) and female sexuality, or the various instances of textual-historical "gaps," some in the form of a dramatic radio interruption (e.g. *FW* 500–1). Universally glorified for its unique post-Babelian medley of tongues, *Finnegans Wake* wishes to remind us on well over fifty separate occasions that "silence" is an important constituent of, and necessary background to, any linguistic activity.

I shall retrace briefly how these suspensive textual figures can be seen in conjunction with the problematic of (the origin of) language as indissociable from, and even capable of returning to, silence. Set against a background of oft-parodied linguistic or philosophical theories or models, the Wakean dynamics of language and silence informs the thematics underpinning the text's narrative fabric: the division and dissemination of the (male) Logos, the quasi-alchemical operations turning word into flesh or vice versa, the silence versus vocalization of the feminine, or the ironic use of linguistic-cultural gender stereotypes (e.g. male consonants vs. female vowels).[3] Voicing silence or silencing the voice: such is the *Wake's* double bind, which this short critical odyssey will adumbrate, before some reflections on how Joyce's "final" text, in mapping the performative aporias of the figuration of language against a ground of silence, prefigures the "rhetoric of silence" increasingly evoked by later critics as the necessary performative dimension and duty of post-war literature.

The secret(ion) of silent origins[4]

There is no better place to approach the relationship between language and silence in the cyclical structure of *Finnegans Wake* than at the point of its ending-as-(re)beginning, when the first half of the "first" sentence loops back, after a silent interruption, to the second half. About the novel's disclosure, Joyce famously remarked:

> In *Ulysses* ... in order to convey the mumbling of a woman falling asleep, I wanted to finish with the faintest word that I could possibly discover. I found the word *yes*, which is barely pronounced, which implies consent, abandonment, relaxation, the end of all resistance. For *Work in Progress*, I tried to find something better if possible. This time I discovered the most furtive word, the least stressed, the weakest in English, a word which is not even a word, which barely sounds between the teeth, a breath, a mere nothing, the article *the*.
>
> quoted in Gillet 1958: 111

In Heideggerian fashion, although avowedly following Vichian signposts appropriate for our reading of *Finnegans Wake*, Edward Said has established a dialectical relation between a more historical, human, active beginning, "*the first step in the intentional production of meaning*," an identification after the fact, and a more secret, sacred, unreachable, passive antecedent or origin:[5]

> In attempting to push oneself further and further back to what is only a beginning, a point that is stripped of every use but its categorization in the mind as beginning, one is caught in a tautological circuit of beginnings about to begin ... Because it cannot truly be known, because it belongs more to silence than it does to language ... it is therefore something of a necessary fiction.
>
> Said 1975: 76–7

The word "origin" itself may be traced back to the Indo-European root *er- (ar* in Skeat, Joyce's usual source for etymology), "to move, set in motion," and its extended form *rei-*, to flow, run, and thus may be said to have implied "originally" a displacement, a flow and flowing out, Joyce's "riverrun."[6] The derived Latin form *origo*, from *oriri*, to rise, logically came to mean at once "beginning," "source," "origin," in a perpetual tension of priority that the *Wake's* language and narrative attempts to capture. Thus, *Finnegans Wake*, at once cyclical and deferred, "blur[s] the distinction between beginning and beginning-again, or writing and rewriting, or positive text and interpretation" (Said 1975: 222); or, in the words of another critic, "begets only beginnings but invalidates all origins" (Rabaté 1984: 79). When, at the end of Book IV, water (Δ) is sucked up into cloud only to drop again as ⊣ (*FW* 628.11), the *Wake's* continuous linguistic integument is ruptured by the silence-as-return, from which language arose and to which it is condemned to revert. Before the (re)beginning, at the origin before source on the last leaf of the text, ALP's stuttering fear of shedding her leaves or *leaving* (dying) turns into a metaphor for the text's own wish to be remembered, not to die (*FW* 628.06–07). ALP's drifting towards her "riverrun" primes the text's linguistic return, mixing textual, sexual, and fluvial origin-and-ending.

Language, sex, and water are also conspicuously intermingled in the washerwomen's garrulous talk about HCE's scurrilous life in "Anna Livia Plurabelle" (*FW* I.8), where they are busy washing his dirty linen, literally as well as figuratively. Their diluted "lavguage" (*FW* 466.32) turns into an ever-widening barrage of words which streams away from the source (*FW* 196.01), the first drop as well as the first letter uttered after the question following the dumb's access to speech at the end of *FW* I.7, the "O" or zero point. A metaphor for the babbling river Liffey (ALP) along whose course the chapter unfolds, the undammed spate of words will eventually prevent the washerwomen from hearing the tale of the origin ... but also from washing off the stains of HCE's guilt and sin, until the two processes become discontinued at nightfall, when the two banks drift apart. Deferring vindication and exoneration, ALP as an embodiment of linguistic babble/babel carries the sinful flow of the text: "Sinflowed, O sinflowed!" (*FW* 481.09), a deluge or sin river of words (German *Sintflut* or Dano-Norwegian *syndflod*) reminiscent of the consummation of the original sin in the Garden of Eden with the feminine rise to language (Genesis 3.2–3). Later on, the text will combine names for river, water (including Arabic *Bahr-el-Abiad*: The White Nile), and father (the sexual begetter) in several post-Babelian languages with Babel and the gate of tears (Bab-el-Mandeb), retracing the birth of language in alphabetical order: "A and aa ab ad abu abiad. A babbel men dub gulch of tears" (*FW* 254.16–17). No sooner has the quest(ion) of "original sinse" (*FW* 239.02)—the common origin of sin and sense since time immemorial, since "to begin = to sin" (VI.B.1 149 [*JJA* 29])—been broached than questing the sexual-linguistic sin at the origin of paternity and language already metaphorizes into a quest for the origin of water (ALP) in language (*aleph*, the first letter of the Hebrew alphabet), a quest for the source of the nil, for the source of the Nile (French *Nil*, pronounced like "nil") or Coleridge's Alph.

Very early in the *Wake*'s genesis, Joyce got interested in the quest for the source of the Nile, an age-old crux which has fascinated mankind since the Romans.[7] Indeed, several Joyce scholars have registered the striking family likeness that the name ALP bears to Alpheus, the sacred river of Arcadia described by Plutarch, and Coleridge's Alph in "Kubla Khan" (the dream setting and atmosphere run parallel in both the Joycean and Coleridgean creations), and how the question of linguistic origins and the quest for the source of a sacred archetypal river meet in Alph(eus) and alphabet.[8] Going up the Nile in *Finnegans Wake*, then, means retracing the historical investigation of its source or nil back to its delta both as letter and sex (cf. the diagram in *FW* 293), and operates as a metaphor for the inquiry into the rise of language from a silent, hidden, unfathomable source.

Joyce's ambivalent motif should be seen within Western literature's long-standing tradition, recalled by Irwin, "of imaging the origin of poetry, or imagination, or language as a remote, hidden, or inaccessible fountain that is the source of a periodically overflowing river."[9] ALP, long for Δ and short for Alph, like Coleridge's shortened version of the mythological Alpheus, bears the root involved in the process of linguistic-fluvial *de-rivation*. Her bed (French *lit*) is the "allaphbed" (*FW* 18.18) which carries along the first letter of the Hebrew and Greek alphabets (aleph, alpha) of the biblical language, whose alphabet lies at the origin of all Western alphabets. In her name and bed/womb, she conceals all the other letters to come, including the countless versions of the Letter or "mamafesta" (*FW* 104.04), woven of letters buried in *litter* (*alvus* also means "excrements"; cf. *FW* 600.07), as well as the hero's French letter, indicative of coming and unbecoming. As the flow of derivation, she will soon bear the Hebrew word-source *abba*, father, or, if capitalized, God the Father, also one of the names for the Nile now turned into a male principle (Irwin 1980: 83), who will in turn bring forth the alphabet as well as father language, and will later inaugurate the filial relationship in a baptismal flow: "whad ababs his dopter?" (*FW* 314.30; daughter + Norwegian *døpe*: to baptize).

The quest for the Protean source of the Nile goes under several guises and is always conducted in a catechistic mode. Each time, the pattern is roughly the same; I shall focus on the "first" major textual occurrence as it has also been glossed by Joyce himself:[10]

> Ex nickylow malo comes mickelmassed bonum ... Only for that these will not breathe upon Norronesen or Irenean the secrest of their soorcelossness. Quarry silex, Homfrie Noanswa! Undy gentian festyknees, Livia Noanswa?
>
> *FW* 23.16–21[11]

Out of nil(e) comes nothing, because (paradoxically) too much; the question put to the source, deemed to be lost and silent, presupposes a unique origin in Victoria Nyanza (i.e. Lake Victoria), the source of the White Nile only (through the Albert Nyanza), and thus fails to obtain an answer in keeping with the terms of the quest. As Joyce himself commented, "the source of the Nile [is] later supposed to represent $\sqcup + \Delta$." "Noanswa" could provide a definite solution (Nyanza) but the duality which it silently encrypts (another couple: Victoria and Albert) turns it into a "no answer" within a quest for a unique origin. On a deeper "existential" level, the misconstrued silence ("no answer") should have been interpreted as a real indication of where linguistic answers come from: the "woid" (*FW* 378.29). In this primordial "woid," void and Word are not yet differentiated, as the parodic reworking of mixed theories of linguistic origin and evolution on *FW* p. 378 indicate, following a mock allusion to "smotthermock Gramm's laws" (*FW* 378.27–8), maternalized (mother) Grimm's phonetic laws concerning the sound shifts between voiced and mute or voiceless consonants (cf. "Pawpaw, wowwow!" and, earlier, "MAW MAW," *FW* 308.R1):[12]

> In the buginning is the woid, in the muddle is the sounddance, and thereinofter you're in the unbewised again ... Silence in thought! Spreach! ... Pawpaw, wowwow!
>
> *FW* 378.29–33

In this Vichian-Joussean language rewriting the canonical opening of John 1.1 ("In the beginning was the Word") as contaminated by a bug from a void, dance as gesture has given way to the dance of sounds: the written sentence is said to be muddled up by its phonic instability or sound dance ("in the muddle is the sounddance") which are blended together in the third and last stage of linguistic derivation according to Giambattista Vico and Father Marcel Jousse (see Weir 1977, Milesi 1988, and Burns 2000). As in Vico's etymological networks for "myth" and "logic" in his *New Science* (§ 401), silence precedes speech, both having been inseparable at the dawn of time. In Samuel Beckett's concise wording

This writing that you find so obscure is a quintessential extraction of language and painting and gesture, with all the inevitable clarity of the old inarticulation. Here is the savage economy of hieroglyphics.

Beckett 1972: 15

Just as Victoria Nyanza is located upstream from Albert Nyanza, the source of the Albert Nile which receives the Victoria Nile from Lake Victoria, the "original" female nil(e) secretes the masculine principle, "Caughterect" (*FW* 600.14) as Joyce's guilty version of the Logos should be, also the Nile cataracts shaping an erect 1. In the "Lessons" chapter (*FW* II.2), whose central exercise is the construction of the geomater's sexual delta, the two complementary figures of the whole Creation are combined in the introduction to the ten (1+0) Kabbalistic questions on the essence of God, all featuring "wh...?" suggestive of the Tetragrammaton YWHY: "Ainsoph, this upright one, with that noughty besighed him zeroine" (*FW* 261.23–4). The Nile quest and its dialectical answers thus provide a thematic variation on the more general why?/(no)answer binary pattern which runs throughout *Finnegans Wake*, and offer further insight into the undecidability of the outcome of the linguistic quest. All answers returned to a "why" in *FW* 597.09–23 give rise to yet more questioning until the final defeated "Such me," which articulates the crucial paradox of identity in a novel tensed between source and course: search me/such [is] me.

Vocalization, vowelization, and the "loud silence" of female identity

Several notebook entries testify to Joyce's awareness of the fictional potential of stereotyped gender constructions of language, some of which he implemented in the *Wake*'s narrative-linguistic fabric. At the juncture of the "Mime" and the "Lessons" (*FW* II.1 and II.2), the children's call to their "Mummum" (*FW* 259.10), after an aspirate vocalized sequence ("Ha he hi ho hu"), fades over into the grammatical muddle opening *FW* II.2 and its concern with orientation and origin—"UNDE ET UBI" (*FW* 260.R1)—as well as its translation in the central text: "Whence ... where" (*FW* 260.08–09). Thus, the chapter announces itself as, among other things, an inquiry into the origin and displacement of discourse from several angles, and will feature especially Issy the young girl's attempt to substitute a "gramma's gramma" for a more male-oriented grammar (see Milesi 1989).

Within the context of the "Mime," the aspirate vowels may be read as a propitiatory homage to the divine afflatus of the thundering Lord ("Loud"), the *pneuma* (Greek) or *ruah* (Hebrew) at the source of language (the end of *FW* II.1 abounds in Hebrew words). The sequence is reworked in *FW* 267.18–21, de-aspirated and with the significant addition of the two semi-vowels instead: "Adamman, Emhe, Issossianusheen and sometypes Yggly ogs Weib. Uwayoei! So may this sybilette be our shibboleth that we may syllable her well." The one and only comment comes from Issy, and the young girl's wish to make herself vocal is both spelt out and denied in the string of "silents selfloud" (*FW* 267.17; German *Selbstlaut*: vowel), the independent woman in her being made silent as the semi-vowels betray her still semi-vocal nature. Here the crux is the instability of letters denoting identity: w(hy), y, and I (e.g. "sybilette" and Issy's signature in the title of the section: "Singalingalying. Storiella as she is syung"; cf. also *FW* 159.17, 408.15–16).

The passage plays out the fiction of her dual identity,[13] couched in artificial language, mythology, and Ossianic forged texts ("Issossianusheen"). But it is also a failed linguistic rite of passage, the "shibboleth" which the foreign Ephraimites mispronounced "Sibboleth" and which thus turned into the "passing place" of their execution as they were trying to cross the Jordan (Judges 12.4-6), a "password" which she cannot syllable well, owing to her sibilant nature (Issy as Eve—Irish *Emhe*—snake). Her only "way" (concealed in the near-unpronounceable "Uwayoei") of uttering the alien sound, not unlike a secret sacred (sibylline) name, is in "silents selfloud": (mum)mum's the word, or "Shshshsh!" (*FW* 148.32; one should remember at this point Issy's characteristic lisping, especially in her role as Sylvia Silence; see Benstock 1982 and 1989: 601–2). With its double *u* or *w*, the "Mummum" that rounds off the mummers' Mime silently spells the mixed nature of the feminine "demivoyelles" (*FW* 116.28; cf. also *FW* 53.02–03: "dumb as Mum's mutyness"). Oscillating between silence and voice ("selfloud"), the semi-vowel w.y of female identity, in parodic contrast with the aspirates and consonants of the male Logos, ask "I … why?" and lack the divine afflatus of the Logos' ineffable Tetragrammaton YHWH which the stuttering wh… at the start of the "Lessons" (cf. "where," "when") and the ten Kabbalistic "Wh… is he?" questions in *FW* 261.28–31 otherwise suggest. In the following chapter (*FW* II.3), a musical passage will harp back on the need to tone down (soft pedal) the name of the mother ("A mum") by religious silence (amen) when singing out her vowels (French *vocalises*: singing exercises):

> Let everie sound of a pitch keep still in resonance … now full theorbe, now dulcifair, and when we press of pedal (soft) pick out and vowelise your name. A mum.
>
> *FW* 360.03–07[14]

Towards a postmodern rhetoric of silence

As end meets beginning on either side of the "final" interruption, Joyce's thematization of the impossible origin turns into a problematic of finality, that of the text, history, as well as of hermeneutics since the narrative disclosure loses the end-as-origin of the linguistic flux into a beginning that has always already begun anew. Yet, in between, the text periodically comes to a standstill: the pivotal switch from the last back to the first page is anticipated by several other similar glitches or stoppages in the textual (w)hole, as when, in the year 0 or "ginnandgo gap" of the Norse Eddas "between antediluvious and annadominant" (i.e. BC and AD, before the flood and during the flow), the scroll is made to vanish (e.g. *FW* 14.16–18), when the action is discontinued by the slamming of a door (*FW* 20.17–18, 334.29–31, etc.), or in the variously spelt silence preceding speech (*FW* 14.06, 334.31, 501.06). Combined with the hero's momentous fall, those textual gaps and silences have been interpreted as an articulation of the inexpressibility of loss, the "loss of loss itself," "the remnant of a catastrophe ... whose quintessence is unrecoverable" (see O'Callaghan 2016: 140).

Such rifts in the tissue of the *Wake*'s fictional universal (hi)story, penned between the two world wars, can be seen to record those deeper hiatuses in history when humanity periodically grinds to a halt—what Philippe Lacoue-Labarthe, deriving the concept from Hölderlin's remarks on Sophocles' *Oedipus Rex* and *Antigone* and applying it to the historical situation after Auschwitz, called a "caesura": "that which, within history, interrupts history and opens up another possibility of history, or else closes off all possibility of history" (Lacoue-Labarthe 1990: 45). Thus, "The silence speaks the scene" (*FW* 13.02–03) in *Finnegans Wake*, and its hermetic eruptions, including in the major interruption at the end-rebeginning, mediate the hermeneutic irruption of the re-reader in a cyclical process of historical repetition famously described by Karl Marx, after Hegel: "the first time as tragedy, the second as farce" (Marx 1979: 103).

It is on such a more general hermeneutic note, invited by Joyce's textualization of silence as the ground from which language-as-figure emerges and to which it periodically returns,[15] that I would like to dwell by way of a long "conclusion." I will take my cue from Susan Sontag's remark, felicitous to a Joycean ear, in her time-honored yet timelessly relevant essay "The Aesthetics of Silence," that "the efficacious art-work leaves silence in its wake" (Sontag 1969: 23). It is, after all, the simultaneous, spatial Wakean pun, tapping the resources of unvoiceable variable typefaces, that thwarts full access to speech and turns *Finnegans Wake* into an essential dumbshow wresting long-forgotten words from silence and oblivion. Poised unwittingly on the threshold of the postmodern era not seen merely as the age of entropy (Thomas Pynchon) but also as that which understands the deeper resonances of silence,[16] Joyce's late modernity in *Finnegans Wake* would thus be tantamount to an ultra-classicist "(re)turn."

About the different forms of "eloquent silence," Sontag remarks that

> As language points to its own transcendence in silence, silence points to its own transcendence—to a speech beyond silence.
>
> . . .
>
> Something takes place in time, a voice speaking which points to the before and to what comes after an utterance: silence. Silence, then, is both the precondition of speech and the result or aim of properly directed speech.
>
> Sontag 1969: 19, 23

Originally published in 1967, Sontag's essay captured the *Zeitgeist* of post-war angst that dragged on into the tormented 1960s, which saw an increasing interest in the potential of silence as a form of aesthetic crisis, political protest, or deeper speech, among other interconnected metaphors such as exhaustion, entropy, or apocalypse used to translate common felt perceptions of the contemporary.[17] More urgently, the diagnosis of what Lyotard will famously call the "postmodern condition" stemmed from the ethical realization of the inadequacy of inherited modes of representation and aesthetic expression in a post-Holocaust world, which for instance informed George Steiner's collection of essays written from 1958 to 1966 titled *Language and Silence*: "The world of Auschwitz lies outside speech as it lies outside reason" (Steiner 1967: 146).

"After Auschwitz"—to use Adorno's now celebrated phrase echoed by several other thinkers (Jean-François Lyotard, Maurice Blanchot, etc.)—there is a "sense of a death in language, of the failure of the word in the face of the inhuman" (Steiner 1967: 71); at best one can only attempt to ward off apprehensively, in a faltering idiom or idiolect (one made up of a cacophonous polyglottism in the *Wake*'s prefiguration of a world in disarray), the various modalities of total human annihilation (the Holocaust, the threat of nuclear apocalypse). If, according to Aristotle, man was a living being having the word/Logos (*zoon logon ekhon*), the post-human condition reverts to the (pre-human) silence of the "last word" (Blanchot) in a sort of new Adamic apocalypse—conflated in "*The abnihilisation of the etym*" (*FW* 353.22; after Buckley's murder of the Russian general) with annihilation by the atom, hence the return *ab nihilo* to language's kernel of truth or etymon (see also *FW* 77.27: "adamelegy"). Published, through a quirk of history, in the year when the world was teetering on the edge of an impending catastrophe, the half-silent nothing of the *Wake's* watershed can be made to coincide retrospectively with humanity holding its breath on the cusp of a historical narrative's momentous backlash. Or in the grave undertones of Norman Brown, spoken in other times of "felt ultimacies" and "final solutions":

> To restore to words their full significance, as in dreams, as in *Finnegans Wake*, is to reduce them to nonsense, to get the nonsense or nothingness or silence back into words; to transcend the antinomy of sense and nonsense, silence and speech.
>
> Brown 1966: 258[18]

Of all the new radical critics of the 1960s, Ihab Hassan, for whom *Finnegans Wake* marked an epochal turning point in literature's orientation towards postmodernity,[19] pursued most insistently the critical implications of a resurfacing of the unsaid in what he called a "literature of silence" ("Silence develops as the metaphor of a new attitude that literature has chosen to adopt toward itself" [Hassan 1967: 15]), and, in a later collection of essays, went as far as to give ten "discrete definitions" of this aesthetic-critical metaphor of "negative silence" (Hassan 1971: 13–14).[20] But the most poignant insistence on the silent horizon of all writing can be found, well before it gained critical attention and almost fashionable appeal, in the work of Maurice Blanchot, *a contrario* from the short war-time essay "The Silence of Writers" (1941) onwards, in which he then encouraged writers to resist yielding to impotent silence "in the midst of the general catastrophe" (Blanchot 1995a: 27). Bringing out the apophatic quality of literary language and *désœuvrement* (literally: "un-working") of writing even more forcefully than Sontag in "The Aesthetics of Silence,"[21] Blanchot has subsequently recognized and expressed the passive affirmation of writing as disaster, a non-present "silent, harmless return," in an enduring reflection on and practice of writing, one of whose best-known terse moments was expressed in *The Writing of the Disaster*: "To *keep* silence, this is what we all want unknowingly when we write" (Blanchot 1995b: 6, 122; second translation modified). Thus, in "The Death of the Last Writer," the writer "is someone who imposes silence on . . . speaking, and a work of literature is . . . a rich dwelling-place of silence"; "If . . . all literature were to cease speaking, what would be lacking would be silence, and it would be that very lack of silence which would perhaps reveal the disappearance of literary speaking" (Blanchot 1995d: 152, 152–3).

Trying to approach the unapproachable, the scandalous disaster of writing in whose absent center an "original rumour" speaks silently, Blanchot's *écriture neutre* forces us to think, in the footsteps of Heidegger's denunciation of inauthentic speech (*das Gerede*; Blanchot's *parlerie* or *parole vaine*)—but also, sadly, in the wake of the German philosopher's yielding to such nationalist empty rhetoric[22] and his taciturnity about its consequences—the paradoxical and painful eloquence of what even the barest of writing and most tenuous of voice cannot exhaust: the ineffable which, whether foreclosed or courted, lurks within and beyond literature, "the most irrepressible speech, the speech that knows neither boundary nor end, has for its origin its own impossibility" (Blanchot 1997: 118). Here is what Blanchot has to say about empty speech:

> To chatter is not to speak. Prattle [*parlerie*] destroys silence while preventing speech. When one chatters, one says nothing true, even if one says nothing false, for one is not truly speaking.
>
> . . .
>
> To chatter is not yet to write . . . To speak with neither beginning nor end, to give speech to this neuter movement which is, as it were, all of speech, is this to make a work of chatter, is this to make a work of literature?
>
> Blanchot 1997: 124, 126

As in the washerwomen's prolix gossip in "Anna Livia Plurabelle," "chatter"[23] can only lead us astray and away from the truth, and eventually spends itself in a sterile "noanswa" rather than disclosing an eloquent silence. In a review essay originally titled "Plus loin que le degré zéro" (1953), which set up a dialogue with *Degree Zero Writing*, Barthes' own first attempt at elaborating a utopian *écriture blanche* or *écriture neutre*, Blanchot had observed that

> To write without "writing", to bring literature to that point of absence where it disappears, where we no longer have to fear its secrets which are lies, that is "writing degree zero", the neutrality which every writer deliberately or unwittingly seeks, and which leads some to silence.
>
> Blanchot 1995c: 147–8

The "disastrous," quasi-Nietzschean silent return of Blanchotian writing, passive, past, yet "passencore" (*FW* 3.04–05), brings us back to the polyglottal utopia of *Finnegans Wake*, on whose suspensive structure it can be read as a discreet gloss: "If the book could for a first time really begin, it would, for one last time, long since have ended" (Blanchot 1995: 36). Paying homage to one of those eloquently silent writers, Blanchot muses in "Mallarmé's Experience":

> Writing begins only when it is the approach to that point where nothing reveals itself, where, at the heart of dissimulation, speaking is still but the shadow of speech, a language which is still only its image, an imaginary language and a language of the imaginary, the one nobody speaks, the murmur of the

incessant and interminable which one has to *silence* if one wants, at last, to be heard.

Blanchot 1982: 48[24]

In the interstices between voiced silence and silenced voice, the textual implementation of a "rhetoric of silence" maps out the dialectic of figural language and silent ground merging into each other like the continuous track of a Möbius strip or Hofstadter's *recursive* figure (Hofstadter 1979: 67), which both so appropriately describe the *Wake*'s Vichian coils of *ricorsi storici*. It goes beyond the final horizon drawn by the celebrated closure of Wittgenstein's *Tractatus*—"Whereof one cannot speak, thereof one must be silent"—in order to approach the evanescence of the word in its incommensurate relation to the world. It must risk being led astray or "seduced" (Latin *seducere*) by the sirens' song, which "once heard, would open an abyss in each word and would beckon those who heard it to vanish into it" (Blanchot 2003: 4; Part I: "The Song of the Sirens"), but whose greatest deception was perhaps, like Joyce's "Sirens" chapter in *Ulysses*, that they might never sing to us but rather merely sign in graphic silence.[25]

To "conclude" again, I shall silently juxtapose Dylan Thomas's appropriately titled poem "In the Beginning" (and its inaugural three-pointed star), written when Joyce was likewise grappling with the word/void and the Nile/nil, and, one last time, Blanchot in *The Work of Fire*:

> In the beginning was the word, the word
> That from the solid bases of the light
> Abstracted all the letters of the void.

Thomas 2014: 59[26]

> In the beginning, I do not speak to say something, but there is nothing which demands to speak, nothing speaks, nothing finds its being in speech and the being of speech is nothing.[27]

Notes

1   See, in particular, Milesi (1985 and 1996). For a more recent, holistic study of the *Wake*'s Babelian vein in the context of Joyce's universalist cosmopolitics of language and search for its lost gestural-visual monogenesis, see also Schotter (2010).

2   See, in particular, Rabaté (1991). More recently, Annika Lindskog (2014) has investigated what a reading of silence as a form of representation reveals about the

modernist novel as a subgenre, and in particular how a scrutiny of the early drafts of *A Portrait of the Artist as a Young Man* uncovers radical changes in Joyce's conceptualization of silence. Let us not forget of course that silence is one of the three "arms," alongside exile and cunning, that Stephen Dedalus allows himself to use as his defence in *A Portrait*.

3 In *Grammar and Gender*, Dennis Baron observes that "[o]ne gender stereotype, popular until recently, assumes that the speech of women and, by extension, the feminine, romance languages abound in vowels, while the speech of men and the masculine, Germanic tongues are predominantly consonantal" (1986: 67), and refers to Swift's fake experiment in *A proposal for correcting, improving and ascertaining the English tongue* (1712), according to which men wrote consonantal strings sounding like "High Dutch" while the vocalic series of women resembled Italian. Baron further quotes Max Müller's *Lectures on the science of language* (2nd series, 1864): "Several languages divide themselves from the first into two great branches; one showing a more manly, the other a more feminine character; one richer in consonants, the other richer in vowels; one more tenacious of the original grammatical terminations, the other more inclined to slur over these terminations, and to simplify grammar by the use of circumlocutions."

4 For a fuller account of the following motifs, especially the role of the quest for the Nile as metaphor in Joyce's text, see Milesi (1990).

5 Said (1975: 5; italics not mine; see also 29, 174–5, 316, 357, 372). Cf. Heidegger (1968: 152): "The beginning of Western thought is not the same as its origin. The beginning is, rather, the veil that conceals the origin ... The origin keeps itself concealed in the beginning."

6 *The American Heritage Dictionary of the English Language*, s. v. "origin," and p. 1515 (Appendix of Indo-European roots); Skeat 1888, s. v. "origin."

7 See, for example, Irwin (1980).

8 See especially Heath (1973 and 1982: 139).

9 See Irwin (1980, 78, 81–2) for a Coleridgean parallel.

10 *SL* 321–2 (letter to Harriet Shaw Weaver dated May 13, 1927).

11 See also *FW* 89.26–7, 202.18–21, 598.05–09.

12 For a more complete unpacking of the various linguistic theories mocked on this page, see Brown (1983: 4).

13 Issy is often abbreviated as "I" or "Is" in Joyce's *Finnegans Wake* notebooks, in a mixture of first- and third-person enunciative agencies; cf. *FW* 75.11, 570.29, 620.32. Joyce may have wanted to record Issy's split entity via the two Spanish verbs for "to be" in "ser estar ⊣" (VI.B.23 [*JJA* 34] 29).

14 For a fuller treatment of female vocalic motifs, especially connected with I.O.U and "yes" or *oui*, see Derrida (2013), Rabaté (1991: 158–64), and Milesi (1994: 140–3).

15 In Rabaté's words, "Silence begs the question of textual hermeneutics, for its
   disturbing effect is the epiphany of meaning" (1991: 200).

16 In that respect, this essay can be read in opposition to reading *Finnegans Wake*, as
   Roy Benjamin (2013: 670–1) does, "in the context of the postmodernist project of
   incorporating noise into the very fabric of meaningful form. As a self-generating,
   stochastic system, the *Wake* opposes both totalitarian reification and entropic
   dissolution by continually adjusting its signal to noise ratio."

17 Other significant landmarks include Norman O. Brown's Phi Beta Kappa Address,
   "Apocalypse" (1961); Leslie Fiedler, "The New Mutants" (1965); Robert Alter, "The
   Apocalyptic Temper" (1966); John Barth, "The Literature of Exhaustion" (also 1966);
   Earl Rovit, "On the Contemporary Apocalyptic Imagination" (1968); and Frank
   Kermode, *The Sense of an Ending* (also 1967).

18 "Felt ultimacies" and "final solutions" were used by John Barth to describe the feeling
   of helplessness in an age of cultural unrest in "The Literature of Exhaustion" (1967),
   reprinted in Barth (1984: 67, 71).

19 See his essay on "*Finnegans Wake* and the Postmodern Imagination," collected in
   Hassan (1975: 77–94) (Joyce's comment on the last silent word of the *Wake* is
   recalled on p. 68).

20 See, more generally, the introductory essay, "PRELUDE: Lyre without Strings"
   (12–23).

21 See, for instance: "As the activity of the mystic must end in a *via negativa*, a theology
   of God's absence, a craving for the clouds of unknowing beyond knowledge and for
   the silence beyond speech, so art must tend toward anti-art, the elimination of the
   'subject' . . . and the pursuit of silence" (Sontag 1969: 3–4).

22 To my knowledge, Len Platt was the first to make a convincing rapprochement
   between the rise of National Socialism's rhetoric of Aryan purity in language and
   race and the *Wake*'s timely counter-politics of linguistic transnationalism. See Platt
   (2007: 14–41) and also Schotter (2010: 101–2).

23 The vintage prototype of the post-war experimental novel exposing the irresistibility
   of chatter (*bavardage*)—but also its perils: its unbearably verbose narrator eventually
   gets pummelled by one of those whom he buttonholes—is Louis-René des Forêts's
   Le Bavard (1946), a *récit* prefaced by Maurice Blanchot, in which "meaning" is
   ultimately created beyond the surface language of the chatterbox's empty
   performative speech about the logorrheic compulsion to speak. As an adolescent, des
   Forêts had purchased a copy of *Ulysses* from Adrienne Monnier, who had asked a
   man by her side to cover the book with crystal paper. Later, Monnier revealed to the
   keen buyer that the man was none else than Joyce himself . . .

24 For an excavation of such an intermittent tradition of silence, on the more modern
   side of which one could adduce Beckett's minimalist theatre of the unsaid, the
   "fullness" of silence in John Cage's "4'33"" performance or even an aged Pound

declaring "*tempus loquendi, tempus tacendi*" (etc.), see, for instance, Peterkiewicz (1970).

25 See, in particular, the "Sirens Without Music" section in M. Beja et al. (1986: 57–92), especially J.-M. Rabaté's "The Silence of the Sirens," and Milesi (1992).

26 Originally published in *18 Poems* (1934).

27 Quoted in Hassan (1991: 19); compare with Blanchot (1995e: 324; "Literature and the Right to Death").

References

Alter, R. (1966), "The Apocalyptic Temper," *Commentary* (June): 61–6.

Baron, D. (1986), *Grammar and Gender*, New Haven, CT: Yale University Press.

Barth, J. (1967), "The Literature of Exhaustion," *Atlantic Monthly* (August): 29–34.

Barth, J. (1986), *The Friday Book: Essays and Other Non-Fiction*, London: Johns Hopkins University Press.

Beja, M. et al. (1986), *James Joyce: The Centennial Symposium*, Urbana: University of Illinois Press.

Benjamin, R. (2013), "Noirse-Made-Earsy: Noise in *Finnegans Wake*," *Comparative Literature Studies* 50, no. 4: 670–87.

Benstock, S. (1982), "The Genuine Christine: Psychodynamics of Issy," in S. Henke and E. Unkeless (eds), *Women in Joyce*, 187–8, Brighton: Harvester.

Benstock, S. (1989), "Apostrophizing the Feminine in *Finnegans Wake*," *Modern Fiction Studies* 35, no. 3: 587–614.

Blanchot, M. (1982), *The Space of Literature*, trans. and intro. A. Smock, Lincoln, NE, and London: University of Nebraska Press.

Blanchot, M. (1995a), "The Silence of Writers," trans. M. Holland, in M. Holland (ed.), *The Blanchot Reader*, 25–8, Oxford: Blackwell.

Blanchot, M. (1995b), *The Writing of the Disaster*, trans. A. Smock, new edn, Lincoln, NE, and London: University of Nebraska Press.

Blanchot, M. (1995c), "The Pursuit of the Zero Point," trans. I. Maclachlan, in M. Holland (ed.), *The Blanchot Reader*, 143–51, Oxford: Blackwell.

Blanchot, M. (1995d), "The Death of the Last Writer," trans. L. Hill, in M. Holland (ed.), *The Blanchot Reader*, 151–6, Oxford: Blackwell.

Blanchot, M. (1995e), *The Work of Fire*, trans. C. Mandell, Stanford, CA: Stanford University Press.

Blanchot, M. (1997), *Friendship*, trans. E. Rottenberg, Stanford, CA: Stanford University Press.

Blanchot, M. (2003), *The Book to Come*, trans. C. Mandell, Stanford, CA: Stanford University Press.

Brown, C. (1983), "*FW* 378: Laughing at the Linguists," *A Wake Newslitter* 2 (March): 4–5.

Brown, N. O. (1961), "Phi Beta Kappa Address 'Apocalypse,'" *Harpers Magazine* (May): 46–9.

Burns, C. (2000), *Gestural Politics: Stereotype and Parody in Joyce*, Albany, NY: SUNY Press.

Derrida, J. (2013), "*Ulysses* Gramophone: Hear Say Yes in Joyce," trans. F. Raffoul, in A. J. Mitchell and S. Slote (eds), *Derrida and Joyce: Texts and Contexts*, 41–86, Albany, NY: SUNY Press.

des Forêts, L. R. (1946), *Le Bavard*, Paris: Gallimard.

Fiedler, L. (1965), "The New Mutants," *Partisan Review* 32, no. 4: 505–25.

Gillet, L. (1958), *Claybook for James Joyce*, trans. and intro. G. Markow-Totevy, London: Abelard-Schuman.

Hassan, I. (1967), *The Literature of Silence: Henry Miller and Samuel Beckett*, New York: Alfred A. Knopf.

Hassan, I. (1971), *The Dismemberment of Orpheus: Toward a Postmodern Literature*, New York: Oxford University Press.

Hassan, I. (1975), *Paracriticisms: Seven Speculations of the Times*, Urbana and Chicago: University of Illinois Press.

Heath, S. (1973), "Trames de lecture," *Tel Quel* 54: 4–15.

Heath, S. (1982), "Joyce in Language," in C. MacCabe (ed.), *James Joyce: New Perspectives*, Sussex: Harvester; Bloomington: Indiana University Press.

Heidegger, M. (1968), *What Is Called Thinking?*, trans. Fred D. Wieck and J. G. Gray, New York: Harper and Row.

Hofstadter, D. R. (1979), *Gödel, Escher, Bach: An Eternal Golden Braid*, Brighton: Harvester.

Irwin, J. (1980), *American Hieroglyphics: The Symbol of the Egyptian Hieroglyphics in the American Renaissance*, Baltimore, MD, and London: Johns Hopkins University Press.

Kermode, F. (1967), *The Sense of an Ending: Studies in the Theory of Fiction*, Oxford: Oxford University Press.

Lacoue-Labarthe, P. (1990), *Heidegger, Art and Politics: The Fiction of the Political*, trans. C. Turner, Oxford: Basil Blackwell.

Lindskog, A. (2014), *Silent Modernism: Soundscapes and the Unsayable in Richardson, Joyce, and Woolf*, Lund: Centre for Languages and Literature, Lund University.

Marx, K. (1979), *The Eighteenth Brumaire of Louis Bonaparte*, in *Karl Marx Friedrich Engels Collected Works*, Vol. 11: 1851–1853, London: Lawrence & Wishart.

Milesi, L. (1985), "L'idiome babélien de *Finnegans Wake*: Recherches thématiques dans une perspective génétique," in C. Jacquet (ed.), *Genèse de Babel: Joyce et la création*, 155–215, Paris: CNRS.

Milesi, L. (1988), "Vico . . . Jousse. Joyce. . Langue," in C. Jacquet (ed.), *James Joyce 1: "Scribble" 1: Genèse des textes*, 143–62, Paris: Lettres Modernes.

Milesi, L. (1989), "Towards a Female Grammar of Sexuality: The De/Recomposition of 'Storiella as she is syung,'" *Modern Fiction Studies* 35, no. 3: 569–86.

Milesi, L. (1990), "Metaphors of the Quest in *Finnegans Wake*," in G. Lernout (ed.), *European Joyce Studies 2: Finnegans Wake: Fifty Years*, 79–107, Amsterdam and Atlanta, GA: Rodopi.

Milesi, L. (1992), "The Signs the Si-rens Seal: Textual Strategies in Joyce's 'Sirens,'" in D. Ferrer, C. Jacquet, and A. Topia (eds), *Ulysse à l'article: Joyce aux marges du roman*, 127–41, Tusson: Éditions du Lérot.

Milesi, L. (1994), "Italian Studies in Musical Grammar," in C. Jacquet and J.-M. Rabaté (eds), *James Joyce 3: "Scribble" 3: Joyce et l'Italie*, 105–53, Paris: Lettres Modernes.

Milesi L. (1996), "*Finnegans Wake*: The Obliquity of Trans-lations," in M. Beja and D. Norris (eds), *Joyce in the Hibernian Metropolis: Essays*, 279–89, Columbus: Ohio State University Press.

O'Callaghan, K. (2016), "'behush the bush to. Whish!': Silence, Loss, and *Finnegans Wake*," in O. Kosters, T. Conley, and P. de Voogt (eds), *A LONG THE KROMMERUN: Selected Papers from the Utrecht James Joyce Symposium*, European Joyce Studies 24, 140–52, Amsterdam: Brill/Rodopi.

Peterkiewicz, J. (1970), *The Other Side of Silence: The Poet at the Limits of Language*, London: Oxford University Press.

Pickett, J. and Kleinedler, S. (eds) (2011), *The American Heritage Dictionary of the English Language*, 5th edn, Boston and New York: Houghton Mifflin Harcourt.

Platt, L. (2007), *Joyce, Race and "Finnegans Wake*," Cambridge: Cambridge University Press.

Rabaté, J.-M. (1984), "Lapsus ex machina," in D. Attridge and D. Ferrer (eds), *Post-structuralist Joyce: Essays from the French*, 79–102, Cambridge: Cambridge University Press.

Rabaté, J.-M. (1991), *James Joyce, Authorized Reader*, Baltimore, MD, and London: Johns Hopkins University Press.

Rovit, E. (1968), "On the Contemporary Apocalyptic Imagination," *American Scholar* 37, no. 3: 453–68.

Said, E. W. (1975), *Beginnings: Intention and Method*, Baltimore, MD: Johns Hopkins University Press.

Schotter, J. (2010), "Verbivocovisuals: James Joyce and the Problem of Babel," *James Joyce Quarterly* 48, no. 1: 89–109.

Skeat, W. (1888), *An Etymological Dictionary of the English Language*, Oxford: Clarendon.

Sontag, S. (1969), "The Aesthetics of Silence," in *Styles of Radical Will*, 3–34, London: Secker and Warburg.

Steiner, G. (1967), *Language and Silence: Essays 1958–1966*, London: Faber and Faber.

Thomas, D. (2014), *The Collected Poems of Dylan Thomas: The New Centenary Edition*, ed. J. Goodby, London: Weidenfeld & Nicolson.

Weir, L. (1977), "The Choreography of Gesture: Marcel Jousse and *Finnegans Wake*," *James Joyce Quarterly* 14, no. 3: 313–25.

Wolff, F. (1979), "L'enfance de la langue," *Critique* XXXV, no. 387–8: 801–12.

Part Two

The Aesthetics of Silence

5

"Fragments of shapes, hewn. In white silence: appealing": Silence and the Emergence of a Style from *Giacomo Joyce* to *Ulysses*

John McCourt

Silence and censorship

Towards the end of *A Portrait of the Artist as a Young Man*, Stephen Dedalus delineates his personal future and indicates how he intends to proceed as an artist:

> I will tell you what I will do and what I will not do. I will not serve that in which I no longer believe, whether it call itself my home, my fatherland, or my church: and I will try to express myself in some mode of life or art as freely as I can and as wholly as I can, using for my defence the only arms I allow myself to use—silence, exile and cunning.
>
> P 246–7

Although much of what the fictional Stephen will or will not do corresponds to what James Joyce himself had already done—or was already doing when he was writing these words—it would be misguided to apply them unquestioningly to Joyce himself as if he were directly setting out his own agenda or his own intended stance and his consequential behavior. At the same time, it would be absurd today—with the benefit of much political, cultural, and critical hindsight—to suggest that Joyce did not serve his home, fatherland or church; by refusing to stay silent he served them all from afar: from what he calls "the safe side of distance!" (*FW* 228). He did so on his own terms, through sometimes searing criticism of the political, economic, and religious powers in the country and through his complex literary responses to the social realities of the Ireland in which he grew up and which he saw developing in his absence. In Ireland, whatever recognition or thanks that he would get for so doing would come, for the most part, only belatedly, partially, and posthumously. Joyce's adult life would be spent in physical if not psychological exile while his writings offer many illustrations of how he lived and applied various meanings of "cunning" (variously translatable as "knowing," "skillful," "ingenious," "curious," "crafty," "artful," "deceitful").

In no real sense did Joyce keep the word given by Stephen with regard to silence. Or rather, we might say that he kept his word too well—he never ceased to write—and so punctured the silence that kept a lid on so much that was suppressed or repressed or went unspoken or was left unsaid both in private conversation and in public discourse in Ireland. And that, very simply, is why he created such alarm in conservative Ireland which, through censorship, reduced so many of its writers after Joyce to silence. And yet, rigid censorship, as poet Austin Clarke commented in 1947, was not particularly needed as a possible Irish readership was small and self-selecting:

> It is idle to suggest that the bulk of Irish people—in the manner of most people everywhere—is interested in serious literature. Most men and women care less about literature than they care about Minoan plumbing; and it is, perhaps, legitimate to assume that a stringent censorship, of the type with which Ireland is familiar, affects severely only the relatively small minority of readers who either are highly cultivated or highly interested.[1]

Joyce did not need to be censored into silence in Ireland (in fact *Ulysses* was never banned there because it was a such a minority taste that it did not need to be). In his own lifetime and in the two decades the followed, his works, when acknowledged, were usually greeted with the silence of indifference (they were more warmly welcomed in France and in the U.S.A.). But Joyce, even if he craved readers, wrote with a long temporal horizon in mind; his novels are today more popular in Ireland than they have ever been, and seem to resonate and engage ever more loudly and effectively with the larger political, social, and religious issues affecting the country.

Voicing noise

On one basic level, Joyce's works are bursting with silence's opposite—noise—with sounds that show the author taking the original Latin verb, "sonare," literarily. The sounds in Joyce's works are abundant and variegated: they range from the "Pok!" made by one of the two bottles of stout in "Ivy Day in the

Committee Room" to the "pick, pack, pock, pock" sounds of balls hitting cricket-bats in *A Portrait of the Artist as a Young Man*; from the "Crush, crack, crick, crick" (*U* 3.19) of Stephen's footsteps on the beach on Sandymount Strand in "Proteus" to the troublingly repetitive "jingle"—"jinglejaunty" (*U* 11.290), "jing" (*U* 11.457), "jiggedy jingle" (*U* 11.579), and "jingly" (*U* 11.606)—of Boylan's jaunting-car in "Sirens."[2] Often, however, noises are in competition with each other while what happens silently can be seen to be more effective, at least in the mind of the reader. In "Sirens," the noisiest episode in *Ulysses*, Bloom breaks wind while reading Irish patriot Robert Emmet's speech from the dock and his famous last words, "When my country takes her place among the nations of the earth, then and not till then let my epitaph be written. I have done":

> Seabloom, greaseabloom viewed last words. Softly. *When my country takes her place among.*
> Prrprr.
> Must be the bur.
> Fff! Oo. Rrpr.
>   *Nations of the earth.* No-one behind. She's passed. *Then and not till then.* Tram kran kran kran. Good oppor. Coming. Krandlkrankran. I'm sure it's the burgund. Yes. One, two. *Let my epitaph be.* Kraaaaaa. *Written. I have.*
> Pprrpffrrppffff.
> *Done.*
>
> U 11. 1284–91

Ironically, Emmet's once uttered words, evoked or voiced here through Bloom's silent reading, compete and eventually merge with Bloom's own deflating bowel sounds which are themselves silenced by the noise of a passing tram. What remains in the reader's mind is not so much the words but Bloom's publicly unheard and vulgarly efficacious bodily comment "Pprrpffrrppffff."

Voicing silence

For all the difficulties in voicing sound and noise through the written word, the writer can trust the reader to imaginatively "hear" what is written; voicing silence is, of course, an even more complicated proposition. Silence cannot be voiced; it can merely be described or evoked by a writer who can hope to rely on the reader to notice it. Often in narrative as in real life, silence is little more than the presumed or articulated backdrop to sound or speech, functioning almost like a platform upon which speech is erected. We find this in the following example:

"In the silence of the soft grey air he heard the cricket bats from here and from there: pock" (*P* 45). Here the silence conveys something peaceful or even something neutral. Elsewhere, however, silence acquires a more definite personality of its own. In *A Portrait*, as Stephen struggles to escape from the "cold silence of intellectual revolt," silence is rendered as something that almost assumes a personality, that expresses an emotion. Thus Stephen is disturbed by his mother's "listless silence" (*P* 164), encouraged by Cranly's "listening silence" (*P* 178), and revels in a moment of somewhat self-indulgent "thought-enchanted silence" (*P* 213) after pronouncing on Aquinas to Lynch. In other cases, again in *A Portrait*, the silence is something less reassuring and this permits sound to travel ominously to the ears of the young boys, signalling the corporal punishment being inflicted on other pupils:

> That was a sound to hear but if you were hit then you would feel a pain. The pandybat made a sound too but not like that. The fellows said it was made of whalebone and leather with lead inside: and he wondered what was the pain like. There were different kinds of sounds. A long thin cane would have a high whistling sound and he wondered what was that pain like.
>
> *P* 45

In the scene in *A Portrait* where the young Stephen, his glasses broken, visits the rector of Clongowes, silence is repeatedly evoked, a silence which never fails to make the already vulnerable young boy feel uncomfortable:

> His heart was beating fast on account of the solemn place he was in and the silence of the room: and he looked at the skull and at the rector's kind-looking face … The rector looked at him in silence and he could feel the blood rising to his face and the tears about to rise to his eyes … The rector looked at him again in silence.
>
> *P* 56

The reiterated textual evocation of silence swells or prolongs the moment, stretches the subjective or inner time as lived by Stephen (and, by extension, the reader) in a manner that recalls Bergson's idea of the *durée*[3] even as the prose moves forward.

Breaking silence

We find countless descriptions of subjective silence in Joyce's writing. Joyce knew how to exploit the pregnant, silent pause before a key moment in a text or in the unfolding of a plot. The central moment in "The Sisters" is introduced by a silence that "took possession of the room" (*D* 17), ushered in by a prolonged pause that evokes "a silence" which grows in intensity until it becomes "the silence." It is as if the silence itself becomes, for a time, the protagonist of the scene. Or, to cite Joyce's own words in *Finnegans Wake*, "The silence speaks the scene" (*FW* 21. 2–3).

> A silence took possession of the little room and, under cover of it, I approached the table and tasted my sherry and then returned quietly to my chair in the corner. Eliza seemed to have fallen into a deep revery. We waited respectfully for her to break the silence: and after a long pause she said slowly . . .
>
> *D* 17

The reader is directly involved in the respectful wait of the "long pause," in the silence, that is, that grows and takes possession of the room before Eliza is ready or able to break it:

> It was that chalice he broke . . . That was the beginning of it. Of course, they say it was all right, that it contained nothing, I mean. But still . . . They say it was the boy's fault. But poor James was so nervous, God be merciful to him!
>
> *D* 17

Ellipses punctuate her revelatory words. They convey silences of indeterminate length that weigh as heavily as anything she actually manages to utter. Even when the silence is broken, crucial information remains silenced, unsaid. This, it should be stressed, is not Joyce engaging in surreptitious or silent censorship; rather he is realistically reflecting the self-policing based on a common idea of decency (a mix of conservative Irish Catholicism and a hangover of late Victorian values) that would have been the norm in turn-of-the-century Dublin. There are certain things that Eliza cannot say, but there are also certain things a literary text in early twentieth-century Dublin (or London) must not say as Joyce learned so well in the seven-year struggle to get an integral version of *Dubliners* into print. The text renders the sense that what remains silent and unsaid is as significant as what is outwardly declared. Furthermore, there is an intuitive understanding among the small group as to the precise nature of what is actually not stated.

Similarly, in "An Encounter," a moment of prolonged silence heralds the boys' epiphanic realization about the real nature of the less than reassuring "old josser" that they have met. Joyce, being Joyce, does not explain what is intended by the word "josser," a slang word dating from the late nineteenth century and suggesting, variously, an old man worthy of contempt, a fool, but also, at least in Australian English, a clergyman who is slightly "off." Again, the silence functions as a signal to the alert reader that something significant is about to happen. This sensation is reinforced by what almost seems like a slowing down of the action through the use of words and phrases like "a long while," "paused," "slowly," "remained," "a silence of a few minutes." The emphasis on silence causes the scene to evolve almost in slow motion:

> After a long while his monologue paused. He stood up slowly, saying that he had to leave us for a minute or so, a few minutes, and, without changing the direction of my gaze, I saw him walking slowly away from us towards the near end of the field. We remained silent when he had gone. After a silence of a few minutes I heard Mahony exclaim:
> —I say! Look what he's doing!
> As I neither answered nor raised my eyes Mahony exclaimed again:
> —I say . . . He's a queer old josser!
>
> *D* 26

Just how much time passes in silence before Mahony exclaims? It is "a few minutes" rather than "a few seconds" and clearly more than long enough for the boys to see exactly what it is the "old josser" is up to. Time enough too, for a reader to intuit its seriousness and, in the light of what emerged at the end of the twentieth century with regard to the Catholic Church's sex scandals in Ireland, its shocking relevance.

Silence and gesture

Joyce also portrays silence as an opportunity, a space for a protagonist to escape into the solitude, amplitude, and freedom of his own thoughts (or indeed into her own thoughts—with Molly Bloom's monologue, which is only "heard" through the imagination of the reader, facilitated by the silent, sleeping Bloom, the supreme example of this). We find something similar, albeit on a far smaller scale, in "Araby," where silence is the necessary condition for the young boy's soul to take flight:

> At night in my bedroom and by day in the classroom her image came between me and the page I strove to read. The syllables of the word Araby were called to me through the silence in which my soul luxuriated and cast an Eastern enchantment over me.
>
> *D* 32

Unfortunately for the boy, the deeply evocative, almost rapturous silence that facilitates his dreams is transformed through the disappointment of his late arrival at the now troublingly silenced bazaar with its closed stalls and its darkened hall. Thus, he finds himself in a hugely anticlimactic "silence like that which pervades a church after a service" (*D* 34). Similarly contrapuntal and oppositional uses of silence can be found elsewhere in Joyce's fiction.

In "Araby," the young boy is affected by both the girl's words and her gestures, each of which has an equally powerful effect over him: "But my body was like a harp and her words and gestures were like fingers running upon the wires" (*D* 31). In *A Portrait*, however, Stephen's pivotal encounter with the bird girl takes place in a silence that is never broken by mere words. Joyce thus conveys a communicational power that is beyond words, which involves physical communication, body language, gesture, all of which takes place in the context of a mutually enclosing veil of silence:

> She was alone and still, gazing out to sea; and when she felt his presence and the worship of his eyes her eyes turned to him in quiet sufferance of his gaze, without shame or wantonness. Long, long she suffered his gaze and then quietly withdrew her eyes from his and bent them towards the stream, gently stirring the water with her foot hither and thither. The first faint noise of gently moving water broke the silence, low and faint and whispering, faint as the bells of sleep; hither and thither, hither and thither; and a faint flame trembled on her cheek.
>
> *P* 171

She is "in quiet sufferance of his gaze," she "quietly" withdraws her eyes and it is the "gently moving water" that "broke the silence, low and faint and whispering." What is exchanged between Stephen and the bird girl is wordless and gestural but deeply significant and indicative of why Stephen will later claim in "Circe" that "gesture, not music not odour, would be a universal language" (*U* 15.105–6). What the reader participates in, watching the silent scene between Stephen and the girl unfold, is analogous to watching a short silent film. The water can no more whisper through the prose than it can make itself heard on the silent screen. But the centrality of gesture and the body as the vehicles of communication should not go unnoticed and would doubtless be appreciated by phenomenologists for whom there is no simple division between body and mind. Rather they see thoughts and feelings as sensuous, corporeal, embodied. Again, in this case, the swooning evocativeness of the silent bird girl vision is contrapuntally followed at the opening of the fifth chapter by Stephen's anticlimactic silent and solitary meal of "watery tea" and "fried bread" (*P* 174).

Before this moment of deflation, however, we cannot but notice that the girl's movements reveal her self-awareness, her heightened consciousness of being watched even as she, more surreptitiously, watches back. Gesture was the principal means of conveying meaning for the silent film actor. Not for nothing would film pioneer Georges Méliès state in a 1907 article that "in the cinematograph ... gesture is everything."[4] At first look, the reader might think that the silence that links Stephen and the girl is broken by Stephen's words but a more careful inspection reveals that it is his soul that speaks while the silence endures and intensifies until the image of the girl becomes too powerful:

> —Heavenly God! cried Stephen's soul, in an outburst of profane joy.
>
> He turned away from her suddenly and set off across the strand. His cheeks were aflame; his body was aglow; his limbs were trembling. On and on and on and on he strode, far out over the sands, singing wildly to the sea, crying to greet the advent of the life that had cried to him.
>
> *P* 171–2

For Stephen, the entire gestural exchange is framed and facilitated by a silence which keeps it at a remove from the dreaded banality of words. This escape from words, aligned with a consciousness of the power of gesture and image was already present in Joyce's writing as early as *Stephen Hero*, in the moment in which Stephen takes refuge from his peers in "a disdainful silence." Silence for the Stephen of Joyce's two early novels of formation is the prerequisite for words, for writing, but it is also the prerequisite for thought, for emotion, for exchange, for epiphany as well, sometimes, as their means. Determined to avoid "the hell of hells," the region, that is, "wherein everything is found to be obvious," Stephen emulates "the saint who formerly was chary of speech in obedience to a commandment of silence." Accordingly, he will be "the artist who schooled himself to silence lest words should return him his discourtesy" (*SH* 33):

> He said to himself: I must wait for the Eucharist to come to me: and then he set about translating the phrase into common sense. He spent days and nights hammering noisily as he built a house of silence for himself wherein he might await his Eucharist ...
>
> *SH* 30

Visualized silence

Giacomo Joyce is Joyce's most silent text. It is silent for various reasons including the fact that, although it appears finished, Joyce, in a rare act of self-censorship, chose not to publish it or even to give it a title. This was unusual for Joyce who rarely finished or appeared to have finished a text only to abandon it to the silence of non-publication. And yet the "silent" text that we came to call *Giacomo Joyce* came into print only posthumously and, in the meantime, could be heard only occasionally, reverberating in the pages of Joyce's other works. It both echoes and is echoed in *A Portrait* and *Ulysses*, sandwiched, as it was, between the two.

More importantly, more than other Joyce texts, it gives ample space to silence between its frames or paragraphs which convey, at times, a series of "still-life" vignettes. The format of Joyce's *Giacomo* text highlights white space, and if the space between words is silence, then this is the most silent text that Joyce has written. The manuscript contains an unusual amount of white space between the paragraphs of varying length. The paragraph-sized white expanses vary in length but are not accidental. They deliberately contribute to the reading experience of this text. This is why Clare Wallace, among others, has referred to *Giacomo Joyce* as "a visual object" noting that "the spaces or gaps between the segments of writing function to produce a highly visual rendering of the processes of desire" (Wallace 2006: 215). In the individual frames of this fragmentary poem-in-prose, silent gesture is also at the forefront of what is a succession or amalgam of contrived, carefully conceived and compiled images, a complicated series of *mise-en-scène* for the most part devoid of words or verbal exchanges. This is a work in which the spoken word itself, as represented by the "Yes: a brief syllable," is reduced and takes secondary place, for once, as other forms of non-verbal communication are foregrounded. Thus, the cursory "Yes" is followed and put into the shade by "A brief laugh. A brief beat of the eyelids" (*GJ* 1).

This is a process that will be repeated and sometimes accentuated in *Ulysses*, especially in "Circe." In his notes for this episode, Joyce wrote "art of gestures," thus underlining the importance of movement, body language, and gesticulation.[5] "Circe" is also punctuated by stage directions—often richly descriptive of gesture—which at times overshadow the moments of speech. Similarly, the episode is notable for what we might term its "silent speech": Stephen's dead mother is pictured "uttering a silent word" and is followed by a "choir of virgins and confessors" who "sing voicelessly" (*U* 15.4161) while Bloom's dead son reads "inaudibly" as Bloom "calls inaudibly" after him (*U* 15.4959–62). Bloom "shakes his head in mute mirthful reply" (*U* 15.4912–13).

In *Giacomo Joyce*, the silence–word binary is enacted in a way that is distinct among Joyce's writings. It is communicated not merely by the evocation of silence through descriptive words but also through the physical layout of Joyce's carefully handwritten manuscript, almost as if the white pages represent the silent backdrop against which the corporality of text takes shape and fills itself out as an uneven series of "Signs on a white field" that herald those evoked by Stephen in the "Proteus" episode of *Ulysses*. Something analogous to this physical evocation of silence in *Giacomo Joyce* is to be found in Octavio Paz's description of silence in *The Bow and the Lyre*. For Paz, silence is "the brink of language. And that brink is silence, the blank page. A silence that is a lake, a smooth and compact surface. Down below it, submerged, the words are waiting" (Paz 1973: 13). Similarly, Joyce and his fictional alter egos delve through the silence of their own soul's well, a source which demands the condition of silence if it is to be tapped. This process is reflected in Stephen in *Stephen Hero, A Portrait,* and *Ulysses,* but also in the fleeting, shadowy character of Jamsey as seen in the almost silent frames of *Giacomo Joyce.*

Joyce sees silence as a prerequisite for communication with others but also, and more importantly perhaps, in his epiphanic texts, with the self. He was also very much aware that "[s]ilence remains, inescapably, a form of speech (in many instances of complaint or indictment) and an element in a dialogue," as Susan Sontag phrased it in her essay, "The Aesthetics of Silence" (Sontag 1966: 28). Joyce revels in words, in an insatiable feast of languages, but he is not afraid to embrace and convey silence. He uses silence not only as mere backdrop for words or gestures but as a form of communication in itself, embodying within itself varying tones and achieving a variety of effects within his texts and on his readers. And in *Giacomo Joyce,* he goes beyond conceiving silence in an aural sense, attempting also to convey it through the visual metaphor of the irregular white spaces. This focus on the visual leads back to Joyce's involvement in cinema. From silent movies, but not only, Joyce came to understand that silence may be pregnant with meaning. Watching silent films Joyce would have seen that cinema communicated unheard sounds and meanings of all sorts, mainly through gesture, which was cinema's primary expressive device, but also, crucially, through silence itself and the liberating space it afforded to the viewers' imaginations, a space, this, that would be grossly curtailed by the arrival of the "talkies" in the late 1920s.

Notes

1   Clarke is quoted in an unsigned article entitled "Irish writing," *Irish Times,* February 14, 1947, 5.
2   For a discussion of this, see, among many others, Attridge (2009).
3   See Bergson (1960).

4   See Georges Méliès (1984). His piece is a translation of the article published in *La Revue du Cinema* (October 15, 1929), published originally in the 1907 issue of the *Annual*.

5   Phillip Herring (1972: 288). Joyce was thinking about gestures as early as *A Portrait of the Artist as a Young Man*, in which Stephen makes a "sudden gesture of a revolutionary nature" (*P* 213), "an angry abrupt gesture" (*P* 200), a "vague gesture of denial" (*P* 177), and remembers his "sadly proud gesture of refusal" (*P* 83).

References

Attridge, D. (2009), "Joyce's Noises," *Oral Tradition* 24, no. 2: 471–84.

Bergson, H. (1960), *Time and Free Will: An Essay on the Immediate Data of Consciousness*, trans. F. L. Pogson (1889), New York: Harper & Brothers.

Herring, P. (1972), *Joyce's "Ulysses" Notesheets in the British Museum*, Charlottesville: University of Virginia Press.

Joyce, J. (1989), *Stephen Hero*, ed. T. Spencer, London: Triad Grafton.

Joyce, J. (1998), *Giacomo Joyce*, London: Faber & Faber.

Méliès, G. (1984), "Cinematographic Views," trans. Stuart Liebman, *October* 29: 28.

Paz, O. (1973), *The Bow and the Lyre*, Austin: University of Texas Press.

Sontag, S. (1966), "The Aesthetics of Silence," in *Styles of Radical Will*, 3–34, New York: Farrar, Strauss & Giroux.

Wallace, C. (2006), "'Ghosts in the Mirror'; Perception and the Visual, in *Giacomo Joyce*," in L. Armand and C. Wallace (eds), *Giacomo Joyce Envoys of the Other*, 207–27, Prague: Litteraria Pragensia.

6

Joyce and the Aesthetics of Silence: Absence and Loss in "The Dead"[1]

Teresa Caneda Cabrera

The collection of *Dubliners*, often celebrated as a masterpiece in the genre of the modern short story, stands to this day as an exceptional example of James Joyce's undisputed talent when he was only an incipient writer. In each of the individual stories, Joyce, the developing artist, skillfully produces a pattern of details, incidents, and images which interrelate with one another in order to compose a "vision" of the Irish capital that, according to Terence Brown (1992: 36), also functions "as a kind of metaphor for the spiritual condition of the Irish nation as a whole." Paradoxically, though, this "vision" relies heavily on the young writer's ability to reproduce the audible surface of human communicative exchanges in the city of Dublin since, as readers discover, the protagonists' characterization remains attached to acts of eloquence.[2] Thus, speech, accent, spoken words, and voices resonate in what has been described as Joyce's "intensely accurate apprehension of Dublin life" (Brown 1992: xiii).

And yet, if it is true that, as Joycean scholarship has extensiveley discussed, the depiction of language relations, the interaction between words and the emphasis on speech acts are essential for the audible portrayal through which the writer re-embodies his native city from his exile in the European metropolises of Trieste, Paris, and Zurich, it is not less true that silence is noticeably ingrained in Joyce's work. Pauses in speech, fragmented utterances, incomplete sentences, absences of words and gaps indicate the degree to which the unspoken, the inarticulable, silence itself is tied to a fair representation of Dublin public and private life.

Unsuprisingly, the topic of silence in *Dubliners* has long drawn the attention of well known Joycean critics such as Jean-Michel Rabaté (1982) who, more than thirty years ago, spoke of the "different kinds of silences" in the collection of stories:

... silence can reveal a gap, a blank space in the text, that can be accounted for in terms of the characters who betray themselves by slips, lapses, omissions or in terms of the general economy of the text, silence being the void element which ensures displacement ... Silence can finally appear at the end, the limit, the death of speech, its paralysis.

45

Rabaté's reading has been extremely influential and has paved the way for subsequent explorations of the subversive effects of silence in *Dubliners*. The stories are highly demanding for the reader precisely because they require the production of textual repositories for the unspoken, for that which the text refuses to name. Silence, in other words, plays deceptive games on the reader since, as Laurent Milesi (1997: 112) has aptly remarked, "gaps, overlaps, repetitions, occulted vistas and imaginary visions, call for an articulation as well as, at the same time, frustrate it."

Whereas still drawing on the meta-textual level of post-structuralist approaches, recent critics who have focused on the relevance of silence in *Dubliners* have attempted to gain a broader perspective by introducing the angles of post-colonial theory and memory studies, thus allowing for a contextualized interpretation of the losses and absences "performed" by the text. In a chapter significantly entitled "Death Sentences: Silence, Colonial Memory and the Voice of the Dead in *Dubliners*," Nels Pearson (2005: 142) explains his aim as follows:

> By bringing structural and deconstructive analysis of *Dubliners* into dialogue with both post-colonial theory and Irish history, my larger objective is to encourage further connections between the formal and the cultural/historical dimensions of Joyce's work—between Joyce the evolving modernist and Joyce the evolving post-colonial writer.

Pearson's claim falls in line with the work of relevant Joycean scholars who have also addressed the issue of silence in Joyce's *oeuvre* in terms of its revealing extra-textual implications and ultimately of its contributing to a form of meaning exceptionally significant in the broader literary, cultural, historical, and political context of Ireland. This is the case with Kevin Whelan's essay "The Memories of 'The Dead,'" an exhaustive and lucid exploration of the story which compellingly reveals that the "buried history of the Famine" (Whelan 2002: 59) and the silent evocation of the (Irish) past are embedded in the language of Joyce's text "as an absence" (66). In the same vein, in her recent piece on memory and ethics in "The Dead," a story that "focuses attention on a suppressed past" (Fogarty 2014: 47), Anne Fogarty discusses the inextricable relationship between silence and memory in the story since, as she convincingly argues, "The ellipsis and moments of undecidability that have textured the other stories of *Dubliners* here come to characterize the very operations of memory".

Drawing on all the above, in what follows, I would like to reflect on Joyce's aesthetics of silence in "The Dead" in order to argue that this is a story which, by evading complete articulation and withholding voice, ironically calls attention to the unsayable as the very essence of what the text attempts to communicate. My use of the concept "aesthetics of silence" borrows directly from Susan Sontag's discussion of the modern artist's revolt against the inadequacies of language. Sontag envisions this revolt first as a "quest for a consciousness purified of contaminated language" (1994: 22) later followed by the development of a "program of perceptual and cultural therapy" through which "language can be employed to check language, to express muteness" (23). Thus, Sontag advocates that "silence is likely to remain a viable notion for modern art and consciousness only if deployed with considerable, near systematic irony" (33). Clearly, the issues of modern art, silence, and irony feature prominently in Joyce's modernist *Künstlerroman, A Portrait of the Artist as a Young Man*, where Stephen Dedalus, the aspiring writer, reflects on his estrangement and alienation from English, as he struggles to produce a literary language that may appropriately convey "the reality of experience" (*P* 253). In the same vein, Joyce's protagonist seeks to develop his own aesthetic program precisely at the cost of loss and absence since, as his proclamation implies, the only available modes of expression will be accomplished through "silence, exile and cunning" (*P* 247).

In his essay on "The Dead," Whelan comments also on the significance of the fact that in order to achieve "eloquence" and "narrative self-sufficiency" (2002: 62) Stephen Dedalus must leave his community. The critic contends that this obligatory flight, this necessary absence, is but a reflection of the complexities of post-Famine Ireland and of the equally complex position of the writers who "restlessly sought access to a world elsewhere—the world of Gaelic civilization, dismissed, expunged, unknowable, vanished, whose very absence must be articulated" (62).

Ultimately, the experience of loss and absence embodied by Stephen as he grapples with the problem of artistic representation, is a problem inherent to the task of the modern Irish writer since, as Joyce, himself, observed:

Ancient Ireland is dead just as ancient Egypt is dead. Its death chant has been sung, and on its gravestone has been placed the seal. The old national soul that spoke during centuries through the mouths of fabulous seers, wandering minstrels, and Jacobite poets disappeared from the world with the death of James Clarence Mangan.

CW 173–4

Through his aesthetics of silence in *Dubliners* and *A Portrait* the writer engages in a sophisticated critique of modern Ireland. Thus seen, Joyce's treatment of silence illustrates not only what Sontag identifies as the modern artist's revolt against the inadequacies of language—"seeking to loosen the grip upon consciousness of the habits of lifeless, static verbalization" (22)—but, beyond that, his use of language "to express muteness" (23) is rooted in a penetrating critique of a post-Famine Ireland "haunted by the afterlife of that deeper world from which it was permanently estranged" (Whelan 65).

For Stephen, speaking the acquired language of the Other becomes a painful reminder of one's own loss: "the language in which we are speaking is his before it is mine ... my ancestors threw off their language and took another, Stephen said, they allowed a handful of foreigners to subject them" (*P* 203). His artistic quest turns to be highly problematic and, ironically, his task ends in silence since, except for the failed villanelle, the sketchy and elliptical journal he writes becomes his only viable form of art and mode of expression. Admittedly, Joyce's own artistic trajectory was dominated by the same linguistic anxiety before a similar sense of loss and absence. As Seamus Deane has argued, the writer must come to terms with "the vexed medium of a language which carries within itself the idea of re-presentation in one form of a culture which initially existed in another, earlier form" (1990: 37).

The nineteenth century out of which Joyce's writing emerges has been described as one of the most "intriguing and haunting of all phases of Irish culture ... in which the great mass of Irish people moved from one language to another, from Gaelic to English" (Welch 1988: x). Read in this specific historical and political context of colonization and dispossession which produced a hollowed-out identity, "the death of speech," the gaps and blanks, the silences in Joyce's works further complicate the interpretation of his well-known statement about *Dubliners* as a study of his native city, "an attempt to represent certain aspects of the life of one of the European capitals" (*Letters II* 109) which, being "the 'second' city of the British Empire" (*Letters II* 111), had not been spoken of before and had, thus, remained a silent text. By writing *Dubliners* Joyce seems to break a double silence, as he is, on the one hand, disrupting the status quo of the European literary establishment and voicing Irish experience, as "no artist has given it to the world" (*Letters II* 111). On the other hand, by writing a chapter in "the moral history of

Ireland" (*Letters II* 134), the writer chooses to give a voice to the de-voiced citizens of Dublin, individuals who bore the marks of social and linguistic paralysis.

Indubitably, as Deane has remarked, Joyce found himself in a paradoxical position:

> Dublin was an absence, a nowhere, a place that was not really a city or a civilization . . . It had to be both nowhere and everywhere, absence and presence. Somehow, he had to find the language which would register both aspects of the city. He had to scorn it for its peripherality and praise it for its centrality. Between these two possibilities, his strange language vacillates and develops.
>
> 42

Furthermore, Joyce's writing of most of the stories of *Dubliners*, and particularly "The Dead," happened against the backdrop of exile, loss, and nostalgia at a crucial moment in the literary history of Ireland when the writer felt he was himself becoming an absent presence, a silent voice.

In a talk given at the James Joyce Centre in Dublin, in January of 2014, to commemorate the first hundred years of the publication of *Dubliners*, Declan Kiberd explained that the writing of the stories was for Joyce not only a measure of his own exile from Ireland, but also a way of dealing with Ireland's exile from its own past. Throughout his discussion of "epiphany," Kiberd referred to the epiphanic nature of silence in Joyce's work and remarked that, as the stories of *Dubliners* prove, Joyce was the master of the unfinished sentence:

> . . . we know why, because Joyce had been working as a teacher of English as a foreign language in Italy when he wrote the stories and if you teach a language as a foreign language anywhere, all you hear from your students all day are non-finished sentences.

This reflection on the relationship between silence and foreignness must be interpreted as an astute remark on the paradoxical condition of the unspoken in *Dubliners*, a work through which Joyce attempts after all to give voice to a problematic and alienated Irish experience, since, as Kiberd puts it, he is dealing with Ireland's exile from its own past. The above-mentioned paradoxical condition is brought about by a historical and political dispossession which is accepted from within, as expressed by Stephen in *A Portrait*: "my ancestors threw off their language and took another . . . his language, so familiar and so foreign, will always be for me an acquired speech."

In her discussions of the notion of strangeness within the self, Julia Kristeva (1991) has observed that border crossers become strangers to themselves as they inhabit a painful location, one of displacement and ambiguity where gains come through losses and voice emerges from muteness. Thus, she refers to the movement from one language to another as a dangerous enterprise which entails estrangement, alienation, and loss:

> Not speaking one's mother tongue. Living with resonances and reasoning that are cut off from the body's nocturnal memory . . . Bearing within oneself like a secret vault, or like a handicapped child—cherished and useless—that language of the past that withers without ever leaving you . . . between two languages, your realm is silence.
>
> 15

It is tempting to invoke the convenient metaphor of silence as a "secret vault" for a story like "The Dead," which deals with unfilled absences, repressed voices, unspoken secrets, and uncoffined bodies. In "The Dead," there is not one but many silences functioning strategically on different levels. On the individual level, silence originates from a significant suppression of speech, the things one declines to say or is forbidden to name, as in the case of Gretta's secret past repressed for so long—"Gretta, dear, what are you thinking about. She did not answer nor yield wholly to his arm" (1992: 219)[3]—and Gabriel's silent response as he struggles to come to terms with the disturbing acknowledgment of Gretta's belated disclosure—"Gabriel was silent. He did not wish her to think that he was interested in his delicate boy" (1992: 220).

For Michel Foucault, silence, "the discretion that is required between different speakers, is less the absolute limit of discourse . . . than an element that functions alongside the things said, with them and in relation to them within over-all strategies" (1990: 27). Foucault's notion of silence as a strategy that underlies one's discourse, "functioning alongside the things said," becomes extremely relevant to characterizations in "The Dead." Thus, when Gabriel, who had "murmured lamely that he saw nothing political in writing reviews of books," suddenly retorts, "I'm sick of my own country" (1992: 190) and Miss Ivors, asks him insistently "why," he simply remains quiet.

> —Why? Asked Miss Ivors
> Gabriel did not answer for his retort had heated him
> —Why? Repeated Mis Ivors
> They had to go visiting together and, as he had not answered her, Miss Ivors said warmly:
> —Of course, you've no answer.
>
> 1992: 190

Gabriel's various silent moments throughout the story, as he gradually moves from irritation to bafflement and terror, and from self-centeredness and self-deception to epiphanic self-recognition, ultimately foreshadow the totalizing silence of the ending. After the numerous ellipses that have textured a story characterized by "undecidability" (Fogarty 47), the end of "The Dead" performs silence itself in a closing scene in which nothing is heard but the muted and peaceful stillness of the snow "faintly falling." At this point, Gabriel, who had been observing things from a distance, refusing to participate in Irish life, yields to the stillness made of sounds reaching him from far away, from the past and from the dead. "His soul swooned slowly," we read and "his own identity was fading into a grey impalpable world" where everything solid "was dissolving and dwindling" (1992: 225). Clearly, the language of the final scene, with its soft alliterations and reverberations, enacts the special quality of silence itself at the precise moment when snow falls and sounds curve up and away into the atmosphere and eventually out to space without ever being heard. As Fogarty has discussed, the story acquires a new meaning through the "resonant" echoes which break the silence of the ending:

> Concurrently, the text seems impersonally to decenter itself from Dublin and move out into the terrain of Ireland as a whole, thus sweeping up into its compass all the lingering aftermath of the traumas of Irish history embedded in the snowy landscape it traverses and the dispersed memories of the degradation and losses of Irish native culture and of Irish Catholic History.
>
> 61

Joyce's aesthetics of silence as developed in the rest of the stories of *Dubliners*, also charged with metaphors of paralysis and speechlessness, culminates in "The Dead" where, ironically, much of what really matters remains unsaid. Clearly, for Joyce, the modern artist par excellence, silence, in Sontag's words, "is likely to remain a viable form of communication" (33), particularly in a story which implicitly speaks to the reader by creating silences through blanks, gaps, and omissions in the text. As announced, silence functions strategically on different levels, not only revealing and illuminating the gradual transformations of the protagonists' psyche on the level of the plot but also powerfully engaging with issues of language, identity, and politics in the broader context of Ireland since undisclosed and unspoken aspects of private life are ultimately caught up in the public narrative of history.

During the dinner party, in a conversation about the opera company at the Theatre Royal, Freddy Malins praises the voice of a "negro chieftain" as "one of the finest tenor voices he had ever heard" and insists that "he has a grand voice"

(1992: 199). A scene charged with meaningful silence follows as he sharply asks his listeners, "And why couldn't he have a voice too? ... Is it because he is only a black? Nobody answered his question and Mary Jane led the table back to the legitimate opera" (1992: 199). As Pearson has noted, it becomes extremely significant that it is precisely Malins, a drunk pub-going Dubliner whose own voice is silenced by self-imposed paralysis and which represents the stage Irishman, a sort of "atavistic Irish presence in search of a voice" (162), who is the one who speaks for the condition of oppression and silence of Irish identity. It is precisely through the silences created around things said, as in the case of Malins's remark about the black tenor, that "The Dead" calls attention to the unsaid and, more importantly, to the unsayable, thus retrieving and foregrounding a narrative disrupted by losses and absences.

In her sensitive reading of the story, Fogarty claims that, in "The Dead," history becomes a "spectral trace" (46) and appropriately argues that "[it] enacts an ethics of memory and focuses attention on a suppressed past and the lingering aftermath of the political conflicts that have torn Irish society apart over the centuries" (47). The story, it is well known, is set in the period of the Irish Literary Revival and illustrates Joyce's own internal negotiation and personal conflict in relation to the political and cultural situation emerging in the Ireland of his day, dealing with, among other questions, the theme of estrangement from one's mother tongue. As has been widely discussed in literary and cultural criticism, the imperial exploitation of Ireland had massive repercussions for the Irish language, and for social issues pertaining to religious affiliation, class, and ethnicity. The decline of the Irish language was accelerated by the Great Famine of the nineteenth century, since most of the one million who died of starvation and the millions who left on coffin ships for America were Irish speakers. Although Joyce was born and raised as a native speaker of English, his violently disruptive style demonstrates an attitude towards language that highlights the notion of absences and gaps. Joyce belonged to a generation who sought to reshape Ireland in fundamental ways in the aftermath of the Famine, writing in a form of English that must necessarily carry within itself the trace of an absence, the loss of the natural relationship to the mother tongue. It is precisely in this particular context that silence in "The Dead" may be understood as a discursive dramatization of that loss. Paradoxically, Joyce turns to muteness as the only mode of expression for the experience of a world from which he, like his characters, feels estranged.

In a newspaper article published in 1907, "Ireland at the Bar," originally published in Italian as "L'Irlanda a la sbarra," Joyce writes about the evils of

British imperial rule in Ireland by focusing on the figure of Myles Joyce, a monoglot Irish speaker, unfairly tried before an English-speaking court and executed for a murder he did not commit. For Joyce, he becomes a symbol of the distortion and failings inherent in the problem of representation in Ireland: "The figure of this dumbfounded old man, a remnant of a civilization not ours, deaf and dumb before his judge, is a symbol of the Irish nation at the bar of public opinion" (*CW* 198).

Apparently, Myles Joyce was executed protesting his innocence in Irish until he died and it was later believed that his ghost haunted the Galway jail where he was buried (Whelan 63). Much has been written about the way in which Joyce's fiction, intensely and consistently reverberative, is heightened by the constant imaginative absorption and reworking of previous literary, historical, and cultural sources. Joyce himself hinted to his brother Stanislaus that "The Dead" was "a ghost story" (Whelan 69). Certainly, the text is haunted by several ghosts, "spectral traces" which, like the ghost of Myles Joyce, become the symbol of the lingering voice of the unsayable. There are numerous reverberations through which the text seems to suggest that the ghosts of a troubled past are demanding to be heard in "The Dead," as when Gretta's buried memory of Michael Furey is resurrected by the singing of "The Lass of Aughrim":

> Gabriel said nothing but pointed up the stairs towards where his wife was standing. Now that the hall-door was closed the voice and the piano could be heard more clearly. Gabriel held up his hand for them to be silent. The song seemed to be in the old Irish tonality and the singer seemed uncertain both of his words and his voice.
>
> 1992: 211

A number of Joyce scholars have noted that "The Lass of Aughrim" is itself a reminder of the deep, oral, Irish-language, Jacobite, Gaelic past of the west of Ireland. Among them, Vincent J. Cheng (1995) has argued that, through the "Lass of Aughrim," Joyce inscribes also the "loss of Aughrim," the silenced memory of the dead of the Battle of Aughrim (1691), closely associated with the Battle of the Boyne (1690), and with the subjugation of the Irish by the English. As Cheng points out, Aughrim, like the Lass in the traditional song, "becomes itself a poignant symbol of domination and colonization by imperial patriarchs—that murdered Irish past, the dead ... Men that had fought at Aughrim and the Boyne" (144).

Ultimately, by leading the reader's attention to the silences that exist in the interstices between the sounds of the words uttered by the characters' voices and the lost words of absent voices evoked by elliptical marginal texts like "The Lass of Aughrim," Joyce ironically deploys the only viable mode of expression for the unsayable. Towards the end of the story, it becomes evident that silence works thematically and structurally through the gradual accumulation of ellipses and gaps, potentially speaking for the various losses and absences—the dead evoked in the title. As Fogarty has observed, even Gretta's story, "punctuated by gaps and circular repetitions," is indeterminate and incomplete and, thus, remains "ghostly, Other and elusive" (58). In this respect, if on the level of the plot Michael Furey becomes a spectral presence, "a few light taps upon the pane" (1992: 225) which force Gabriel to turn to the window, his uncanny and haunting presence figures also as a "ghostly" discursive event in Gretta's elusive narrative. Associated with the Irish past and very likely with the lost Irish language, Michael Furey, like Myles Joyce and the dead men that fought at the Battle of Aughrim, belongs to the realm of the void, the unsayable, and as such, they can only be spoken of through the ultimate displacement of language: silence.

As I have been suggesting, in the context of modern Irish literature, the aesthetics of silence has profound implications for narratives like "The Dead" that deal with history and identity and, thus, require to be read as evocations of absence, loss, and dispossession, in themselves idiosyncratic aspects of Irish culture. In this respect, it could be said that Joyce initiates a concern with silence, both as a theme and a formal strategy, which has continued to characterize much of contemporary Irish writing. The obsession with what cannot be spoken has come to occupy such a central position in the Irish literary imagination that it could be argued that the concept of silence itself has been predominant in the literary production of the past few years.[4] Certainly, the notion of silence attached to the ideas of loss and otherness has continued to saturate contemporary Irish narratives. Yet, in post-independence Ireland, many writers seemed to have developed a new version of Joyce's aesthetics of silence with a view to articulate mainly the tensions and contradictions of Irish contemporary culture and to expose the wrongs,[5] often denouncing both private and public dysfunctions of a society in which shocking anomalies have long remained buried and unacknowledged. In this new context, fiction attempts to communicate aspects of Irish life that are "beyond words" and, therefore, silence must speak for the "unsayable."

Notes

1   This essay is part of a research project on Silence in Irish Literature (FFI2017–84619-P) funded by the Spanish *Ministerio de Economía y Competitividad* and

ERDF and the ED431D2017/17 *Rede de Investigación de Lingua e Literatura Inglesa e Identidade* III, *Xunta de Galicia.*

2   For a study of Joyce's use of Irish oratory, see Bevis (2007).

3   References in this essay are to *Dubliners*, intro. and notes T. Brown, London: Penguin (1992).

4   For a detailed discussion of the topic of silence in contemporary Irish Literature, see Beville and Dybris McQuaid (2012).

5   For a study of the richness and diversity of post-independence narrative which specifically addresses the issues of unresolved political and cultural debates, see Harte and Parker (2000).

References

Beville, M. and Dybris McQuaid, S. (2012), "Speaking of Silence: Comments from an Irish Studies Perspective," *Nordic Irish Studies* 11, no. 2: 1–20.

Bevis, M. (2007), *The Art of Eloquence: Byron, Dickens, Tennyson, Joyce*, Oxford: Oxford University Press.

Brown, T. (1992), "Introduction," in J. Joyce, *Dubliners*, vii–xlviii, London: Penguin.

Cheng, V. J. (1995), *Joyce, Race and Empire*, Cambridge: Cambridge University Press.

Deane, S. (1990), "Joyce the Irishman," in D. Attridge (ed.), *The Cambridge Companion to James Joyce*, 31–53, Cambridge: Cambridge University Press.

Fogarty, A. (2014), "'I Think He Died for Me': Memory and Ethics in 'The Dead,'" in O. Frawley and K. O'Callaghan (eds), *Memory Ireland: James Joyce and Cultural Memory*, 46–61, Syracuse, NY: Syracuse University Press.

Foucault, M. (1990), *History of Sexuality*, Vol. 1, trans. R. Hurley, New York: Vintage.

Harte, L. and Parker, M. (2000), *Contemporary Irish Fiction: Themes, Tropes, Theories*, London: Macmillan.

Joyce, J. (1992), *Dubliners*, intro. and notes T. Brown, London: Penguin.

Kiberd, D. (2014), "*Dubliners*: The First Hundred Years," talk delivered at the James Joyce Centre, Dublin, January 6, https://www.youtube.com/watch?v=A5qhK7LH6co (accessed July 31, 2017).

Kristeva, J. (1991), *Strangers to Ourselves*, New York: Columbia University Press.

Milesi, L. (1997), "Joyce's Anamorphic Mirror in 'The Sisters,'" in M. Power and U. Schneider (eds), *New Perspectives on Dubliners*, 91–113, Atlanta, GA: Rodopi.

Pearson, N. (2005), "Death Sentences: Silence, Colonial Memory and the Voice of the Dead in *Dubliners*," in C. Jaurretche (ed.), *Beckett, Joyce and the Art of the Negative*, 141–70, Amsterdam and New York: Rodopi.

Rabaté, J.-M. (1982), "Silence in *Dubliners*," in C. MacCabe (ed.), *James Joyce: New Perspectives*, 45–72, Bloomington: Indiana University Press.

Sontag, S. (1994), "The Aesthetics of Silence," in *Styles of Radical Will*, 3–34, London: Vintage.

Welch, R. (1988), *A History of Verse Translation from the Irish, 1789–1897*, Totowa, NJ: Gerrards Cross.

Whelan, K. (2002), "The Memories of 'The Dead'," *Yale Journal of Criticism* 15, no. 1: 59–97.

7

"Affirmation and negations invalidated as uttered" in *Ulysses* and *How It Is*

Sam Slote

In his book *Joyce Effects*, Derek Attridge elegantly deconstructs the all too common characterization of the "Penelope" episode as having a fluid style.[1] Contrary to the varied application of fluvial metaphors to an understanding of "Penelope," he claims that "*Ulysses* makes no such association [between flow and femininity]" (Attridge 2000: 111). This unequivocal claim is not completely accurate even if Attridge's critique of the fluvial reading of Molly's thoughts is a necessary corrective. And so, the question asked in "Ithaca" apropos the water from Bloom's tap, "Did it flow?" (*U* 17.163), might be answered with a "no" with respect to Molly. However, there is a question and answer unit within "Ithaca" that is pertinent to Molly and its pertinence is announced overtly:

> What special affinities appeared to him to exist between the moon and woman?
>
> Her antiquity in preceding and surviving successive tellurian generations: her nocturnal predominance: her satellitic dependence: her luminary reflection: her constancy under all her phases, rising and setting by her appointed times, waxing and waning: the forced invariability of her aspect: her indeterminate response to inaffirmative interrogation: her potency over effluent and refluent waters: her power to enamour, to mortify, to invest with beauty, to render insane, to invite to and aid delinquency: the tranquil inscrutability of her visage: the terribility of her isolated dominant implacable resplendent propinquity: her omens of tempest and of calm: the stimulation of her light, her motion and her presence: the admonition of her craters, her arid seas, her silence: her splendour, when visible: her attraction, when invisible.
>
> *U* 17.1157–70

This is an excellent example of one of Joyce's capricious lists. The general sentiment that unites these individual entries—or at least some of them—is a yoking together of various clichés about the moon and clichés of womanhood on a general, abstract level; for example, "her splendour, when visible: her attraction, when invisible" and "her omens of tempest and of calm." Other qualities enumerated here, while pertinent to both moon and woman, apply differently, such as "the forced invariability of her aspect." Apropos the moon, this refers to the fact that the moon always presents the same side towards the earth because it takes the same time for it to revolve around its own axis as it does to orbit around the earth. When applied to women, it would mean something a bit different. Some units posit a different manner of consociation between matters selenian and matters feminine: "her potency over effluent and refluent waters." On the one hand, this refers to the moon's control over earthly tides and, on the other hand, to menstruation. Both these cycles are linked, and so, *pace* Attridge, *Ulysses* does make an association between flow and femininity, in this one instance at least.

The phrase "her indeterminate response to inaffirmative interrogation" is an interesting statement to come within the catechestical "Ithaca" since many of this episode's questions could be characterized as inaffirmative interrogations and many of its answers indeterminate responses. This phrase also provides an interesting premonition of "Penelope." If "Ithaca" is an exercise in abstraction, then "Penelope" might seem to be an expression of the direct and unequivocal in that it is punctuated by determinate responses that follow from (mostly) unasked questions, that is, Molly's resounding and repeated yeses. However, these yeses are less unequivocal than they might seem and are, in their own way or ways, also indeterminate responses.

Like the soul, Molly's yes is not simple: it is complex and promiscuous precisely because Molly's perspective is multifarious and ever-changing. As an example, the episode begins with her remembering Bloom's obsequiousness with Mrs Riordan (Stephen's aunt Dante) back when they used to live at the City Arms Hotel, but this train of thought leads her to think "still I like that in him polite to old women" (*U* 18.16). No matter what negative thoughts Molly harbors towards her husband—and she has more than a few—she cycles back to things she likes in him. Her affirmations are not usually consistent. Likewise, her sense of gender solidarity is inconsistent. At one point she thinks, "I dont care what anybody says itd be much for the world to be governed by the women in it" (*U* 18.1434–5); and then just a little bit later, "I hate that in women no wonder they treat us the way they do we are a dreadful lot of bitches" (*U* 18.1458–9). (Of course, these two seemingly antithetical statements are not necessarily mutually exclusive.)

Precisely because Molly's perspective shifts as she affirms different, potentially contradictory things throughout, Derrida proposes that her affirmations are, in aggregate, irresponsible and indeterminate. Each of Molly's yeses is also, potentially, a negation of something else. In "Ulysses Gramophone," he addresses the question of how one might respond to affirmation, specifically to Molly's concluding affirmation. In context, she could be referring to Bloom, as she has just remembered their first date at Howth, or to Boylan, or to going to sleep, or to her childhood in Gibraltar. And so amidst all these possibilities, what exactly is she affirming: "What is being said, written, and what happens/arrives with *yes*?" (Derrida 2013: 72). For Derrida, Molly's yes is an affirmation that affirms itself as an affirmation without any single decidable referent; it is an indeterminate affirmation. In having an undecidable referent, Molly's yes is irresponsible and so Derrida's question is how does one respond to the irresponsible. "Reciprocally, two responses or two responsibilities refer to each other without having any relation between them. The two sign yet prevent the signature from gathering itself. All they can do is call for another *yes*, another signature. And furthermore, one cannot differentiate between two *yes*es that *must* gather together like twins, to the point of simulacrum, the one being the gramophony of the other" (Derrida 2013: 80). To say yes, to affirm the yes, is to listen to the *ouï-dire* (hearsay) and to have and to hear that listening respond. Molly's affirmation is excessive and overflows in affirming itself as an (act of) affirmation.

The yeses in "Penelope" serve a diverse range of functions. The first would be the most evident, a basic statement of affirmation, such as we have in the episode's first line, "Yes because he never did a thing like that" (*U* 18.01). Of course, this category could be refined and nuanced with all sorts of different categories or even values of affirmation. In some cases, the subject of the affirmation is unambiguous and in others there is some equivocation, but, even in cases where the subject can be equivocated, we still have a structure of affirmation, that is, a response to some question, even if it is unasked. The point I want to signal about this particular category of "yes" is that it is semantic in that it offers a positive meaning. A related category would be the citation of past yeses: "he pestered me to say yes" (*U* 18.302), where again the primary force of the "yes" is semantic. In distinction, I am more interested in the *syntaxes* of the "yes" in "Penelope" and here we see a variety of uses, some of which can tend to blur, for this is where the more interesting ambiguities emerge. The first syntactic function would be equivalent to a full stop or caesura, closing off one line of thought before another begins: "of course the woman hides it not to give all the trouble they do yes he came somewhere" (*U* 18.33–4). The converse to this would be the "yes" as copula, conjoining two statements: "Id have to dring it into him for a month yes and then wed have a hospital nurse next thing on the carpet" (*U* 18.19–21). Another example is where Molly thinks of Bloom's odd habit of kissing their hall-door. This serves as a neat example of Bloom's own particular flavor of lapsed Judaism: he kisses the place where the mezuzah should be but isn't, thereby showing obeisance to a missing sign: "didnt he kiss our halldoor yes he did what a madman" (*U* 18.1406).[2] Here the yes answers the question but also works as a conjunction: Bloom did kiss the hall-door and that act was a sign of his, let's just say, eccentricity.

However, the most interesting use of the yes would be as an elision, for example: "that Andalusian singing her Manola she didnt make much secret of what she hadnt yes and the second pair of silkette stockings" (*U* 18.441–2). This echoes a common trait or tic of Bloom's internal monologues: the aposiopesis. The aposiopesis is an interruption and an elision, but unlike the ellipsis, the elided material is not necessarily inferable from the context. An example would be the furtive message Bloom inscribes at the end of "Nausicaa": "I. . . . AM A." (*U* 13.1258, 1264). In this example from "Penelope," the yes masks whatever it is that the Andalusian girl had done. Even if this Andalusian girl was not able to successfully hide what she had done, Molly manages to keep it concealed; although, certainly, guesses are possible. This yes silences precisely that which it purportedly affirms.

Another example of an aposiopesis where the elision is potentially inferable but not in a way that is unequivocal is "Ill change that lace on my black dress to show off my bubs and Ill yes by God Ill get that big fan mended" (*U* 18.900–1). Unless "getting that big fan mended" is some kind of euphemistic expression, the yes here functions as either an element that conjoins two tasks of household maintenance—mending a dress and mending a fan—or it serves as an elision for what will transpire once the dress is mended and becomes more revealing. The dress may be revealing, but the yes is coy and concealing.

In some instances, the yes seems to exhibit all these different syntactic functions: "theyre all mad to get in there where they come out of youd think they could never go far enough up and then theyre done with you in a way till the next time yes because theres a wonderful feeling there so tender" (*U* 18.806–9). Here, the yes both closes off the contemplation of male libido but also continues it into a different register. It is unclear if that "wonderful feeling" refers to either female pleasure or male; presumably the former, but it is not unequivocal. And so, the copula here—conjoining two statements—denotes a copulative function.

The yeses function not unlike punctuation marks; they redress, at least in part, the episode's lack of punctuation. They disambiguate, or, in places, ambiguate various clauses and provide a sense of rhythm for reading:

yes he said I was a flower of the mountain yes so we are flowers all a womans
body yes that was one true thing he said in his life and the sun shines for you
today yes that was why I liked him because I saw he understood or felt what a
woman is and I knew I could always get round him and I gave him all the
pleasure I could leading him on till he asked me to say yes.

U 18.1575–81

The yeses in this passage are deployed strategically for emphasis and pace.
Indeed, it is very difficult to read this passage aloud in a neutral fashion that
obviates a sexual rhythm. This is a key passage in the episode and the book as a
whole in that it signals Molly's sober and equivocal affirmation of Bloom: she
may understand and appreciate that he can empathize with women, that he is a
"womanly man" (*U* 15.1799) who "understood or felt what a woman is," but she
also knows that she can always outsmart him. Different, even contradictory
senses are both yoked together and isolated. Each term is silenced by what comes
next. As conjoining elements, the yeses, in effect, make this passage and, indeed,
the whole of "Penelope" into something like a very long list, albeit a list that is not
entirely paratactic since the yeses also indicate subordinate clauses. The term
polysyndeton means an overabundance of conjunctions and so the polyvalence
of "Penelope" is enabled through and orchestrated by its polysyndetic yeses. In
effect, "Penelope" does not so much flow as *stutter*.

This leads me to my main point about Molly's multifarious yeses: they enable
discourse, her discourse, to continue through a kind of series of polysyndetic
disjunctive conjunctions. The yeses link because they are incomplete: they
indicate the copula of continuing discourse. At one point Molly thinks, "yes
because a woman whatever she does knows where to stop" (*U* 18.1438–9). This
is an odd comment in the context of an almost continuous block of unpunctuated
text since it certainly might seem that Molly does not know when to stop. Her
yeses motivate discourse, but, of course, not ad infinitum.

Derrida notes that the Irish language weighs over "Penelope" because the
language lacks words for *yes* and *no* in direct forms (Derrida 2013: 82, n. 9). This
absence of *yes* would make it very difficult to translate "Penelope" into Irish. And
so, what the Irish translators did was to use the word "*seadh*" (Joyce 1991:
1 passim), a purely phatic word devoid of semantic meaning and which is used
to facilitate communication rather than impart information. At best, one might
render *seadh* into English as "un-huh." In this way it is a perfect example of
an "indeterminate response to inaffirmative interrogation." The use of this
indeterminate response to translate Molly's seemingly determinate response
actually indicates something about Molly's yeses in that it helps suggest how

ambivalent these yeses are. As resounding as Molly's yes may be—in its polysyndetic polymorphous perversity as an enabler of the propagation of discourse—it nevertheless partakes of silence. After all, yes is the last word of the episode. The final yes is a conjunction that also works as an aposiopesis: the yes that closes off the text into its final silence. This brings me back to that list in "Ithaca" with which I began. One of the elements jointly associated between the moon and woman is the "the admonition of her craters, her arid seas, her silence."[3] The silence of the moon, its imperviousness to the responsibility of response, is an example of what is called elsewhere in "Ithaca" "the apathy of the stars" (*U* 17.2226). To the "admonition of her silence" one could add "the admonition of her yeses" since the yes enables the perpetuation of discourse, that is, until the end when it affirms the end of affirmation.

And so Molly's yes would be an example of what Beckett's Unnamable calls, as a kind of description of how he is to proceed, "affirmations and negations invalidated as uttered" (Beckett 2010a: 1). For the Unnamable, every step taken is also a step retracted: the path forward is aporetic. The copula is also an aporia. This is, of course, encapsulated in the text's final line: "I can't go on, I'll go on" (Beckett 2010a: 134). The Unnamable's goal, from the start, is to speak himself into silence: "The search for the means to put an end to things, an end to speech, is what enables discourse to continue" (Beckett 2010a: 10). The proliferation of discourse is orientated towards a silence it can never quite achieve. In this, Molly is very close to the Unnamable in that both texts present us with multiple, incommensurable fragments of ratiocination that asymptotically tend towards a silence that never quite comes within the interval of discourse. Both texts continue on through disjunction and incompleteness.

Beckett continued *The Unnamable* in a different vector with the *Texts for Nothing*, the first of which begins, "Suddenly, no, at last, long last, I couldn't any more, I couldn't go on" (Beckett 2010b: 3). This text begins with the seemingly unequivocal affirmation of termination ("I couldn't go on"), which of course is paradoxical since this affirmation is itself a continuation on from *The Unnamable*. Unsurprisingly, the narrative voice subsequently equivocates upon the problematic fate of continuation: "How can I go on, I shouldn't have begun, no, I had to begin" (Beckett 2010b: 3). As with *The Unnamable*, the voice here has always already begun and has begun by deliberating the problem of beginning.[4] And, as with most of Beckett's post-war prose writing, this text was initially written in French and was revised during the course of translating (or rewriting, or going on) into English. The English continuation is thus disjunct with the purported French original. Indeed, the English version of this passage has an interesting difference from the French: "Comment continuer? Il ne fallait pas commencer, si, il le fallait" (Beckett 1958: 115). The English version twists this imperative slightly: in place of the French "si, il le fallait," the English has "no, I had to begin." Unlike the linguistic austerity of the Irish language—which is devoid of yes—the French language is blessed with two flavours of affirmation, si and oui. The "si" and the "no" are each idiomatically appropriate and rhetorically equivalent in that they both affirm the inevitability of continuation: I could not go on, *yes*, I had to go on; or in other words, I could not go on; *no*, I had to go on. Apparently, yes does sometimes mean no. Denial and affirmation are both examples of going on. Or, in other words, going on is what goes on, whether denied or affirmed. Like "Penelope," the text continues by affirmative disjunction.

We see these issues of affirmation and continuation quite starkly in Beckett's last novel, *How It Is*, which, like "Penelope," is bereft of punctuation, although it is set into short paragraphs, or versets, of varying length. The novel presents us with a character, Bom, alone in the dark in the mud, who is joined, for a time, by a companion, Pim, whom he instructs and tortures by carving capitalized words onto his back. The novel ends with an accumulation of yeses of some force. And these yeses certainly seem to suggest the end of *Ulysses* with Molly's polygamous and polyvalent yes, but the yeses at the end of *How It Is* are perhaps somewhat different. If Molly's yes is an affirmation—equivocal as it may be— then the yes in *How It Is* is nothing less than an unqualified rejection. The goal of The Unnamable is here realized: affirmation has indeed become coterminous with denial.

> alone in the mud yes the dark yes sure yes panting yes someone hears me no no one hears me no murmuring sometimes yes when the panting stops yes not at other times no in the mud yes to the mud yes my voice yes mine yes not another's no mine alone yes sure yes when the panting stops yes on and off yes a few words yes a few scraps yes that no one hears no but less and less no answer LESS AND LESS yes.
>
> Beckett 2009: 128

Mired in the mud, exploiting others so that he may enjoy a simulacrum of being alive, of having a finite life, "a different man more universal," Bom affirms an impotent mastery that nonetheless retains sufficient power to exploit. Like Derrida's reading of Molly's yes, Bom's yes affirms itself as an (act of) affirmation, but also as an affirmation of inability. Each of his acts—his torture of Pim, his terminal affirmations—is made to defer the end until such a time as it can no longer continue, that is, until the end can no longer be deferred any longer, such as with the moment of death. This is what Bom finally realizes at the end of *How It Is*, after his final burst of ineffectual affirmation:

> so things may change no answer no end no answer I may choke no answer sink no answer sully the mud no more no answer the dark no answer trouble the peace no more no answer the silence no answer die no answer DIE screams I MAY DIE screams I SHALL DIE screams good good good end at last of part three and last that's how it was end of quotation after Pim how it is.
>
> Beckett 2009: 129

If Molly's yes—in all its ambivalences and equivocations—is like Nietzsche's "great Yes to life" (Nietzsche 1969: 226), an indeterminate affirmation of all modalities of life, good and bad, then Bom's is the great Yes to death, which is to say that they are much and more or less the same thing.

Notes

1   The first example (of many) Attridge cites is perfectly representative of this general tendency: "The rarity of capital letters and the run-on sentences in Molly's monologue are of course related to Joyce's theory of her mind (and of the female mind in general) as a flow" (*JJII* 376; cited in Attridge 2000: 93).

2   Compounding this sense of Bloom's lapsed Judaism, in "Nausicaa" he confuses the mezuzah with tephilim, small boxes containing parchments of scripture, that are affixed to leather straps and worn during prayer: "And the tephilim no what's this they call it poor papa's father had on his door to touch" (*U* 13.1157–8).

3   The syntax of this entry requires some clarification. Joyce sets off each element within the list with colons: the colon is thus the copula that conjoins each element within the list. (Note that Joyce's use of the colon as a separator is more common in French than in English.) On the Rosenbach manuscript, Joyce set off the various elements with commas, thereby creating a problem for compound elements that would include internal commas (such problems of identifying hypotactic elements within lists are common in the various lengthy lists in *Finnegans Wake*). Joyce changed the commas to colons on the page proofs (*UCSE* 1546). Since it's possible that Joyce might have inadvertently skipped updating the commas to colons in the passage "the admonition of her craters, her arid seas, her silence," this passage could be read either as a single, sylleptic unit (which, unpacked, would read as "the admonition of her craters, the admonition of her arid seas, the admonition of her silence"), or as three discreet entries ("the admonition of her craters; and her arid seas; and her silence"). Since the previous unit in the list is more unambiguously a triple syllepsis ("the stimulation of her light, her motion

and her presence"), it seems likely that this unit is a syllepsis that follows from the word "admonition."

4　The Unnamable phrases this problem of having always already begun in his typically paradoxical manner: "The best would be not to begin. But I have to begin. That is to say I have to go on" (Beckett 2010a: 2).

References

Attridge, D. (2000), *Joyce Effects*, Cambridge: Cambridge University Press.

Beckett, S. (1958), *Nouvelles et Textes pur rien*, Paris: Minuit.

Beckett, S. (2009), *How It Is*, ed. Édouard Magessa O'Reilly, London: Faber.

Beckett, S. (2010a), *The Unnamable*, ed. Steven Connor, London: Faber.

Beckett, S. (2010b), *Texts for Nothing and Other Shorter Prose, 1950–1976*, ed. Mark Nixon, London: Faber.

Derrida, J. (2013), "Ulysses Gramophone: Hear Say Yes in Joyce," trans. François Raffoul, in A. J. Mitchell and S. Slote (eds), *Derrida and Joyce: Texts and Contexts*, 41–86, Albany: State University of New York Press.

Ellmann, R. (1982), *James Joyce*, rev. edn, New York: Oxford University Press.

Joyce, J. (1991), *Uilséas*, Vol. 12, trans. Séamas Ó hInnéirghe and Breasal Uilsean, Belfast: Foillseacáin Inis Gleoire.

Nietzsche, F. (1969), *Ecce Homo*, trans. Walter Kaufmann, in *On the Genealogy of Morals and Ecce Homo*, 199–344, New York: Vintage.

8

"Shut up he explained": Joyce and "scornful silence"

Morris Beja

I take my title from the moving and profound remark about the need for silence in Ring Lardner's short novel *The Young Immigrunts*, where the child narrator tells about a car trip during which his father is increasingly frustrated and infuriated:

> Are you lost daddy I arsked tenderly.
> Shut up he explained.

Lardner 2006: 332

In James Joyce, too, there is something definitely off-putting about quietness, a connection between the "scornful silence" of Stephen at the beginning of *Ulysses* ("Stephen listened in scornful silence," *U* 1.418) and separation, distance, aloneness, alienation, indifference, desperation, exile. In "The Sisters," Eliza condescendingly says of her brother, the late Father Flynn, "—Ah, poor James! . . . He was no great trouble to us. You wouldn't hear him in the house any more than now" (*D* 16). Now, that is, that he's "gone" (*D* 16). Mr. Crofton, in "Ivy Day in the Committee Room," is "silent for two reasons. The first reason, sufficient in itself, was that he had nothing to say; the second was that he considered his companions beneath him" (*D* 130–1). In "The Dead," Gabriel responds to Molly Ivors' repeated demand that he explain why he is "sick" of his own country with stony, even resentful—scornful—silence (*D* 189). But in *Dubliners* the epitome of such distance and cut-off-ness and alienation is surely the end of "Eveline," as Eveline, completely silent, gives Frank "no sign of love or farewell or recognition" (*D* 41).

In *A Portrait*, Stephen feels, in the "silence of the evening," "the vast indifferent dome and the calm processes of the heavenly bodies" (*P* 172)—while the characters of *Ulysses* live in what is called in "Oxen of the Sun" "clouded silence: silence that is the infinite of space" (*U* 14.1078–9). In "Proteus," as Stephen reflects, "I am lonely here," he wonders, "What is that word known to all men?"—and his immediate next words to himself are, "I am quiet here alone" (*U* 3.434–5).

The alienating silence can be, as well, painfully reproachful. In "Oxen of the Sun," again, we read of a "vision" that comes "shrouded in the piteous vesture of the past, silent, remote, reproachful" (*U* 14.1353–5). The vision echoes Stephen's dream of his mother in "Telemachus," where "Silently, in a dream she had come to him after her death, her wasted body within its loose brown graveclothes giving off an odour of wax and rosewood, her breath, that had bent upon him, mute, reproachful, a faint odour of wetted ashes" (*U* 1.102–5). Evocatively, the vision and the dream echo as well Joyce's own dream of his mother recorded in one of his manuscript epiphanies, where "She comes at night when the city is still; invisible, inaudible . . ."[1]

Not surprisingly, given how Joycean silence seems connected with aloofness and remoteness and reproach and distance and coldness and exile, silences are pervasive in the play *Exiles*, where typical stage directions repeatedly demand "some moments in silence": "*He stares before him for some moments in silence, as if dazed*"; "*He rises and goes to and fro some moments in silence. Then he goes towards the porch and leans against the jamb.* ROBERT *watches him*"; "*He looks at* RICHARD *for some moments in silence*"; "*They both look at each other coldly in silence for some moments*"; once, the scene directions indicate, they even "*look at each other for some minutes in silence*" (*E* 76, 82, 85, 125, 78). Those are just a few examples in the play.[2]

In drama you have to wait until Samuel Beckett and Harold Pinter to hear such deafening silences. It is no wonder that Pinter was so fascinated by *Exiles*, and directed productions of it twice. But in terms of modernist fiction, one may also note the profound connections between alone-ness and silence, exile and distance, and alienation and silence, in Virginia Woolf—as in *The Waves*, where all the characters dwell on what Neville, for example, sees as the "Loneliness and silence" surrounding Percival, or where Bernard tells us that "Drop upon drop . . . silence falls. It forms on the roof of the mind and falls into pools beneath. For ever alone, alone, alone,—hear silence fall and sweep its rings to the farthest edges . . . I, whom loneliness destroys, let silence fall, drop by drop" (Woolf 1993: 96, 145).

Particularly intriguing are such connections between silence and alienation within Joyce's epiphanies, especially the manuscript epiphanies he wrote and collected, and which provide perhaps the ultimate examples of the revelatory power of what is "*un*said"—the *Wake*'s "aristmystic unsaid" (*FW* 293.18). The manuscript epiphanies are filled with gaps, gaps that are graphically indicated by Joyce's liberal use of dots, of ellipses, which are never, of course—we're talking about James Joyce, after all—used arbitrarily. Like the single huge dot at the end of "Ithaca," they forcefully evoke silence. Or, as in the eponymous epiphany in *Stephen Hero*, inaudibility:

> The Young Lady—(drawling discreetly) ... O, yes ... I was ... at the ... cha ... pel ...
> The Young Gentleman—(inaudibly) ... I ... (again inaudibly) ... I ...
> The Young Lady—(softly) ... O ... but you're ... ve ... ry ... wick ... ed ...
> *SH* 211

Such ellipses also pervade, for example, the first story in *Dubliners*, "The Sisters," in which, annoyed and "angry" as he is with old Cotter—"I crammed my mouth with stirabout for fear I might give utterance to my anger," forcing himself to be mute—the narrator nevertheless confesses, "I puzzled my head to extract meaning from his unfinished sentences" (*D* 11). The annoyance and frustration Joyce's characters experience in the face of those "unfinished sentences" persist— as in *Finnegans Wake*, where one of the proposed titles for the Mamafesta is "*The Suspended Sentence*" (*FW* 106.13–14).

For of course we find evocative gaps in the published works as well as the epiphanies. In the *Wake*, Shaun complains about "them bagses of trash which the mother and Mr Unmentionable (O breed not his same!) has reduced to writing" (*FW* 420.3–5). "Mr Unmentionable" brings to mind—at least to my mind— Samuel Beckett's *The Unnamable*, where the speaker wonders if he can conceivably "speak and yet say nothing, really nothing" (1958: 303) and then of course goes on to speak: to speak about not speaking, about silence and nothingness. Actually, the value of silence is something of which all the Unnamable's avatars, from Molloy on, seem conscious. As Molloy derisively says, "... you would do better, at least no worse, to obliterate texts than to blacken margins, to fill in the holes of words till all is blank and flat and the whole ghastly business looks like what it is, senseless, speechless, issueless misery" (13). But it is in *The Unnamable* that the theme of silence fully resounds in all its deafening decibels: "Yes, in my life, since we must call it so, there were three things, the inability to speak, the inability to be silent, and solitude, that's what I've had to make the best of" (396).[3]

Art Spiegelman's *Maus II* recognizes the paradoxes here, when the mouse quotes Beckett as saying that "Every word is like an unnecessary stain on silence and nothingness," then pauses—in silence—before going on, "On the other hand, he SAID it."[4] Uncontrollably, the Unnamable desperately continues talking—talking against the silence, as it were: "the silence is outside, outside, inside, there is nothing but here, and the silence outside, nothing but this voice and the silence all round . . ." (410). Yet, as he himself puts it on the first page of *The Unnamable*, he is "obliged to speak. I shall never be silent. Never" (291). If he *were* able to stop, then presumably the longed-for silence would or could take over—and he would not have to "go on," in the famous or infamous trope of "going on," or not being able to go on, or having to go on, that occurs through so much of Beckett's work:

> VLADIMIR: Well? Shall we go?
> ESTRAGON: Yes, let's go.
> *They do not move.*
>
> 1954: 61

So silence is, well, not easy to talk about. In fact, it is not always completely silent.

No, it never is. For example, John Cage's musical composition, *Four Minutes Thirty-Three Seconds*, consists of a bit over four and a half minutes of silence—except, of course, that it doesn't: for, as Cage observed, "There is no such thing as silence. Something is always happening that makes a sound."[5] Similarly, film theorists have long realized that it takes a sound film truly to render silence.[6]

In *Ulysses*, the narrator of "Cyclops" contemptuously claims, "I declare to my antimacassar if you took up a straw from the bloody floor and if you said to Bloom: *Look at, Bloom. Do you see that straw? That's a straw.* Declare to my aunt he'd talk about it for an hour so he would and talk steady" (*U* 12.893–6). And yet, among all the glib talkers we see on Bloomsday, Bloom is after all relatively restrained, and knows how to be quiet.

Leopold Bloom knows about the need for silence.

Notes

1 Epiphany 34, *The Workshop of Daedalus*, 44.
2 Cf. "Eumaeus": "There ensued a somewhat lengthy pause" (*U* 16.601).
3 Cf. the Unnamable to the "two separate Quentins" in Faulkner's *Absalom, Absalom!* "talking to one another in the long silence of notpeople, in notlanguage" (9).
4 The mouse to his "shrink" in *Maus II* (*Complete Maus*, 205). For the Beckett quotation, see Gruen (1969: 210).
5 Quoted in Sontag (1969: 10).
6 See, for example, Des O'Rawe (2006).

References

Beckett, S. (1954), *Waiting for Godot: Tragicomedy in Two Acts*, New York: Grove Press.

Beckett, S. (1958), *Three Novels: Molloy, Malone Dies, The Unnamable*, New York: Grove Press.

Faulkner, W. (1951), *Absalom, Absalom!*, New York: Random House.

Gruen, J. (1969), "Samuel Beckett Talks about Beckett," *Vogue* 154 (December): 210–11.

Joyce, J. (1965). *The Workshop of Daedalus: James Joyce and the Raw Materials for A Portrait of the Artist as a Young Man*. Ed. Robert Scholes and Richard M. Kain. Evanston, Illinois: Northwestern University Press.

Lardner, R. (2013), *Stories and Other Writings*, New York: Library of America.

O'Rawe, D. (2006), "The Great Secret: Silence, Cinema and Modernism," *Screen* 47, no. 4: 395–405.

Sontag, S. (1969), "The Aesthetics of Silence," in *Styles of Radical Will*, 3–34, New York: Farrar, Straus and Giroux.

Spiegelman, A. (1997), *Maus II*, in *The Complete Maus*, New York: Pantheon.

Woolf, V. (1993), *The Waves*, Oxford: Blackwell.

Part Three

Writing Silence

9

The Silent Author of James Joyce's Dictated Letters

William S. Brockman

Beginning from the Great War years through the late 1930s James Joyce dictated, rather than wrote himself, many dozens and perhaps hundreds of letters. At times, medical problems involving his eyes impeded his sight sufficiently that he could not read or write for days or even weeks. Through the course of the final two decades of his life, the reasons for dictation became more complex, with Joyce using his amanuenses as intermediaries between himself and his correspondents to maintain privacy or to evade direct contact to express sensitive topics that might have been offensive were they to have been communicated directly. Joyce used any number of amanuenses, including family members (Giorgio, Lucia, and Nora Joyce all provided services), friends, casual acquaintances, and, eventually in the 1930s, Paul Léon, who as lawyer, advisor, and devoted friend conducted much of Joyce's day-to-day letter writing.

The voice of a letter writer is generally unambiguous. A letter is, for the most part, communication between two people or at least two entities. A letter is generally fixed in time and expressive of its time—hence the common practice of dating letters. The writer's voice is emphatic. While a writer might well choose a variety of voices among different recipients, and might even vary the voice within an individual letter, there is usually only a single voice represented at a time.

The act of dictation from a writer to a scribe for transmission to a recipient would seem simply to expand horizontally the simple one-to-one audience, but in fact it complicates the relations. Dictated letters, directed to a private audience, differ significantly from dictated manuscripts, the latter intended for eventual publication. An individual letter is in itself the end product. While letters might be revised (though Joyce rarely did this) or copied, they represent a direct narrow transmission from sender to recipient. Manuscripts, on the other hand, are intended for dissemination and generally revised by the author—in Joyce's case, heavily.

Joyce's authorial silence or at least evasiveness in the dictated letters corresponds to analogous situations in the published works. Of the many cards, letters, and telegrams in *Ulysses*, there are numerous examples of such authorial ambiguity. For example, in "Sirens," the narrative voice guides the character Bloom through a sham of writing a business letter to disguise the imaginary Henry, author of a love letter to Martha: "Bloom dipped, Bloo mur: dear sir. Dear Henry wrote: dear Mady" (*U* 11.860). The ambiguous authorship of the letter that floats through *Finnegans Wake* certainly has features in common with the joint authorship of many of Joyce's dictated letters.

Without the editorial reworking that goes into a manuscript intended for publication, the authorial voice of a letter is inflected by an amanuensis with tone, vocabulary, language, or content. In this chapter, I would like to look at some examples of letters dictated by Joyce, following—to the degree that the surviving evidence allows—their changes in voice from Joyce's as originator to the amanuensis's as transmitter. Moreover, I would like to pose a question: when is Joyce's voice—or one of his voices—present in these dictated letters, and when is it overruled by that of the amanuenses, and hence silent?

Ophthalmological problems, particularly iritis in his left eye, plagued Joyce on and off for a good part of 1917 during his years in Zurich; he underwent an iridectomy in August of the year. It was also the time of his first significant use of amanuenses to write his letters. He drew upon acquaintances in the city, Antonio Battara and M. Gal, neither of whom is mentioned in the Ellmann biography.[1] The former was a press representative and journalist from Trieste with an office on Bahnhofplatz, directly across the street from Zurich's main railroad station. Triestine newspaper editor Silvio Benco identified him as "my friend . . . who was [Joyce's] companion in his Swiss exile" (Benco 1930: 379). Battara was prominent in Trieste before the war; in 1913 he was elected first president of "l'Associazione della Stampa Italiana a Trieste," and Joyce could well have come to know him then. Battara was responsible for at least two letters, both in French, dictated by Joyce. The first of these was a handwritten letter dated February 17 to Harriet Weaver, informing her simply that Joyce was ill ("malade"), asking to see any reviews in the English press of the recently-released English edition of *A Portrait of the Artist as a Young Man*, and promising to pay for his own copies of the novel as soon as the doctor allowed him to take care of his affairs himself.[2] On February 28 Battara wrote to Weaver's lawyers Slack, Monro, Saw, noting that Joyce had been ill for several weeks, acknowledging that he was profoundly moved by the generosity of his anonymous benefactor (i.e. Weaver, who through the firm had pledged a gift of £200), and promising that he would write as soon as the doctor would allow.[3]

Both of these letters bear the office address of Battara. French was most likely the one language that Battara and Weaver would have shared. In a month of profound events for Joyce in relation to Weaver—the publication and the gift— he was unable to communicate directly with her in his own voice, but was reduced to employing the second-hand words of an amanuensis. It was not until weeks later, on March 6, that Joyce was able by himself to write Slack, Monro, Saw to express his gratitude and enclose a letter to the benefactor.[4] Battara's letters are formally polite, befitting the occasion and reflecting the presence of a third party in the correspondence, but the gratitude shown in Joyce's own letter of thanks contrasts significantly.

Another acquaintance came to Joyce's aid at the same time, one less prominent than Battara and identified only as M. Gal in the extant letter written by him. Gal was a dealer in "Haushaltungsartikel," or household goods, who lived within blocks of the Joyces on Seefeldstrasse and who may well have supplied some of their domestic needs. In a flowery hand, Gal wrote to Grant Richards on February 27, 1917, noting that Joyce had been ill for three weeks and promised copies of the English edition of *A Portrait*. Further, he informed Richards that Joyce's agent would be sending a copy of *Exiles* (this apparently did not happen for some time, as he made the same promise in subsequent letters in March and April).[5] Like Battara, Gal wrote from his own address. Whether this situation represented live dictation by Joyce or notes taken at Joyce's flat and composed later into letters is not clear. Gal's restrained letter in French makes a telling comparison with a letter written by Joyce in English just a week later which reiterates the same information but in a more demanding tone.[6] Richards was a notoriously casual businessman, and it is likely that he responded to neither communication. The relatively flat style in these letters written by Zurich friends makes distinguishing Joyce's intentions fairly simple.

Throughout the summer of that year Nora served as amanuensis; being closer to Joyce, her own voice mingled with his. Despite his operation in late August, at least minimal communication needed to be maintained with agent Pinker, editor Pound, and publisher Weaver; Nora was responsible for at least four letters from late August through mid-September (though on September 5, Joyce was able to dash off to Claude Sykes a couple of limericks and an invitation to pay a visit to the Augenklinik). Nora usually wrote in the first person, adding Joyce's own words or at least messages at the end. For instance, on September 15, 1917 she wrote, "He was very glad indeed to hear the good news in your letter and thanks you for your kind and generous patronage of his <u>Ulysses</u>."[7]

On January 23, 1919 a short stint of iritis led Joyce to employ a third Zurich acquaintance, Antoine Chalas, whom he later referred to as "a Greek friend of mine."[8] The address on Chalas's letter was that of a hotel right around the corner from the Kronenhalle restaurant, which was to become a favorite of the Joyces. Chalas's letter, again in French, and again to Harriet Weaver, noted that Joyce had been ill for six days, asked her to contact Pinker regarding a proposed Italian translation of *A Portrait*, and reported that Joyce had just sent "Wandering Rocks" (with the episode's title given in Greek letters, perhaps a collusion between author and amanuensis) to the typist.[9] Three out of the four sentences in the short letter begin "Mr. Joyce," as if Joyce had simply spoken out several sentences which Chalas transformed into the third person. Joyce reported in a letter to Weaver of February 25, 1919 that Chalas had also written on Joyce's behalf to Richard Aldington (*JJII* 454).

With the Joyce family's move to Paris in 1920, most of the dictation work for Joyce's almost annual eye problems was taken over by the now-teenaged Lucia, and with her new responsibilities the interplay of voices between author and amanuensis became more complex and at times humorous. Lucia wrote to Harriet Weaver from Nice on October 29 and November 6, 1922 to report a relapse of Joyce's iritis.[10] Both letters began "My father thinks," continue to relate facts in Lucia's own voice, and conclude on a typically Joycean note with dire weather reports. An iridectomy in June 1924 was the occasion for a letter by Lucia dated June 16 replying in French to Edouard Dujardin, who had written just days before to Joyce.[11] She wrote that her father, having just had an operation on his eyes, had asked her to let him know how much he appreciated his "gentile lettre." Referring to her father in the third person, she thanked Dujardin "de tout son coeur" for an invitation to meet with George Moore and wished him success with the new edition of his *Les Lauriers sont coupés*: "Il me charge de vous dire combien il vous est reconnaissant des bonnes paroles que vous lui avez envoyées." Joyce's habitually deferential tone to Dujardin comes through even in Lucia's words: "cher monsieur" is repeated three times in the short letter, which closes with an elaborate "l'assurance de mes salutations distinguées."

Letters to Frank Budgen that Joyce dictated to Lucia in 1933 read as if she was writing down every word that he said. The humor is distinctly Joyce's own, and phonetic uncorrected spellings suggest the rush of live dictation. A letter dated September 3 gives Budgen advice on finding a publisher for a German translation of his *James Joyce and the Making of Ulysses*.[12] Lucia wrote:

We are just back from Geneva and my father sends you the following suggestions. Keep a close hold on your American wright. The Continental wrights he believes he can arrange for you with the Albatross Press who have published him . . . Have nothing to do with Tauchnitz but have a copy sent to Mr. Daniel Brody Rheiverlag 35a Koniginstrasse Munich his german publishers. He says if all the germans have gone daffed by then [a reference to the Nazi takeover and book burnings earlier that year] a Swiss firm might do the translation . . . The Zimmerleuten one [a Zurich guild hall] is now quiet chic with the french chef named Michel who can serve you Kangarooschwanzsuppe which is a change from the Zurich cuisine at wartime. The frase of the latin mass which you could not read is on Ulysses page I. The old catholics Augustiner Kirche are a good example of a Mooks gone Gripes. They separated from Rome in 71 when the infallibility of the pope was proclaimed a Dogma . . . [misspellings as in the original][13]

Following the initial sentence in the first person (Lucia's voice) is a mix of what one guesses are Joyce's literal admonitions ("Keep a close hold . . . Have nothing to do . . .") interspersed with reported approximations ("he believes . . . He says . . ."). Some words seem distinctly Joyce's, such as "daffed" (i.e. daft). The evolution of menus at the Zimmerleuten is undoubtedly Joyce's memory; Lucia, who had turned ten during the war, wouldn't have remembered such detail. The conflation of Zurich's Augustiner Kirche with "Mookse gone Gripes" is undoubtedly Joyce's construction, rendered perhaps not-so-precisely in the sentence by Lucia. Another letter from the same year begins "My father says" and then goes on to quote the first words of the Roman Catholic Mass in German followed by a parenthetical "compare Ulysses."[14] A four-page letter from April 5 cheerfully mingles information that only Joyce, not Lucia, could have known ("The principal bistro, he says, was the Mullingar Inn, of which in W.i.P. the big man is assumed to be landlord") with her own ("You will be glad to hear that my letters for Chaucer's A.B.C. poem have been accepted").[15]

The dictations to Lucia in 1933, when Joyce did indeed suffer from a series of on-and-off eye problems, did however portend a new role for his dictation. Joyce's use of Sylvia Beach as an amanuensis led into more complicated relationships in the letters as Joyce began to use dictation as a mask rather than a vehicle in times of ill health. The German translation of *Exiles—Verbannte—* was published in Zurich in 1919. Joyce had signed a contract with Rascher Verlag that promised a payment from author to publisher before any royalties would accrue. The books were printed, Joyce was billed—and then, failing to pay, he departed Zurich with the family to return to Trieste and apparently left no forwarding address for Rascher. The firm carried the debt for years. Contact in

1926 from Rhein Verlag to Rascher regarding publication rights for German translations of *Ulysses* led Rhein to Shakespeare and Company and apparently a query to Sylvia Beach regarding the debt. The answer that Rhein received was concocted by Joyce to be sent under Beach's name. Joyce's draft of the letter remains, and though Beach's letter is unavailable, a letter from Rhein to Rascher transcribed the entire text.[16] It is a highly indignant communication, claiming that Rascher did nothing to promote the book, accusing the firm of never providing statements (the publisher had no idea of where Joyce was), and maintaining that in any case the amount that Joyce had agreed to pay in 1919 was far too much.

Joyce's drafting of this letter shows him to have been in charge of the reply, but also unwilling to be answerable to Rascher by not even signing his name or providing his own address. The transcription of Beach's letter leaves out Joyce's threat of legal action present in the draft—most likely dropped by Beach to avoid raising the possibility of retaliatory action by Rascher. Rascher followed with a polite letter to Joyce in care of Shakespeare and Company affirming Joyce's obligation.[17] Another letter sent the following year expressed disappointment that Joyce had not replied.[18] Joyce's intransigence prevailed, and the matter apparently remained unresolved.

In the early 1930s, Beach's assistant, Myrsine Moschos, became Joyce's resident amanuensis at Shakespeare and Company. He used her in a similar way, with Joyce playing the ventriloquist in order to avoid direct expression. An example is a letter to Harriet Weaver of January 29, 1933 under Moschos's name. She thanks Weaver in Joyce's name for sending a wreath to George Moore's funeral adding that "Mr Joyce is very vexed" that his name did not appear in the newspaper "as for once he wanted his name to appear." Joyce was probably still smarting from the publicity that his marriage received in July 1931, but unwilling to refer explicitly to that memory.[19] The report of Joyce's vexation put a rhetorical distance between his emotion and its report, allowing his "vexation" to be expressed without the potential slight to Weaver that a direct accusation might have caused.

One of the more egregious examples of Joyce's stepping aside from direct responsibility in correspondence occurred in a letter written by Lucia to Italo Svevo's widow on January 25, 1931 as she was planning for posthumous publication of the English translation of *Senilità* (*As a Man Grows Older*).[20] Joyce had promised Livia Svevo his assistance after Svevo's death three years earlier in promoting Svevo's work. But this letter, responding to a request from the widow to write an introduction to Svevo's novel, was answered (and signed) by Lucia:

A long time ago he [Joyce] made it a rule that he would not write a preface to his own or another's book or notes of explanation or give an interview or deliver a lecture. He has in fact refused several times offers for highly paid lecture-tours in german, english and american cities to say nothing of France. He says, moreover that a preface from him would damn the book in the eyes of readers in England and America for whom he is still a pariah and by whom his present method of writing is considered "una vera senilità."

Ultimately, Stanislaus Joyce, fulfilling the role of "his brother's keeper," stepped in to write the introduction to Svevo's book. By avoiding direct address, Joyce himself hid behind Lucia's explanation of his "rule," as if he the author had no voice in the matter. However, this "rule" seems to have been more of a ruse: his protests seem to be more of an excuse for silence than an artistic justification.

Joyce's dictations in the 1930s were largely to Paul Léon. Léon's role as intermediary has been acknowledged for many years.[21] His wife's memoir summarized the situation plainly: "Paul was there to handle every situation, to smooth over all sorts of misunderstandings, to protect Joyce from gate-crashers and intruders" (Noël 1950: 8). Léon could act "as a persona which Joyce could use when he wished to describe his own state of impatience or anger or upset" (Fahy 1993: 8–9). At least dozens of examples of letters dictated by Joyce and signed either with his or with Léon's name during this time are sprinkled with "Mr Joyce believes" or "Mr Joyce asks." In retrospect, it is difficult and in some cases impossible to assign responsibility to either Joyce or Léon for many letters and indeed even to paragraphs or sentences within individual letters. Many letters written over Léon's signature would restate Joyce's instructions in Léon's own words (as Joyce expected him to do) and expand upon Joyce's message with his own opinions. During the 1930s Joyce and Nora and sometimes Lucia were frequent travelers, either to vacation spots in the south of France or to extended stays in London or to Zurich for consultations with ophthalmologist Vogt. Regardless of the distance, Joyce and Léon remained tethered via frequent telegrams or brief postcards. More extensive letters from Joyce would give Léon instructions for correspondence with publishers or other business relationships, but also for communication with those close to him, especially Harriet Weaver.

Drafts of these letters in Léon's hand suggest that Joyce would in a single session dictate a series of sketches to several recipients that he intended Léon to flesh out. A two-page set of notes in Léon's hand from late 1933 is organized by headings with recipients' names: "Parisienne," "Reece," "Morley," and "Miss Weaver."[22] The curt flavor of the notes and the repeated reference to legal action for copyright infringement suggest Joyce dictating in a self-protective flurry. This was not a period of eye problems for Joyce; dictating the letters was a way of avoiding direct communication with the recipients. To focus on one of these examples, the Reece referred to above was John Holroyd Reece, a co-founder of the Albatross Press which published the 1932 edition of *Ulysses* in Germany under the Odyssey Press imprint. The notes for the letter to Reece begin "Mr Joyce has instructed his London solicitors to precede [sic] at once by way of a legal injunction against the anonymous group of pirates and he will take similar measures, quiet [sic] independently of his agents in London, against any person who attempts to publish Ulysses privately semi privately or publicly partly or wholly in England." While the draft message is framed in the third person ("Mr Joyce"), the vehemence, beginning with the word "pirates," is clearly Joyce's own. The hostility inherent in this draft is typically Joycean, echoing the language used in, for instance, his outrage at the *Frankfurter Zeitung*'s innocently mistaken attribution of an article by a Michael Joyce to James Joyce.[23] In contrast, Léon's own letters are invariably genteel, cautious, and polite.

The last weeks of 1932 were extraordinarily stressful for Joyce. Though *Ulysses* was selling well and other publications were in the works, the family continued to be enveloped in financial problems. Moreover, Lucia's psychological condition worsened, as Joyce documented in vivid detail in letters to Weaver. In a letter to Weaver from November 25, he minced no words in complaining of the strains put on others from Lucia's erratic behavior and of his central role in the family drama: "I tread on thistles of envy, suspicion, jealousy, hatred and so on and so on . . . as usual I am the fellow in the middle of the rain holding out both hands . . ."[24] On December 4 Paul Léon wrote briefly to Weaver that Joyce had asked him to write to thank her for a recent letter. "He has been living for the last fortnight under the strain of very trying circumstances and therefore been unable to write to you himself. As soon as he collects himself the energy he will write to you."[25] It was the occasion of a dramatic choice of epistolary silence for Joyce. On December 12, Léon ended a signed handwritten letter to Weaver, mostly speculating about publishing opportunities for *Ulysses*, with the following:

> Mr Joyce asks me also to write to you that he needs <u>immediately</u> £100.- from the amount he has given his solicitors powers of attorney to sell as he has a payment to make on his flat for the 15th. Will you kindly instruct Messrs Monro Saw & Co to send him the money c/o me. The reason why Mr Joyce doesn't write to you himself is that the state of his personal affairs at home have brought upon him a strain which has made him come very near a collapse. The only strength he draws on is his work which he continues through thick and thin every afternoon.

In the last two days he seemed to have recovered a little—at least I hope so—but it takes a great strength from him to be able to withstand the storms which he has to weather at home.[26]

This was followed two days later by another:

Mr Joyce wishes me to write you in greater detail about the state of the situation at his home and the state of health of his daughter. His position is the more strained because he is alone of the opinion that his daughter should be kept home and everything done in order to occupy her mind and help her to pass through the difficulties of her present condition ... You can imagine therefore what strained atmosphere reigns at his home and how much he must suffer from it especially wounded in his feelings as a father. He has assumed therefore an attitude of rather rough aloofness and tries to ignore outbursts and storms but he suffers from it very deeply and last week he had two lacrimose [sic] collapses.[27]

These letters express an undeniable drama. They cannot be considered dictated letters, for though they were written at Joyce's request, the prose is Léon's. But assigning the urgency and rhetorical melodrama clearly and distinctly to either author or amanuensis is impossible. The demanding voice evident in the underlined "immediately" is probably Joyce's—or is it? Is "immediately" underlined to create an insistent tone intended to put pressure on Weaver? Does this insistence originate with the same man who has "come very near a collapse"? In the letter of December 12 Joyce apparently draws strength from his work "through thick and thin" every afternoon—noble sounding, but perhaps too noble. The "storms" that he weathers seem more like purple prose than straightforward reporting of the stresses. The "lacrimose collapses" are stilted language for what nevertheless must have been emotionally-wrought scenes— but given that Léon likely was not present for these, in whose language are they being described? Who wrote these letters?

Joyce's break with Léon in late 1939 left him without the epistolary shield. His correspondence from 1940 and 1941 following publication of *Finnegans Wake* and in the increasing turmoil in Europe was a direct and emphatic recovery of his unmediated voice in the months before his death. Joyce's postal correspondents in these late months consisted almost solely of family members, friends, and occasional government officials. In numerous letters and postcards to friends Paul Ruggiero, Louis Gillet, and others, written from Vichy France, he attempted desperately—in his own voice and unambiguously—to provide for Lucia's care and to find a refuge for himself and other family members. In the termination of his own writing for publication and in the dwindling of demands from agents, editors, publishers, lawyers, and bankers, Joyce found a way to discontinue the silence of dictated letters and to express himself—urgently and clearly—in a sincere and undisguised voice.

Notes

1 Information on Battara, Gal, and, later, Chalas, is taken from *Adressbuch der Stadt Zürich für 1917* (Zürich: Art. Institut Orell Füssli), 1917.

2 Antonio Battara, ALS February 17, 1917 to Harriet Weaver, British Library Add MSS 57345. Unless indicated otherwise, all the correspondence is unpublished.

3 Antonio Battara, ALS February 28, 1917 to Harriet Weaver, British Library Add MSS 57345.

4 James Joyce, TC March 6, 1917 to Slack, Monro, Saw and Co., British Library Add MSS 57345.

5 M. Gal, ALS February 27, 1917 to Grant Richards, Beinecke Library, Yale University.

6 James Joyce, ALS March 7, 1917 to Grant Richards, Beinecke Library, Yale University.

7 Nora Joyce, ALS February 28, 1917 to Harriet Weaver, British Library Add MSS 57345.

8 James Joyce, ALS April 30, 1919 to Benjamin Huebsch, *Letters* I.

9 Antoine Chalas, TLS January 23, 1919 to Harriet Weaver, British Library Add MSS 57345.

10 Lucia Joyce, ALS to Harriet Weaver, British Library Add MSS 57346.

11 Lucia Joyce, ALS June 16, 1924 to Edouard Dujardin, Harry Ransom Center.

12 This was not published until decades later as *James Joyce und die Entstehung des Ulysses*, translated by Werner Morlang (Frankfurt am Main: Suhrkamp, 1977).

13 Lucia Joyce, TLS September 3, 1933 to Frank Budgen, Beinecke Library, Yale University.

14 Lucia Joyce, ALS [1933] to Frank Budgen, Zürich James Joyce Foundation.

15 Lucia Joyce, ALS April 5, 1933 to Frank Budgen, Zürich James Joyce Foundation.

16 [James Joyce], AL [1926] to "Messieurs," University at Buffalo James Joyce Collection; Rasher & Cie, TLS March 22, 1926 to Rhein Verlag, Zentralbibliothek Zürich.

17 Rascher & Cie, TLS April 9, 1926 to James Joyce, Zentralbibliothek Zürich.

18 Rascher & Cie, TLS August 10, 1927 to James Joyce, Zentralbibliothek Zürich.

19 Myrsine Moschos, ALS January 29, 1933 to Harriet Weaver, *Letters* I.

20 Lucia Joyce, ALS January 25, 1931 to Livia Schmitz, Museo Joyce Trieste. My thanks to Erik Schneider for bringing this to my attention.

21 One of the earliest examples of Léon's correspondence on behalf of Joyce was in a letter of February 3, 1932 to Sylvia Beach in which Léon identifies himself as Joyce's lawyer interested in contract negotiations regarding *Ulysses* (Crispi 2012: 30).

22 Paul Léon, notes, 1933, National Library of Ireland.

23 For example, "In my opinion the whole thing is a deliberate and malicious forgery." James Joyce, ALS August 16, 1931 to Harriet Shaw Weaver, British Library Add MSS 57350.

24 James Joyce, ALS November 25, 1932 to Harriet Shaw Weaver, British Library Add MSS 57351.

25 Paul Léon, ALS December 4, 1932 to Harriet Weaver, British Library Add MSS 57351.

26 Paul Léon, ALS December 12, 1932 to Harriet Shaw Weaver, British Library Add MSS 57351.

27 Paul Léon, ALS December 14, 1932 to Harriet Shaw Weaver, British Library Add MSS 57351.

References

Benco, S. (1930), "James Joyce in Trieste," *Bookman* 72, no. 4: 375–80.

Crispi, L. (2012), "*Ulysses* in the Marketplace: 1932," *Joyce Studies Annual*: 29–65.

Fahy, C. (1993), "The James Joyce/Paul Léon Papers in the National Library of Ireland: Observations on Their Cataloguing and Research Potential," *Joyce Studies Annual* 4: 3–15.

Noël, L. (1950), *James Joyce and Paul L. Léon: The Story of a Friendship*, New York: Gotham Book Mart.

10

"Secrets, silent … sit" in the Archives of Our Publishers: Untold Episodes from Joyce's Italian Odyssey

Sara Sullam[1]

Preparatory to anything else

Virginia Woolf described the course of female literary tradition as "strange spaces of silence" (2008: 133). The phrase applies well to the reception of the works of James Joyce in Italy. In this chapter, I explore what was "silenced" and why during the first five decades of Joyce literary presence in Italy, and how those silences (invoked in my title, U 2.170) shaped the perception of Joyce's works within the Italian context. That is, using materials available in the archives of two Italian publishers, Cederna and Mondadori, and working at the intersection of literary history, cultural translation studies, and book history, this chapter employs "silence" in a metaphorical sense to illuminate two relevant untold episodes from the history of reception of Joyce's works in Italy. The theoretical and methodological premise that underpins my discussion embraces the interdisciplinary perspective that emerged over the past few decades as reception studies have enjoyed a resurgence, establishing a common ground for framing literary history in a broader scope.[2] Studies on the reception of foreign authors have successfully intersected with cultural translation studies on the one hand, and book history on the other, two disciplines that are being increasingly integrated to present a wider and more empirically-grounded approach to processes of literary transfer. From this perspective, publishers' archives have become a crucial site of investigation and research, allowing scholars in the field of modernist studies to illuminate the materiality of modernism's transnational dimension and thus highlight the "network relations amongst diverse texts within a wider sphere of modernist publishing" (Wilson et al. 2014: 223). The abundant archival material that is increasingly being made available to scholars of literature and translation studies has launched a new line of studies that take an integrated approach to the history of translations and literary transfer; its complex methodological and theoretical framework is still being fully elaborated.[3]

Such an integrated approach proves very fruitful when it comes to studying the reception of modernist authors, particularly of Joyce who was exquisitely transnational in his writing (Melchiori 2000, Zanotti 2013) and had "uncanny talent as self-publicist" (Bulson 2001: 12). After Gianni Cianci's 1974 pioneering study on the reception of Joyce in Italy (which, due to its publication date, could not rely on archival material), Serenella Zanotti (2013) has reconstructed the initial reception of *Ulysses* in literary journals during the 1920s and 1930s on the basis of archival evidence, with particular attention to the role of Joyce's *impresari*.[4] But considering Joyce's ties with Italy, the publishing history of his works after the Second World War still remains to be uncovered,[5] influenced as it is by the belated, in comparison to other European countries, publication of *Ulysses* in 1960. This chapter will focus on two episodes in particular: the publishing history of Joyce's critical writings and the publishing history of his letters. First, I will bring to light the unsuccessful plan to publish a volume containing Joyce's essays. Second, I will investigate the consequences of the "long silence" around *Ulysses* and its belated translation by investigating the construction of the "Joyce character" as it was influenced by Joyce's *Letters*.

A book on Joyce and Italy: Cederna and Joyce's critical writings

Joyce's critical writings were a relatively late discovery: unlike his fellow-modernists T. S. Eliot or Virginia Woolf, Joyce has not been considered a critic. In English, his critical essays were published in book form long after his death, when Richard Ellmann and Ellsworth Mason issued *The Critical Writings of James Joyce* in 1959, the same year that Ellmann published the first edition of Joyce's biography. The early articles written for the Irish and the Triestine press that, according to Melchiori (2000: 109–11), Joyce intended to publish in 1914 with Italian publisher Formiggini, had been scattered after his death and remained unknown to most Joyce scholars. Mason's contact with Stanislaus Joyce dates back to 1952,[6] and before that date, Joyce the essayist lingered in silence. But a small Milanese publisher, Cederna, had actually planned to bring out a volume of Joyce's essays back in 1949: his failed enterprise sheds light on a less explored—if not unknown—chapter in Joyce's publishing narrative.

Cederna was a small and short-lived enterprise (1946–51) that belonged to a group of publishers committed to renewing Italian culture, often through translations, in the immediate aftermath of the Second World War (Ferretti 2004, Piombo 2010). Such small enterprises were usually established by very young people—in Cederna's case, the founders were both twenty years old—who in the interwar period acted as middlemen between the literary journals (crucial sites for the Italian reception of modernism) and bigger publishers. In most cases, the bigger publishers took over the catalogs of the smaller publishers once they failed and were forced to shut down. Since most of their projects never saw the light of day, the most interesting data in cases such as Cederna's are the "silent" data, ones that point to what did *not* get published; they can only be recovered by archival research framed within the bigger picture of the reception of Joyce in Italy.

While the first wave of Joyce reception in Italy occurred in the 1920s and the interwar period (characterized by the intense activity of literary magazines; Zanotti 2013), Cederna's attempt to publish Joyce's critical wrings can be seen as the second wave that spans 1946 to 1960, that is, from the year in which the main actor in the Italian publishing field, Mondadori, secured the translation rights for most of Joyce's works and for the publication of the Italian *Ulysses*. These fourteen years are characterized, on the one hand, by the "*Ulysses* enterprise"[7] and, on the other hand, by the work of smaller competitors like Cederna or Scheiwiller collaborating with alternative Joycean networks. The only tangible results of such attempts were Cederna's 1949 edition of *Pomes Penyeach* and the "Proteus" episode of *Ulysses* and Scheiwiller's 1960 edition of *Chamber Music*. If carried out, Cederna's Joycean projects would have been pioneering, not only for Italy, but for Joyce's publication history more in general.

In addition to *Pomes Penyeach*, Cederna had in store a volume containing a selection of Joyce's critical writings and Carlo Linati's translation of *Dubliners*, parts of which he had already received. Cederna's middleman in the case of critical writings was not Linati, but Renato Poggioli. A Florentine and a founder in 1946 of the literary magazine *Inventario*, devoted to the translation of foreign literature, Poggioli was at that time professor of Slavic and Comparative Literature at Harvard, where he had been introduced to Harry Levin. Poggioli became the middleman between Levin and Cederna when it came to the translation of Levin's 1941 monograph on Joyce, to which Cederna intended to add an Italian bibliography on the writer. As we gather from the correspondence with Cederna preserved at the Centro Apice at Milan University, Levin, informed by Poggioli about Cederna's commitment, was actually keen on granting the rights to the small publisher. The deal, though, had to be done with James Laughlin, chief editor of *New Directions*, who decided to accept Mondadori's higher offer. Through Levin, however, Poggioli came into a direct contact with John Slocum, who was at work on his seminal bibliography of Joyce. That is, Poggioli was in touch with the most informed person on Joyce's writings, with the exception of Stanislaus, who, until his death in 1955, acted as the gatekeeper of all minor Joyceana and who would share them only with Mason and Ellmann.[8] What is of interest here is that Mason's contact with Stanislaus dates, as mentioned earlier, to 1952, while the Slocum–Poggioli–Cederna connection dates back to 1949. The contact with Slocum was undoubtedly an asset for a small publisher like Cederna, who thus knew much more about Joyce's essays than Mondadori (advised by Linati), or Richard Steele, Joyce's London agent.

It was to Linati that Mondadori turned in 1948 for information about Joyce's critical writings as soon as he became aware of their existence:

> Dear Professor,
>
> We would be very grateful if you could kindly enlighten us as regards the situation of James Joyce's work, especially as far as his "Essays" are concerned.
>
> We know that he wrote several essays, but his English publishers say that no volume has ever been published in England.
>
> Given your deep acquaintance with Anglo-Saxon literature, we think that you shall be able to provide us with all necessary information.[9]

At the same time Mondadori inquired with Steele:

> As regards the essays we know for sure that Joyce wrote many of them, but we do not know if they have been published in England and in France in a single volume. We are inquiring on the subject with Italian scholars and we would kindly ask you to do the same in English literary circles.[10]

Neither Linati (who remained silent on the essays) nor Steele were of much help to Mondadori. In fact, the publisher seems to be clueless about Cederna as the publication venue of Joyce's critical writings, as we learn from his letter to Steele:

> As regards the essays, we have made inquiries but we were not able to find one single edition. It could be, as you say, that a certain number of essays were published in Italian cultural magazines, but we think it is impossible, at the present moment to find out the names of the magazines. In this case too, therefore, the best thing would be to draft an agreement for all the essays you are aware of.[11]

The issue was never settled: Steele did not provide any further information and Mondadori gave up on the project. Joyce's *Scritti italiani* was not to be published until 1977, while a selection from his critical writings in English was published in 1992, in the "Meridiani" volume edited by Franca Ruggieri.[12] Back in 1949, though, Cederna knew the titles of Joyce's essays very well. Thanks to Poggioli.

After establishing contact with Cederna for Levin's book, Poggioli contacted the publisher with an ambitious proposal to bring out Joyce's essays and criticism full ten years before Ellmann and Mason's 1959 edition of the *Critical Writings*. Here is what Poggioli wrote to Cederna:

> As concerns your project for a volume on Joyce and his Triestine years, it could contain the following materials:
>
>> the articles-conferences published in the Piccolo della Sera (Swift, Parnell, Synge) to be located and collected;
>> the satire against Irish culture published by Joyce when in Pola;
>> the James-Joyce [sic] correspondence with Harry Levin's preface, already featured in Inventario, to be possibly integrated with further materials to be included in the volume;
>> Svevo's conference, which he published on il Convegno after Joyce's death;
>> Stanislaus' recollections, already featured in Letteratura;
>> Silvio Benco's article, already featured in Pegaso.
>
> In this way, the whole text, if we except part of the correspondence with Svevo and the Pola satire (with parallel text) could appear in Italian.
>
> In the event of a bilingual edition, a viable option if we reached an agreement with American or English publishers, who might have an interest in granting us the rights provided that they distribute the book in England and America, we should have the following translated:
>
>> Joyce's articles;
>> Benco's essay;
>
> Whereas we could use our English versions for:
>
>> The correspondence with Svevo and Harry Levin's introduction;
>
> We could ask the following American publishers and magazine editors to grant us the right to use their English version of the following titles:
>
>> Svevo's conference on Joyce (James Laughlin di New Directions, New York)
>> Stanislaus' recollections (Hudson Review di New York).[13]

Poggioli's initial idea was to publish a bilingual and transnational volume under a triple imprint: the Cederna–Inventario–Joyce Society. Further, he also suggested that Cederna republish Synge's *Riders to the Sea* in the Joyce–Vidacovich's translation in a bilingual edition, with an introduction by Harry Levin. Poggioli specified that "Foreign Joycean admirers might be willing to buy his version if published with the English parallel text of Synge's play."[14] Cederna reacted enthusiastically and wrote to his literary agent, Erich Linder, sketching the plan of his "Joycean volume":

> The Joycean volume I have in mind should contain:
>
> > *Ibsen's new Drama*
> > *The Day of the Rabblement*
> > *James Clarence Mangan*
> > *Un poeta irlandese*
> > *L'anima dell'Irlanda*
> > *The Holy Office*
> > *Gas from a Burner*
> > Italian translation of Synge's *Riders to the Sea* (with Synge's original
> >   text—ask for copyright)
> > Joyce's articles published in the *Piccolo della Sera* in 1907. Nino Frank and
> >   James Joyce's translation of *Anna Livia Plurabelle*.
>
> As an appendix we could have some of the most important critical essays on Joyce (for example the one by his brother Stanislaus)
>
> . . .
>
> It would be interesting to add also the letters to Linati and Svevo, which we could obtain through Poggioli-Slocum (the latter is the owner).[15]

The volume, though, never materialized. This was partly due to Laughlin's eventual refusal to grant the copyright for Levin's book, which put a halt to Cederna's Joycean plans, but also due to the fact that the small publisher had to close down in 1951. His planned Joycean volume, however, represents a relevant episode in the history of Joyce's transnational and Italian reception: it adds a kind of 'prologue' to the "Stanislaus vs. the critics" narrative (Kelly 1998), backdating to the actual circulation of Joyce's essays, in particular those in the *Piccolo*. Within the Italian literary field, Cederna's volume would have represented the transition between the first wave of Joycean reception in literary magazines, and the second wave that saw Joyce as a "modernist classic." Furthermore, Cederna's volume contained a lot of "Irish matter," which would have been made available to a much wider public than just the readers of the interwar period magazines. Indeed, the Italian public would have become acquainted with the most "political" Joyce and that would have certainly influenced the reception of *Ulysses*.

Unraveling episodes of publishing history that have hitherto remained unknown can help us establish missing links, illuminate the presence of wider transnational networks in the geography of modernism, and address significant silences and gaps, as well as delays, in the reception of a given author.

We'll simply have to dress the character: Italian Joyce before and after *Ulysses*

Considered within a larger process of Joycean reception, Cederna's ambitious attempt to publish Joyce's early essays may have failed because of the heavy reliance on people who had connections with Joyce when he was still alive. In contrast, Mondadori's publishing plan included active participation of numerous young academics, such as Glauco Cambon, Carlo Izzo, and Giorgio Melchiori, and poets such as Eugenio Montale (as requested by Joyce's heirs). They acted as advisors to the publisher, helping him to "dress the character" of the Italian Joyce as he was already becoming a "classic," even though the artistic voice of his *Ulysses* was still metaphorically silent, his works having yet to be translated into Italian. When the Italian translation of *Ulysses* finally came out in 1960, critic and writer Oreste del Buono wrote that "our readers might take advantage of the delay with which they receive *Ulysses*, for they know that the book itself is no more at issue, that Joyce has become a classic: readers shall therefore approach him without being suspicious, without being irritated, which will allow them to appreciate the great reading adventure right from the start" (1960: 77).[16] "The book itself is no more at issue," but how was the approach to the publishing of *Ulysses* managed and the character of Joyce, the classic modernist, constructed? The publication history of Joyce's letters, as it emerges from the papers preserved at the Mondadori Foundation, provides a significant insight into how the initial silencing of *Ulysses* shaped the reception of Joyce's private writings in the Italian context.

If we reconstruct the early phase of Mondadori's publication plans (1957), we see how the "silence" around *Ulysses* shaped the decision about translating the first volume of Joyce's letters edited by Stuart Gilbert. Claudio Gorlier, a great popularizer and a keen critic of Joyce's works, wrote in his December 1960 article, "Studi su Joyce," that "Joyce appears in Italian with *Ulysses* (while, in

Hollywood, people talk of a movie adaptation, following a comedy that has now been published, *Ulysses in Nighttown*) when a sound critical 'corpus' on his work has become established" (Gorlier 1960: 121).[17] Gorlier's "critical corpus" included Ellmann's 1959 biography of Joyce, William Y. Tindall's 1959 *Reader's Guide to James Joyce* (which would be translated into Italian the following year with Umberto Eco's bibliographical note), Levin's 1941 *James Joyce*, and Sylvia Beach's 1957 *Shakespeare and Company*. The letters, of course, would add to this corpus, easing the task of reading *Ulysses*.

Mondadori received Stuart Gilbert's volume of *Letters* in 1957 and immediately sought counsel from Elio Vittorini and Fernanda Pivano, two of his most important advisors who had already been involved with *Ulysses*, and from Glauco Cambon, the university professor who was well acquainted with the American academia. While the publication of the letters was part of Mondadori's larger Joycean plan, the question in 1957 was, should the letters be published before or after *Ulysses*? Expectations for the Italian translation of the great modernist novel were mounting, but the question remained: how would a volume of letters fit into the bigger picture? Glauco Cambon, who guaranteed Gilbert's scholarly reliability, was the first to offer a solution: he would rather have the letters published after *Ulysses*, since they could function as a kind of guide to many aesthetic stances of the novel:

> The book is a selection from the abundant correspondence of the Irish writer, one of great interest since it follows Joyce's career from the beginning of the century through his Triestine years, to Zürich and Paris ... Further, the preface by Stuart Gilbert, among the most reliable exegetes of *Ulysses*, provides substantial information. The correspondence tackles several literary issues, still, it would be advisable to publish it after the translation of *Ulysses*, otherwise it might remain confined within specialists' circles.[18]

The explicit mention of "Trieste–Zürich–Paris" is a clear reference to the geography of *Ulysses*: the focus was no more Joyce the Italian, but Joyce the European writer, Joyce the author of *Ulysses*. Vittorini was also of the opinion that the letters should follow *Ulysses*. Fernanda Pivano, however, thought that the letters could whet curiosity about Joyce as a character (his biography had not yet been published in Italy), particularly since *Ulysses*, though not yet available in Italian, had already been fueling the debate:

> Vittorini suggests we have the volume out only after the publication of Ulysses. As to me, I think that the very expectation around Ulysses is generating a curiosity around its author, which might be dramatically dampened by the

actual publication of the book. This is why I think we should benefit from the current interest around the work.[19]

It must be remembered that in those years Italy was finally receiving modernist literature, fostering interest in the modernist writers' private lives: for example, in 1959 Mondadori would publish the translation of Virginia Woolf's *A Writer's Diary*. But, ultimately, the translation and publication of Gilbert's volume of letters gave way to *Ulysses* that came out in 1960, by which time Ellmann had already established himself as the main actor in the Joycean field (Kelly 1998: 141–75). The *Letters*, however, made it into the mainstream press: in 1959—the year in which Mason and Ellmann's *Critical Writings of James Joyce* and Ellmann's biography also came out—Agostino Lombardo, university professor and literary critic, wrote a long review of both the essays and the letters in the popular *Il Mondo* magazine.

Lombardo was rather critical of Gilbert's choice to exclude some letters—for example Joyce's correspondence with Svevo, or the letters of his Triestine years—but was on the whole positive on the great importance of the volume, which he considered as complementing the scant biographical material on Joyce. Lombardo wrote that "More than for any other writer of our times, for Joyce art merges with life," which is why Joyce's correspondence "is indispensable to scholars" (Lombardo 1959).[20] Joyce's "character" was therefore necessary to fully grasp the gist of *Ulysses*. In fact, the publishing odyssey of *Ulysses* occupies the greater part of the review. The last quote in Lombardo's review is from Joyce's February 22, 1932 letter to T. S. Eliot (*Letters I*, 315), where Joyce declines the offer to publish *Ulysses* in installments in *The Criterion*:

> "As regards the proposal to publish episodes of *Ulysses* in the *Criterion Miscellany* I am against it. First it implies that I have recognised the right of any authorities in either of Bull's islands to dictate to me what and how I am to write. I never did and never will. Secondly the episodes are of unequal length, thirdly I think that at least seven of the eight episodes would not pass the censor ... Fourthly *Ulysses* is a book with a beginning, middle and an end and should be presented as such ..."
>
> Here the main and most significant feature of the collection becomes clear. A precious collection, for many reasons: it sheds light on several *loci* of Joyce's work, it illustrates his composition method, illuminates most of his sources; at the same time, it allows us to gain clearer insights into the writer's personality.
>
> Lombardo 1959[21]

This must have sounded well to the Italian public. In fact, the issue of publishing Gilbert's edition of letters resurfaced when *Ulysses* finally came out. This time, however, it was Richard Ellmann who, through his literary agent in Italy, Erich Linder, took advantage of the "event" created by the publication of *Ulysses* to trace the still missing "Italian letters" for his edition of the correspondence. He wrote to Mondadori:

> Dear Mr. Mondadori,
>
> Erich Linder has informed me of your kind intention to give notice of my edition of Joyce's letters in EPOCA, and I deeply appreciate your support. Mr. Linder has asked me to specify which kind of information to include in your notice. I am not sure if it is a letter that you have in mind, or some other form of writing. In any case, I have prepared the following text, which I think should suit the purpose:
>
> "To the Director:
>
> I am preparing the edition of James Joyce's letters, which will be published in England and in the States. I am particularly interested in copies of the letters addressed by Joyce to his Italian friends, whom he met during the ten years that he spent in Trieste, or later in Zürich or Paris. I will be grateful to anyone among your readers who will be able to tell me where to find those letters.
>
> Sincerely yours,
>
> Richard Ellmann"
>
> The letter could be preceded or followed by a note explaining that who is writing is a well known American critic, professor of English and author of a biography of Joyce published by Oxford University Press.[22]

We do not know whether Ellmann eventually found any letters. When his volume of Joyce's correspondence came out in 1966, however, Mondadori resumed his long-dormant plans to publish Joyce's letters, entrusting the editing and translation to Giorgio Melchiori (chosen over Claudio Gorlier and Agostino Lombardo). Roberto Fertonani, scholar of German literature and one of the main editors in the house, compared Joyce's correspondence to Umberto Saba's, for its measure and scope, and wrote to Melchiori, asking whether they should publish the whole correspondence contained in Faber's volumes or just a selection; what criteria to follow in selecting the letters; and whether Mondadori would envisage two editions, one unabridged (to be published in the Classici Contemporanei series) and one abridged.[23]

Melchiori answered after two months, apologizing for his delay, saying, "it is a big issue and I changed my mind several times on what I intended to say."[24] Melchiori advised Mondadori to publish only a selection—albeit a vast one—of the letters, with generous annotations. As to the criteria for selection, he wrote:

(a) leave out all the letters dealing exclusively with business matters.

(b) leave out all (or almost all) letters addressed to Joyce (many in the Faber volume), including only extracts or summaries when necessary to understand the answers.

(c) include all letters or parts of them revealing Joyce's character, his idiosyncrasies, his attitude towards his own or other people's work, the vicissitudes of his private life, the debates he took part in;

(d) include those letters (or parts of them) containing judgments and impressions on people, place, books and readings.

(e) the main thread must be necessarily and thoroughly geographical, which means we'll have to include letters that, even without any literary or personal interest, are relevant to the vicissitudes of the Joyce family and provide information on Joyce's economic and health conditions, on matters related to publishing etc.[25]

Melchiori further wrote:

> ...considering that specialists and scholars who want to have all materials available are of course able to read them in the original, it seemed to me that the "public" for the correspondence will be rather composed by readers of Joyce interested in gaining first-hand insights on the writer's personality and biography.[26]

The letters were therefore, in a way, to provide an alternative reading to Ellmann's biography,[27] published in Italy by a relatively new entrant in the literary field, the publisher Feltrinelli.[28] Mondadori eventually opted for a single volume of the letters and, in 1969, after he entrusted Melchiori with the translation and editorship of the volume, he also asked him (upon Giansiro Ferrata's suggestion) to include "the elements needed to follow the making of his major works."[29] The book came out in 1974, by which time Joyce had become fully established on the Italian literary scene, influencing—more or less directly—many Italian writers (Zanotti 2004). On the occasion of the 1982 centenary, Mondadori published Luigi Schenoni's partial translation of *Finnegans Wake*, which made it into the Italian bestsellers list during that summer. The translation of the *Wake* is still to be completed. But that is another story, still in the making.[30]

Notes

1 I wish to thank the Italian James Joyce Foundation for the Giorgio Melchiori Special Grant that I was awarded in order to carry out my research for this chapter. I also thank the Centro Apice and the Fondazione Arnoldo e Alberto Mondadori for

allowing me to work with and to quote from the materials preserved on their premises. Finally, I'm grateful to Gianni Antonini of Cederna Edizioni, and to the heirs of Richard Ellmann, Carlo Linati, Giorgio Melchiori, Fernanda Pivano, and Renato Poggioli for granting me the right to publish from their relatives' correspondence.

2   I am referring mainly to the project, led by Elinor Shaffer, on the reception of British and Irish authors in Europe.

3   On the integration of translation studies with book history, see Billiani (2007), Bachleitner (2009), and Levie (2009). For a concrete example of such an approach, see Sisto (2014), in particular the introduction to the volume that features the methodological framework of the study, bringing together a sociological-bourdieusian stance with Even-Zohar's polysystem theory. Also relevant are the British Library workshops on literary archives: *Archival Uncertainties: International Conference on Literary Archives* (April 4, 2016) and *The Translator Made Corporeal: Translation History and the Archive* (May 8, 2017).

4   See also, especially on the Linati–Joyce connection, Pasquero (2012).

5   For *Ulysses* and the translation of Joyce's poems, see, respectively, Sullam 2013 and 2014.

6   On the subject, see Kelly (1998: 142–8), in particular 143: "Stanislaus provided Mason with a neglected store of Joyceana—Joyce's book reviews and his articles for the Italian paper *Il Piccolo della Sera.*"

7   For a detailed account, see Sullam (2013).

8   On the subject, see Kelly (1998: 142–8).

9   Fondazione Arnoldo e Alberto Mondadori (henceforth FAAM), Milano, Archivio storico Arnoldo Mondadori Editore (henceforth AsAME), Sezione Alberto Mondadori, folder Joyce, Alberto Mondadori to Carlo Linati, Milan, March 5, 1948, typewritten.

Caro Professore,

> Le saremmo immensamente grati se Lei volesse cortesemente illuminarci circa la situazione delle opere di James Joyce, specialmente per quanto si riferisce ai "Saggi."
> A noi risulta che l'autore ha scritto diversi saggi ma i suoi editori inglesi dicono che in Inghilterra non è mai stato pubblicato un volume che comprende tali opere.
> Poiché sappiamo che Lei è profondo conoscitore di tutta la letteratura anglosassone, pensiamo che possa fornirci tutti i chiarimenti possibili.

10 FAAM, AsAME, Sezione Alberto Mondadori, folder Joyce, Alberto Mondadori to Richard Steele, Milan, March 5, 1948, typewritten.

> Per quanto riguarda invece i saggi, noi sappiamo da fonte sicura che Joyce ne ha scritti parecchi, ma non sappiamo se siano stati pubblicati in Inghilterra e in Francia in un volume unico. Stiamo facendo delle ricerche in questo campo

presso letterati italiani e Vi preghiamo, da parte vostra, di fare lo stesso negli
ambienti letterari inglesi.

11 FAAM, AsAME, Sezione Alberto Mondadori, folder Joyce, Alberto Mondadori to
Richard Steele, Milan, April 21, 1948, typewritten.

Per quanto concerne i saggi, abbiamo fatto parecchie ricerche ma non siamo stati
capaci di trovare una singola edizione. Può darsi che, come dite, un certo numero
di saggi sia stato pubblicato da giornali italiani a scopo culturale, ma sarebbe
assolutamente impossibile, ora, sapere il nome di tali giornali. Anche per queste
opere la soluzione migliore sarebbe stendere con noi un contratto per tutti i saggi
che conoscete.

12 A complete translation of Joyce's critical writings has been published in 2016: James
Joyce, *Lettere e saggi*, ed. Enrico Terrinoni, Milan: il Saggiatore.

13 Unimi, Apice, Fondo Casa editrice Cederna, Serie 1, Corrispondenza, UA 113
(Renato Poggioli), letter of Renato Poggioli to Gianni Antonini, Florence,
September 1, 1949, typewritten.

Rispetto al volumetto progettato intorno a Joyce e al suo soggiorno triestino, esso
potrebbe contenere i seguenti materiali:
gli articoli conferenze sul Piccolo della Sera (Swift, Parnell, Synge) da rintracciare
e raccogliere;
la satira contro la cultura irlandese pubblicata da James Joyce a Pola;
la corrispondenza James-Joyce e la prefazione di Harry Levin, già apparsa su
Inventario, da integrarsi forse con riferimenti agli altri materiali da includere
nel volume;
la conferenza che Svevo lesse e pubblicò sul Convegno dopo la morte di Joyce;
i ricordi del fratello Stanislaus già apparsi su Letteratura;
l'articolo di Silvio Benco già apparso su Pegaso.
In questo modo tutto il testo, eccetto qualche lettera della corrispondenza con
Svevo e il testo della satira polese (con versione a fronte) potrebbe apparire in
italiano.
In caso di un'edizione bilingue, che si potrebbe fare se ci accordassimo con gli
editori americani o inglesi che possono avere un interesse a cederci i diritti
purché siano loro a distribuire la pubblicazione in Inghilterra e in America,
dovremmo far tradurre appositamente:
gli articoli di Joyce;
il saggio di Benco;
potremmo usare le nostre versioni inglesi per:
la corrispondenza con Svevo e l'introduzione di Harry Levin;
potremmo chiedere ai seguenti editori e riviste americane il diritto d'usare la loro
versione inglese dei seguenti titoli:

conferenza di Svevo su Joyce (James Laughlin di New Directions, New York)
ricordi di Stanislaus (Hudson Review di New York).

14 Unimi, Apice, Fondo Casa editrice Cederna, Serie 1, Corrispondenza, UA 113
(Renato Poggioli), letter of Renato Poggioli to Gianni Antonini, Florence, September
1, 1949, typewritten.

Gli amatori stranieri di Joyce potrebbero acquistare volentieri la sua versione se
pubblicata con a fronte il testo inglese del dramma di Synge.

15 Unimi, Apice, Fondo Casa editrice Cederna, Serie 1, Corrispondenza, UA 1 (Agenzia
Letteraria Internazionale), *s.l., s.d.*, typewritten note.

Il volume joyciano che avrei in mente dovrebbe contenere:
Ibsen's new Drama
The Day of the Rabblement
James Clarence Mangan
Un poeta irlandese
L'anima dell'Irlanda
The Holy Office
Gas from a Burner
Traduzione italiana del dramma di Synge *Rider sto the Sea* (questo col testo
inglese di Synge a fronte—chiedere diritti)
Gli articoli di Joyce pubblicati su *Il Piccolo della Sera* di Trieste nel 1907. La
traduzione di Anna Livia Plurabelle dovuta a Nino Frank e a James Joyce.
In appendice al volume si potrebbero aggiungere alcuni fra i più importanti saggi
su Joyce (ad es. quello sul fratello Stanislao)
. . .
Al volume sarebbe interessante aggiungere le lettere a Linati e a Svevo che si
potrebbero forse avere tramite Poggioli-Slocum (quest'ultimo ne è il proprietario).

16 Il nostro lettore è probabilmente favorito dal ritardo con cui gli arriva l'*Ulisse*, sa che
il libro non è più in discussione, che Joyce è ormai un classico: può accostarglisi
senza sospetti e irritazioni, apprezzarne sin dall'inizio la grande avventura.

17 Joyce appare in italiano con *Ulysses* (mentre a Hollywood si medita addirittura di
trarre un film dal romanzo dopo che n'è stata ricavata a suo tempo una commedia,
oggi pubblicata, *Ulysses in Nighttown*) quando un vero e proprio 'corpus' critico viene
definitivamente sistemandosi nei confronti della sua opera.

18 FAAM, AsAME, Segreteria Editoriale Estero, Serie C, envelope 30, folder 12 (James
Joyce), report of Glauco Cambon, May 5, 1957, typewritten.

Questo libro raccoglie in un volume la numerosa corrispondenza dello scrittore
irlandese, che presenta un interesse notevole perché accompagna via via la

carriera di Joyce dall'inizio del secolo agli anni di Trieste, di Zurigo e di Parigi . . .
Infine la prefazione di Stuart Gilbert, che è fra gli esegeti più accreditati di
Ulysses, porta il suo contributo di informazione. Si riscontrano nell'epistolario
questioni letterarie, però sarebbe consigliabile pubblicarlo dopo la traduzione
di *Ulisse*, altrimenti rischia di rimaner confinato a una ristretta cerchia di
specialisti.

19 FAAM, AsAME, Segreteria Editoriale Estero, Serie C, envelope 30, folder 12 (James
Joyce), report of Fernanda Pivano, June 5, 1957, typewritten.

Vittorini propone di farlo uscire solo dopo la pubblicazione di Ulisse.

A me pare proprio che l'attesa di Ulisse susciti intorno a questo autore una
curiosità e un interesse che forse la pubblicazione della traduzione farà molto
smorzare. Per ciò mi sembrerebbe più opportuno sfruttare questo interesse finché
c'è.

20 Più che per ogni altro scrittore del nostro tempo, nell'arte, per Joyce, si risolve la vita
. . . un libro indispensabile allo studioso.

21 E qui si scorge, invero, la nota principale e la più significativa della raccolta. La quale
è preziosa per molti motivi; getta luce su molti luoghi dell'opera joyciana, illustra,
spesso il suo metodo compositivo, indica parecchie delle sue fonti; consente, del pari,
di scorgere con più chiarezza, in tutte le sue pieghe, la personalità dello scrittore.

22 FAAM, AsAME, Segreteria Editoriale Estero, Serie C, envelope 30, folder 12 (James
Joyce), letter of Richard Ellmann to Mondadori, December 2, 1960, typewritten.

Dear Mr. Mondadori,

Erich Linder m'informa della vostra cortese intenzione di pubblicare su
EPOCA una notizia sull'edizione, da me curata, delle lettere di Joyce e io
apprezzo profondamente l'appoggio che mi viene gentilmente da Voi offerto. Il
signor Linder mi chiede di precisare, con esattezza, le informazioni che
dovrebbero essere accolte in tale notizia. Non so bene se Voi pensavate a una mia
lettera, oppure a qualche altra forma di scritto: ho preparato comunque la
seguente lettera che potrebbe forse fare al caso:

"Al direttore,

sto preparando un'edizione delle lettere di James Joyce, da pubblicare in
Inghilterra e negli Stati Uniti. Particolarmente m'interessano copie delle
lettere indirizzate da Joyce ai molti amici italiani e conosciuti nel corso dei
dieci anni in cui si fermò a Trieste, o incontrati poi a Zurigo o a Parigi. Sarò
molto grato a coloro fra i Vostri lettori che potranno dirmi dove queste
lettere possono essere reperite.

Sinceramente vostro,

Richard Ellmann"

La lettera potrebbe essere preceduta o seguita da una nota in cui si dice che lo scrivente è un ben noto critico americano, professore d'inglese e autore di una biografia su Joyce, pubblicata dalla Oxford University Press.

23 See FAAM, AsAME, Segreteria Editoriale Estero, Serie C, envelope 30, folder 12 (James Joyce), letter of Roberto Fertonani to Giorgio Melchiori, Milan, February 2, 1967.

24 FAAM, AsAME, Segreteria Editoriale Estero, Serie C, envelope 30, folder 12 (James Joyce), letter of Giorgio Melchiori to Roberto Fertonani, Milan, April 6, 1967, typewritten.

perchè il problema è veramente grosso, ed ho cambiato più volte io stesso opinione su quanto dovevo dire

25 FAAM, AsAME, Segreteria Editoriale Estero, Serie C, envelope 30, folder 12 (James Joyce), letter of Giorgio Melchiori to Roberto Fertonani, Milan, April 6, 1967, typewritten.

(a) escludere tutte le lettere che riguardano solo questioni di affari.

(b) escludere tutte o quasi le lettere dirette a Joyce (sono molte nei volumi di Faber) limitandosi a estratti o riassunti in nota ove indispensabili per intendere le risposte.

(c) includere tutte le lettere o parti di lettere che rivelino il carattere di Joyce, le sue idiosincrasie, l'atteggiamento verso l'opera propria o di altrui, le circostanze familiari, le traversie della sua vita privata, le polemiche sostenute,

(d) includere quelle lettere e parti di lettere che contengono giudizi e impressioni di uomini, luoghi, libri e letture.

(e) il filo conduttore deve essere necessariamente ed esaurientemente biografico, e ciò comporta l'inclusione di lettere che, pur non avendo alcun interesse letterario o strettamente personale, rendono conto delle vicende della famiglia Joyce, delle sue condizioni economiche e di salute, di questioni più strettamente editoriali ecc.

26 FAAM, AsAME, Segreteria Editorial Estero, Serie C, envelope 30, folder 12 (James Joyce), letter of Giorgio Melchiori to Roberto Fertonani, Milan, April 6, 1967, typewritten

considerando che lo specialista o lo studioso che voglia avere sottocchio tutti i documenti disponibili è ovviamente in grado di leggerseli nell'originale, mi è sembrato che il "pubblico" per l'epistolario tradotto sarà rappresentato piuttosto dai lettori di Joyce curiosi di conoscerne di prima mano la personalità umana e la biografia.

27 We are confronted here with another significant "silence," for it is intriguing that Mondadori should miss the opportunity to publish Ellmann's biography. The papers preserved at the Mondadori Foundation bear no trace of the book.

28 Founded in 1955 in Milan, Feltrinelli hugely contributed to the widening of the public for the novel. In 1957, he issued the first world edition of Boris Pasternak's *Doctor Zhivago* and in 1958 he was the protagonist of another literary case when he published Giuseppe Tomasi di Lampedusa's *The Leopard*, which had previously been rejected by the two main Italian publishers, Mondadori and Einaudi.

29 FAAM, AsAME, Segreteria Editoriale Estero, Serie C, envelope 30, folder 12 (James Joyce), report of Giansiro Ferrata, Milan, May 13, 1969, typewritten.

> gli elementi utili a ricostruire la formazione delle opera maggiori.

30 For an overview on Italian translations, see Bosinelli in Joyce (1996) and Bendelli (2014).

References

Bachleitner, N. (2009), "A Proposal to Include Book History in Translation Studies Illustrated with German Translations of Scott and Flaubert," *Arcadia: Internationale Zeitschrift für Literaturwissenschaft* 44, no. 2: 420–40.

Bendelli, G. (2014), "Sanesi tra le prime versioni italiane di *Finnegans Wake*," in Maria Antonietta Grignani and Anna Longoni (eds), *Autografo 52: Traduzione e Novecento*, 149–65, Novara: Interlinea.

Billiani, F. (2007), *Culture nazionali e narrazioni straniere: Italia 1903–1943*, Florence: Le Lettere.

Bollettieri Bosinelli, R. M. (1979), "Joyce as an Italian Writer: Regarding *Scritti Italiani di James Joyce*, a cura di G. Corsini e G. Melchiori, Milano, Mondadori, 1979," *James Joyce Quarterly* 17, no. 3: 320–3.

Bulson, E. (2001), "Getting Noticed: James Joyce's Italian Translations," *Joyce Studies Annual* 12: 10–37.

Del Buono, O. (1960), "Il suo capolavoro fu dato alle fiamme," *Epoca* (November): 77–81.

Ellmann, R. (1959), *James Joyce*, New York: Oxford University Press.

Ferretti, G. C. (2004), *Storia dell'editoria letteraria in Italia: 1945–2003*, Turin: Einaudi.

Ferretti, G. C. (ed.) (2012), *Protagonisti nell'ombra*, Milan: Unicopli-Fondazione Arnoldo e Alberto Mondadori.

Gilbert, S. (ed.) (1957), *Letters of James Joyce*, New York: Viking Press.

Gorlier, C. (1960), "Studi su Joyce," *il verri* 6, no. 6: 121–5.

Joyce, J. (1974), *Lettere*, trans. (selection) G. and J. Melchiori and R. Oliva, Milan: Mondadori.

Joyce, J. (1979), *Scritti Italiani di James Joyce*, ed. Gianfranco Corsini and Giorgio Melchiori, Milan: Mondadori.

Joyce, J. (1996), *Anna Livia Plurabelle, versione italiana di James Joyce e Nino Frank*, ed. R. M. Bollettieri Bosinelli, intro. U. Eco, Turin: Einaudi.

Kelly, J. (1998), *Our Joyce: From Outcast to Icon*, Austin: University of Texas Press.

Levie, S. (2009), "Transfer and Integration: Foreign Literatures in National Context," *Arcadia: Internationale Zeitschrift für Literaturwissenschaft* 44, no. 2: 229–36.

Lombardo, A. (1959), "Le lettere di Joyce," *Il mondo*, July 2.

Melchiori, G. (2000), "Joyce scrittore italiano," in *James Joyce: Il mestiere dello scrittore*, 99–118, Turin: Einaudi.

Pasquero, M. (2012), "'Mi par di trovarmi di fronte a un fatto nuovo letterario.' Carlo Linati alla scoperta di James Joyce," *Studi irlandesi: A Journal of Irish Studies* 2: 199–254.

Piombo, S. (2010), "Collane di liberazione: Piccole case editrici di cultura a Milano tra il 1945 e il 1947," *Charta* 107: 68–72.

Sisto, M. and Fantappiè, I. (eds) (2014), *Letteratura italiana e tedesca 1945–1970: Campi, polisistemi, transfer*, Rome: Istituto Italiano di Studi Germanici.

Sullam, S. (2013), "Le peripezie di Ulisse nell'Italia del secondo dopoguerra," *Letteratura e letterature* 7: 69–86.

Sullam, S. (2014), "The Translation of Joyce's Poetry in Post-war Italy," in M. Canani and S. Sullam (eds), *Parallaxes: Virginia Woolf Meets James Joyce*, 178–96, Newcastle upon Tyne: Cambridge Scholar Publishing.

Wilson, N. et al. (2014), "The Hogarth Press, Digital Humanities, and Collaboration: Introducing the Modernist Archives Publishing Project (MAPP)," in M. A. Gillies and H. Wussow (eds), *Virginia Woolf and the Common(wealth) Reader. Selected Papers from the Twenty-Third Annual International Conference on Virginia Woolf*, 223–31, Clemson, SC: Clemson University Digital Press.

Woolf, V. (2008), "Women and Fiction," in D. Bradshaw (ed.), *Selected Essays*, 132–9, Oxford: Oxford University Press.

Zanotti, S. (2004), "James Joyce among Italian Writers," in G. Lernout and W. van Mierlo (eds), *The Reception of James Joyce in Europe*, Vol. 2, 311–61, London: Continuum.

Zanotti, S. (2013), *Italian Joyce: A Journey Through Language and Translation*, Bologna: Bononia University Press.

11

The Silence of the Looms: "Penelope" as Translation

Tim Conley

In Robert Fitzgerald's translation of *The Odyssey*, Penelope is called "the quiet queen" (18.201). While this epithet seems justified—compared to the epic's many men who variously boast, flatter, and quarrel, Penelope is no jabberer—it differs significantly from those chosen by other translators.[1] Charles Stein, following Butcher and Lang, calls her "wise" (18.266), Robert Fagles, opting for two adjectives rather than one, judges her "wary, poised" (18.182), and Richmond Lattimore is most literal with "circumspect" (18.159). Homer's term is περίφρων (18.159), which might be translated as "thoughtful" or "cautious," though the Greek word is more interesting than either of these English ones. Cunliffe's eminently useful *Lexicon of the Homeric Dialect* suggests "[o]f great good sense, wise, sage, prudent" (1963: 326). The prefix περί (*peri*) suggests someone with a "roundabout" approach, circumspective, perhaps even one who goes round and round in her thoughts. To this might be compared περιφέρεια, the circumference of a circle, and the spinning or twirling motion of weaving (περί σχεδίην ἐλέλξεν). Penelope's wiles are most famously associated with her nightly unweaving of the shroud, a ploy that is the female counterpart to her husband's with the Trojan Horse. The latter is an act of secretly filling up a vessel in anticipation of confrontation, the former an act of secretly emptying designed to defer confrontation. Ann Bergren points out that such tricks are "the essential form of *mêtis*, the τρόπος 'turning' that binds opposites, manifest in the reversal and the circle, in weaving, twisting, and knotting, and in every joint" (2008: 216).

It is probably unlikely that many readers of *Ulysses* would characterize Molly Bloom as "quiet." Readers have variously demonized or celebrated her for being outspoken to a fault, and the absence of punctuation in the novel's final chapter no doubt helps give the impression—even to those who have not read it, but have heard tell of it—that Molly's is an untrammelled voice, going on and on. Yet the fact is that we hear Molly say relatively little in the novel, and the ambiguities of what is meant by "hearing" and "saying" will come to play a central role in this essay. If "Penelope" may be at least provisionally distinguished as narration, in contrast to the spoken dialogue that Joyce usually marks with a *tiret*, the question of how much Molly says becomes a manageable and perhaps surprising matter of accounting. In "Calypso," we hear Molly speak 130 words— no great sum, and that's generously counting "Mn" as one and "J. C. Doyle" as three words. To this figure might be added those spoken by "Marion Bloom," an apparition, and likewise "Marion's Voice" in "Circe": another 125, by my count, including "O! Weeshwashtkissinapooisthnapoohuck?" (*U* 15.3812–13; taken here as two "words"). Comparison gives such numbers more palpable meaning: Molly's grand total is less than half of all of the words spoken by Nosey Flynn (574 of them) in Davy Byrne's. If Flynn's low count is symptomatic of his being a minor character (as he no doubt is), what reason or excuse do we attribute to Molly's? Could it be that she is, when all is said but not done, a *peripheral* character?[2]

Tracing Homeric "parallels" as such is not my business here.[3] In order to explore and evaluate how the reader "hears" (or does not "hear") the women in *Ulysses*, and particularly Molly Bloom, it is useful to consider Joyce's novel as a kind of translation of Homer—a *translation*, not simply an homage or a parody, and a *kind of translation* because it may not operate by the recognized principles of other translations.[4] Further justification for thinking of this intertextual relationship this way lies in the fact that translation is an act of voicing what is not understood, of rescuing sound from silence. However, a dilemma arises: how to translate silence? Translation is often a matter of expansion and amplification, making explicit and sometimes even exaggerating what is perceived as significant, however nuanced, subtle, or obscure in the original. Silence defies the translator.

Fitzgerald's "quiet queen" may strike us as a translation that is inexact but not inapt. Over and over again in *The Odyssey* there is a movement between the alluring voices of women, voices which often speak a truth that men cannot bear to hear, and the silencing of those voices. (Think of the tempting songs of Calypso, Circe, and the Sirens, all of which Odysseus must hear and resist, or of the nurse Eurycleia, whose throat Odysseus seizes while Athena prevents Penelope from hearing what she excitedly reveals.) How does *Ulysses* translate this theme? Peripherally, by means of what Ezra Pound, complaining of *Finnegans Wake*, called "circumambient peripherisation" (*Letters III* 145). This might be thought of as "talking a lot without saying anything," but Joyce playfully proposes the interchangeability of this formula with its inverse: "not talking at all while saying a good deal." Readers in effect become attentive in the way that translators must, alert as possible to what is emphasized and what is muted as well as to how the text sounds, and what in the text is without sound. We best hear the women in *Ulysses* when we hear their silences.

Calypso

Molly Bloom's very first spoken word, which perhaps is not a word at all, has to be translated:

—You don't want anything for breakfast?
A sleepy soft grunt answered:
—Mn.
No. She didn't want anything.

U 4.55–8

That "Mn" is fascinating not only because it seems to be the contrary of her famous "Yes." It might not be decipherable were it not for Bloom, whom the reader at this moment comes to trust as a cautious but reliable translator of his wife (so far just "she"), but by the end of the novel, when the reader turns back to admire the retrospective arrangement, the characterization of lusty Molly as she who "didn't want anything" sounds ridiculous.[5] Moreover, "Mn," a "grunt" rather than a recognized phoneme from a known language, may be the first and the most compact instant of an untranslatable term in *Ulysses*: nearly every translation of the novel using a Roman alphabet (Catalan, Croatian, Dutch, Finnish, French, German, Hungarian, Irish, Italian, Norwegian, Polish, Portugese, Romanian, Serbian, Spanish, Swedish, Turkish) makes no change to "Mn."[6] Yet it may well be an open question whether, say, a sleepy Dutch or Italian speaker softly grunts in quite the same way that a sleepy French or Turkish one does. Molly's "yes," by striking contrast, is *always* translated: *ja, oui, sí*, and so on.

The chapter of *Ulysses* in which the Blooms are introduced is named after the nymph whose singing and weaving beguile Homer's hero. The name "Calypso" means deception, concealment, secret knowledge. The etymology of "Penelope," the other renowned weaver, is not so certain (perhaps πηνη (*pene*), "threads, weft"), and the secrets of "Calypso" are not entirely or decisively revealed in "Penelope." Some of the most significant (and recurring) information in the novel is first spoken by Molly in "Calypso," though readers have no access to it:

we cannot hear her. Molly's mispronunciation of "metempsychosis" is withheld, unlike the phonetic spelling of the cat's "Mkgnao!" or "Mrkgnao!" (*U* 4.16, 25), and the time of Boylan's visit becomes available to the reader only later, like "met him pike hoses" (*U* 8.112), in Bloom's recollection. This delayed understanding is akin to how Bloom reads the letter from Milly: he first quickly scans it, and then only later is struck by something in it ("What was that about some young student and a picnic?" *U* 4.393–4) and so rereads it more attentively. Hearing is a rather different operation from reading, of course, for sound is not tangible in the way text is, and one cannot exactly "rehear," except by mechanical recording. This is in part why Jacques Derrida refers to Molly's "yes" as "manifest and manifestly marked as a *word*, whether spoken, written, or phonogramed" (Derrida 2013: 72). This word, as a word, has a life of its own.

But "yes" is a word that Molly uses only selectively in "Calypso." Decisive when it comes to declaring which word it is she wants defined and what dirty books she wants brought home, she leaves "yes" unsaid—or else we readers do not hear her use it—on other occasions, either because her attention is elsewhere (i.e. on Boylan) or because she expects her Poldy to know the answer:

> He laid her card and letter on the twill bedspread near the curve of her knees.
> —Do you want the blind up?
> Letting the blind up by gentle tugs halfway his backward eye saw her glance at the letter and tuck it under her pillow.
> —That do? he asked, turning.
> She was reading the card, propped on her elbow.
> —She got the things, she said.
>
> *U* 4.253–60

> —Would you like the window open a little?
> She doubled a slice of bread into her mouth, asking:
> —What time is the funeral?
>
> *U* 4.317–19

Maybe Molly does express assent in some way that is imperceptible to the reader (or, put another way, not noticed or recorded by the narrator, much like the precise time of Boylan's visit), but any such gesture is not a "yes" that we can hear.[7] Maybe Molly says "yes" in her head, which we later discover appears to be a habit, but we have no access to that phenomenon at this point. In fact, Bloom's "yeses" are more frequent and more lyrical than Molly's here ("Be near her ample bedwarm flesh. Yes, yes," *U* 4.238–9), but they are unspoken, and thus anticipate "Penelope."

"you couldnt hear your ears"

Sleepless Molly stands—or rather, reclines—in contrast to Penelope, whose repeated enchantment into unworried sleep is a kind of refrain in Homer. Penelope's silence, at least in these instances, is imposed, but the silences of Molly are of a different kind, and it might be argued that the "ideal insomnia" that inspires, produces, and is demanded by *Finnegans Wake* is prefigured by Molly's going over and over her memories and desires, most of them inexpressible in the respectable light of day.

A proposition for debate: "Penelope" is the only chapter in which nothing is spoken aloud. The closest contender for this distinction is "Proteus," which might well be compared with "Penelope" to measure how porous is the boundary between external stimuli and internal monologue, especially with respect to sound. Most immediately conspicuous among the absent punctuation marks is the *tiret*, and even though desperate readers might wish for a few commas or periods, such pauses would not alleviate the quandary of ascertaining the tone of the words and their origin. Molly appropriates and perhaps mimics the voices of others, to the consternation of some editors and annotators. Robert Gogan's "remastered" edition of *Ulysses*, whose changes to the text's typography and punctuation offer "an easier reading experience" (Gogan 2012: 649), italicizes the entire chapter to convey the understanding that, without exception, Molly is thinking rather than speaking these words. Danis Rose, in offering as an appendix to his "Reader's Edition" an "alternative format" of "Penelope" in which snatches and titles of songs are italicized, displays the same anxiety.

What is to be heard in "Penelope" if it is an "interior" monologue (though "interior" is not a word that Joyce used to describe it in either the Gilbert or the Linati schema)? There are distended words that imply sounds, such as in the observation "frseeeeeeeefronnnng train somewhere whistling" (*U* 18.596). Does Molly hear the train? Do *readers* hear it—or do they only "hear" Molly's approximation (an exercise in harmony? an exercise in parody?), or is it wrong to say that even that approximation is "heard"? This phenomenological puzzle breaks apart into smaller and smaller puzzle pieces the closer one examines it. Molly suggests that the train is "whistling": literally, there is a steam trumpet blowing a warning signal, though "whistling" suggests a human, musical quality. Yet "frseeeeeeeeefronnnng" does not, at least to my ear, sound much like whistling. And if Molly herself is making this "sound," does this mean that she is whistling aloud, or—how *does* one do this?—whistling in her head? Throughout *Ulysses* the limits of auditory mimesis are tested, such as in the rendering of sounds in print: "Kinch" may or may not be convincingly translated as "the knifeblade" (but cutting into what?); the previously mentioned dicta of the cat in "Calypso"; the pealing of churchbells ("Heigho" and "Cuckoo"); Davy Byrne's complex yawn ("Iiiiiichaaaaaaach!" *U* 8.970); and the various colorful expressions of the inanimate, the abstract, and the imaginary in "Circe."

These seem more or less mediated versions of sounds, translations in which the modality of the audible is underscored. Or we might call these indirect "sounds" a sort of periphrasis, and therein hear cognate echoes of περίφρων, whatever it means. If there is reason to be cautious about believing that, for example, a nannygoat's bleat sounds like "Megeggaggegg! Nannannanny!" (*U* 15.3370), then it might be wondered whether the words of "Penelope" are sounds, and what relationship those many words have with a woman who has not said very much in the novel before now. One forceful feminist reading paradigm of "Penelope" can be summed up with the assertion that "Joyce *ventriloquizes* his own notion of what femininity is through the textual construction of 'Penelope'" (Van Boheemen 1999: 269). Molly is, in the most extreme such interpretation, a silent dummy, her voice an illusion. Similar questions about the reality, plausibility, and sovereignty of the voice(s) in the novel pertain to many if not all its female characters, among them Gerty MacDowell, Misses Douce and Kennedy, and the assortment of prostitutes and indignant upper-class ladies in "Circe." "Were the Sirens nothing more than unreal voices," wonders Maurice Blanchot (1981: 106), "voices which were not supposed to be heard?" Such suggestions are, to use a word that is exactly right and exactly wrong, disquieting.

"I could have been a prima donna"

In August 1921 Joyce professed to Frank Budgen that "Penelope" is "probably more obscene than any other preceding episode"—and in this context it ought to be remembered that "obscene" literally means "off-stage," or peripheral—but he went on to judge it "perfectly sane full amoral fertilisable untrustworthy engaging shrewd limited prudent indifferent *Weib*" (*Letters I* 170). This list of adjectives includes at least two translations of περίφρων ("shrewd" and "prudent") though one might make the case that they all could be understood this way, and thus see "Penelope," a portrait of an inconstant and inconsistent woman, as a combination of possible translations (varying in accuracy and degree of embellishment or invention) of Homer's slippery epithet. The unexpected halt at *Weib*, a (Goethean) noun, confuses things: is Joyce describing the chapter (as the grammar of his sentence dictates) or the character? This confusion has occasionally spread to readers and critics. For example, Fr. Robert Boyle (1974: 415) understands this sentence to give evidence that Molly is capable of having another child if she wants to because it calls *her* "'fertilisable,' not 'fertilised.'" The way that roundabout "Penelope" gives readers no small trouble in trying to distinguish who (which "he") is being referred to in any one instant is part of a larger phenomenon. Molly's stream of qualifications, corrections, reversals, calculations, and above all affirmations, washing away any chance of a fixed or restrictive identity, amounts to a disarming diffusion of subjectivity. Little wonder that readers have declared her an incarnation of whatever qualities they find most fascinating (earth mother, slut, everywoman), and little wonder that so many have read her aloud, no more possessing her than possessed by her. Blanchot (1981: 109–10) envisions Odysseus becoming Homer; Joyce invites the reader to become Penelope.

"O Lord I wanted to shout out all sorts of things fuck or shit or anything at all" (*U* 18.588–9). Molly "wanted to"—but didn't. Why not? One can only suggest various possible answers to this, perhaps none of them a full explanation in itself: Molly supposes that Boylan would disapprove of such language from a woman; she is, in the heat of the moment, unable to decide just what expression ("anything at all") is *le mot juste*; she cannot bring herself to utter such words aloud, either in public or private, because for all of her (unspoken) rebellions against repressive social codes, she nonetheless adheres to them in practice. This recognition, however it might be explained, kindles doubt about Molly's future scheme: "I know every turn in him Ill tighten my bottom well and let out a few smutty words smellrump or lick my shit or the first mad thing comes into my head" (*U* 18.1530–2). Molly here is planning to do something spontaneous, and moreover that which she has been unable to do before—very much the sort of symptom of repression that readers generally find pathetic in a character such as Little Chandler ("If he could only write a book and get it published, that might open the way for him ... If he could get back again into that mood," *D* 79; ellipsis added).

"Penelope" is in fact the chapter of the subjunctive (which, suitably enough, follows the matter-of-fact interrogation of "Ithaca"). While certain other chapters more or less overstep the bounds of naturalism into differently shaded realms of wishful thinking and projections of desire ("Proteus" has a brief, speculative representation of Stephen visiting the Gouldings; "Nausicaa" may largely be Bloom's own pornographic voice-over; and "Circe" can claim to be a full-blown fantasia), the book's final chapter is an index of hypothetical futures. What Molly might do, what she would like to do, what might be done with the world—the narrative is made of these. Even the most prurient passages are notional, conditional. Molly schemes:

> I know what Ill do Ill go about rather gay and not too much singing now and then mi fa pieta Masetto then Ill start dressing myself to go out presto non son piu forte Ill put on my best shift and drawers let him have a good eyeful out of that to make his micky stand for him Ill let him know if thats what he wanted that his wife is fucked yes and damn well fucked too up to my neck nearly not by him 5 or 6 times handrunning theres the mark of his spunk on the clean sheet I wouldnt bother to even iron it out that ought to satisfy him
>
> U 18.1506–13

Will Molly iron the sheet or won't she? Unwoven shroud, stained sheet: all a question of what might be done, what revelations might be made, what they might effect. In more than one way, "Penelope" is propositional. (This point lends force to Nietzschean readings, but might also prompt considerations of what an aphorist Molly truly is, and for that matter how Wittgensteinian: she is a weaver of a language game of "what Ill do" and "yes").[8] Molly plans this, imagines that, and of course the chapter concludes on a promise "yes I will Yes" (U 18.1608–9) that suspends time, pointing as it does back (or forward) to her husband's own imagined strategies ("Divorce, not now," U 17.2202) and further on to the refrain of "not yet" in *Finnegans Wake*.[9]

"the wrong things and no stops to say like making a speech"

Staged and filmed performances of "Penelope" paradoxically demonstrate how undramatic the chapter is. They have to compensate for the lack of definite action with recitation; they directly translate all of the words into speech, usually talking to the audience (even if as voice-over). Leopold Bloom of the stage and screen does not articulate each and every word in the novel—or even a sizeable percentage of them—that we understand as his thoughts (all of what Gogan italicizes, though there is room for debate on any given distinction), but Molly is all palaver. Although the cinematic qualities of *Ulysses* have been much commented upon, the notion of it as a *silent* film (cinema as Joyce would have known it) seems to have eluded serious consideration. Even Sergei Eisenstein, who saw a distinction between spoken dialogue and "quivering inner words that correspond with visual images," appears to have thought of *Ulysses* as "a particularly suitable basis for training visual consciousness" in relation to sound film (qtd. in Williams 2010: 159). Can we not imagine *Ulysses* as a silent film? In this connection, I think of a film like *Bed and Sofa* (dir. Abram Room, co-written with Viktor Shklovsky, 1927; *The Jazz Singer*, the first "talkie," appeared the same year). In the film, the female protagonist Lyuda is largely confined to and directly associated with the apartment in which she lives with her husband and, eventually, his friend, two men who change places sleeping on the title's bed and sofa. Though a comedy about sex and modern marriage, the film is also a frank, deeply sympathetic, and psychologically aware portrait of an adulterous wife. The scenes in which Lyuda wordlessly contemplates the room around her and her complicated amorous situations (including a shot of her noticing, with a most momentary smirk, that her seducer, now asleep beside her, still has his shoes on) are carefully orchestrated sequences of very minor gestures and minimal expressions. Taken together, they provide silent insight into her thoughts. Could "Penelope" be thus translated? But would doing so not betray that quintessential *wordiness* of Molly—she who asks for definitions, cherishes "plain words," and who thinks of what bad words she "wanted to say"?

The difficulties of such translation are glaring—how to convey all that Molly is thinking?—but all the same, the utter absence of spoken dialogue as such would seem to alleviate problems that would bedevil any of the other chapters, especially the ones with plenty of gab, song, and ambient noise (again, the salient comparison is with contemplative "Proteus"). An intriguing double bind, then: the silence of "Penelope" must be broken, yet the sense of silence must be conveyed.[10] The problem is directly comparable and perhaps even synonymous with the ineluctable problem of translation: *traduttore, traditore*; to betray faithfully. It is no coincidence that this is exactly what "Penelope" is all about (the loving wife who cheats; the wife who must "translate" what her husband has said to her, beginning with his unexpected request for breakfast in bed next morning). If "Penelope" is to be voiced, at what volume and with what rhythm ought it to be spoken? Are those qualities consistent throughout or do they sometimes shift? Actors have typically adopted a hushed tone, even a whisper, to convey that sense of quiet, but upon its repetition this seems a doubtful device, and, turning again to the text, the thought that Molly Bloom is almost unhaltingly whispering aloud to herself might well inspire concern for her state of mind. Derrida (2013: 74) argues that

> Nothing is less a monologue than Molly's "monologue" even if, within certain conventional limits, one is justified in considering it as belonging to the genre or kind "monologue". But a discourse situated between two qualitatively different

"*Yeses*," two "*Yeses*" in capital letters, thus two gramophoned "*Yeses*," could not be a monologue, at most a soliloquy.

The dramatic gimmick that obviates silence and ambiguity, defines character and outlines action, soliloquy seems apt in that Molly does present opinions and plans in a way that is removed from dramatic action and dialogue. A coinage of St. Augustine, "soliloquy" literally means "talking to oneself" (Skeat 2005: 580). Even if Molly can be said to be "talking," it is no less risky to suppose or assume that she is talking to herself, that she is her only audience. Disappointed with these feeble classifications, we might be tempted to liken "Penelope" to a musical score, but the lack of marked pauses quashes that idea. As in the riddle to which "silence" is the answer, there is no generic designation to be given "Penelope" that does not dispel what it is.

All verbalizations of "Penelope" are unique, because the speaker must make a series of decisions, very like those of a translator, about what is to be sounded and what is to be left in silence, and all such verbalizations are also perforce selective and incomplete, for the same reason. How Joe Hynes manages to read aloud the erroneous spellings in the letter by Rumbold, Master Barber's letter (*U* 12.414–31) is enough of a hermeneutic poser, and the stage directions provided for the dialogue in "Circe" are not exactly instructive (e.g. a feminist speaks "*masculinely*," *U* 15.1465–6, and Lynch's cap speaks "*with saturnine spleen*," *U* 15.2096–7). But "Penelope" is itself a flood of such text-to-speech defects. How does someone reading "Penelope" aloud "sound" the absence of punctuation, the orthographic oddities, the numbers, the prudish dash in "a—e" (*U* 18.490), and the corrective deletions in her routinely misspelled words "symp*h*athy" and "ne*w*phew" (*U* 18.729–31)?[11] Indeed, how does this performer determine a pace, or even manage to breathe? Answer: prudently, warily, thoughtfully, wisely, circumspectly, cautiously, quietly. Take your pick.

Weaving, unweaving

Derrida's characterization of Molly's "yes" and, by implication, all of *Ulysses* as "gramophoned" words points to a mechanical repetition that need not be exclusively associated with the gramophone, or even with machines. The forerunner of the computer that Derrida ultimately imagines ("a computer which has not yet been invented" (2013: 80)—*l'ordinateur à venir*, we might say), a sort of Deep Thought which could take up the complex rhythms of the novel, is the industrial loom of the early nineteenth century. The decision to cross one thread either over or under another is the basis of binary code (which we might think of as a question of "Yes" or "Mn"). Before this, of course, such calculations fell to women's hands, the quiet work of household weaving.[12]

In *The Odyssey*, Penelope's ruse with the shroud is as much a past event (prior to the narrative) as the Trojan Horse is a future event in *The Iliad*. Yet just as George Fredric Franko discerns how "Homer thrice hints to those listeners familiar with the traditional story that [the horse] lurks just beyond the [*Iliad's*] horizon" (2005–6: 121), the story of Penelope's deceit and its discovery is thrice told in *The Odyssey*. Here is Lattimore's version of the second telling, Penelope speaking to the strange visitor she does not recognize as her husband:

> These men try to hasten the marriage. I weave my own wiles.
> First the divinity put the idea of the web in my mind,
> to set up a great loom in my palace, and set to weaving
> a web of threads, long and fine. Then I said to them:
> "Young men, my suitors now that the great Odysseus has perished,
> wait, though you are eager to marry me, until I finish
> this web, so that my weaving will not be useless and wasted.
> This is a shroud for the hero Laertes, for when the destructive
> doom of death which lays men low shall take him, lest any
> Achaian woman in this neighborhood hold it against me
> that a man of many conquests lies with no sheet to wind him."
> So I spoke, and the proud heart in them was persuaded.
> Thereafter in the daytime I would weave at my great loom,
> but at night I would have torches set by, and undo it.

> 19.137–50

First Antinous tells this story to Telemachus, then Penelope tells it to the disguised Odysseus, and finally, Amphimedon, another suitor at the poem's end arriving as a shade in the underworld, tells it to the curious Agamemnon. These are verbatim retellings, the differences between them negligible—these are no subtle "hints" but obvious and mechanical repetition. No gramophone is necessary: only deft hands and the thread of the story.

Although weaving is a very common metaphor for artistic production generally, there may be an ancient basis for a contrary understanding. Benjamin Eldon Stevens (2013: 213) sees in Catullus, for example, a similar connection between the domestic task of weaving and "the subordination, and with it the silence" of women. Pre-industrial weaving is quiet, humble work: the story of Arachne's contest with Athena is startling for exactly this reason. Though triumphant, Arachne is silenced, transformed by the goddess into a spider, which of course will go on to "weave." This pattern in Greek myth recurs: she who is silenced is also, crucially, *not entirely* silenced: Philomela, Cassandra. Indeed, one of the most fascinating scenes in *The Odyssey* is of silenced women given voice:

> So went our talk; then other shadows came,
> ladies in company, sent by Perséphonê—
> consorts or daughters of illustrious men—
> crowding about the black blood.
>   I took thought
> how best to separate and question them,
> and saw no help for it, but drew once more
> the long bright edge of broadsword from my hip,
> that none should sip the blood in company
> but one by one, in order; so it fell
> that each declared her lineage and name.
>
>   Fitzgerald 11.256–66

In the kingdom of the dead, Odysseus gives ear to the stories of Tyro, Antiope, Alcmena, Epicaste, Chloris, Leda, Iphimedia, and many others, so many that he cannot name them all, all "sent by Perséphonê." But why? Odysseus has just spoken with his mother but, finding himself unable to embrace her, wonders whether this might all be an illusion, and his mother assures him that Persephone does not deceive him and pointedly instructs him to bear witness of his experiences to his wife. And this is the cue for these dead women to appear.

Ewigweibliche, the "eternal feminine"—it is a fantasy that has been rightly (and roundly) challenged but which perhaps should not be rejected but instead retranslated, with Joyce's help. The prefigured postponement that is weaving and unweaving, the persistence of desire within the subjunctive and the future tense, and the unceasing calculation of the dialectic between "yes" and "not yet" together urge a Penelopean understanding of the "eternal feminine" as an ever-imminent moment of communication, a way of speaking without spoken words, a way of speaking beyond death, in a silence of one's own.

"forthflowing, wending back"

Hugh Kenner highlights how two paragraphs in "Cyclops" offer two different "translations" of the arrival of Alf Bergan, the first a pastiche of Butcher and Lang's style of rendering Homer, and the next in the amusing vernacular of the chapter's narrator. Kenner makes the point that Homer and by extension the classical world and its legacies are in Joyce's time (and our own) composed of translations: "*Ulysses* is at this level a comment on the age that had allowed its perception of Homer to get into such a state" (Kenner 1955: 191–2). This point certainly strikes its mark, but leaving aside the question of the degradation of learning (just as I have refrained from dismissing or merely chiding Fitzgerald for his "quiet"), I suggest that *Ulysses* is a meta-translation, a translation of translations, with the understanding that translation is by definition a kind of "comment," not just on "the age" but on translation itself. As a translation, it faces the problem of translating what is silent or quiet; as a meta-translation, reading and rewriting Homer's *Odyssey* as a continuous process of discovering new *Odysseys*, it ingeniously engages this same problem by unsettling the reader's certainty about the relation of word to sound.

Molly Bloom is both a translation (of Penelope) and, more bewilderingly, a translator. She translates not only her own history but the history of Homeric translation. Readers of Joyce gradually learn to "think with their ears" (to borrow a memorable phrase from Adorno), but "Penelope" in particular recalibrates this readerly hearing. It takes a singer to remind us that we readers, merely *as* readers, hear nothing; that at best reading is circumauditory, "hearing around" sounds. The risk of the translator is to make heard what is only thought to be heard, to weave without also unweaving.

Notes

1 Fitzgerald's choice cannot be simply put down to the allure of alliteration, for elsewhere he refers to Penelope as "that quiet lady" (16.394). In fact, "quiet" seems to be an *idée fixe* for his translation. Consider this passage:

> In the entrance way they stayed
> to listen there: inside her quiet house
> they heard the goddess Kirkê.
> Low she sang
> in her beguiling voice, while on her loom
> she wove ambrosial fabric sheer and bright,
> by that craft known to the goddesses of heaven.
>
> Fitzgerald 10.240–6

Again, none of the other translators that I have consulted has anything to say about the house being "quiet." A tricky scene of trickery, it is followed by the transformation of the dupes, of which Eurylochos reports, "but I saw cruel deceit, and stayed behind. / Then all our fellows vanished. Not a sound, / and nothing stirred, although I watched for hours" (10.284–6). Did the witness see nothing, or hear nothing? Only Fitzgerald writes "Not a sound": his women seem cloaked in quiet.

2   She is at least circumreferential, a woman of curves and turns: "I knew I could always get round him" (*U* 18.1579–80).

3   Taking a cue from Fritz Senn (1984: 127): "Even though the so-called Homeric parallels, the transposition of characters and situations, have definite purposes, it is sometimes useful not to insist on the strictly parallel nature of the correspondences."

4   One advantage to addressing the novel as a translation is that doing so in no way precludes consideration of all of the other things it may be interpreted as: modern epic, *roman à clef*, satire, etc.

5   In "Memory and Marital Dynamics in *Ulysses*," Jolanta Wawrzycka links "Mn" with Mnemosyne and suggests that Molly displays a less clumsy facility with words than her husband does (2014: 4).

6   A list of exceptions:

    Albanian: "Mm" (*Uliksi*, trans. Idlir Azizi (Zenit, 2004), 74).
    Czech: "Ň" (*Odysseus*, trans. Aloys Skoumal (Prague: Argo, 1993), 49).
    Italian: "Mnn" (*Ulisse*, trans. Gianni Celati (Turin: Einaudi, 2013), 75).
    Portuguese: "Hm" (*Ulisses*, trans. Antônio Houaiss (Rio de Janeiro: Editôra Civilzação Brasileira, 1966), 63); "Hum" (*Ulisses*, trans. João Palma-Ferreira (Lisbon: Edição Livros do Brasil, 2005), 85); "Mnan" (*Ulisses*, trans. Bernardina da Silveira Pinheiro (Rio de Janeiro: Objetiva, 2007), 84). (The 2012 Galindo translation keeps "Mn.")
    Slovenian: "Nn" (*Ulikses*, trans. Janez Gradisnik (Ljubljana: Zalozba, 1993), Vol. 1, 71).

    My thanks to Sam Slote for his assistance in collecting and comparing these various translations.

7   Cf. Derrida (2013: 71): "I say the *yes* and not the word "yes" for there can be some *yes* without a word."

8   Reading "Penelope" as a kind of "philosophical investigation" is both a special sort of delight and worthy of extended study. Its (or do I mean "Her"?) measuring of inherent linguistic fault lines, such as the tricky differences between "emissions" and "omissions" (*U* 18.1170) and between "where" in the world and "where" on one's body (*U* 18.107–10), or the questionable axiom that "a noun is the name of any person place or thing" (*U* 18.1473), might well be separated, numbered, and scrutinized as *pensées* in the Wittgenstein manner.

9   Blanchot concludes "Song of the Sirens: Encountering the Imaginary," the essay of his from which I have been quoting, by contemplating the "presence of a song which

was still to be sung" (112). This song, the promise of the imaginary, is linked to both the *Ewigweibliche* of Goethe and "the ambiguity of time": "[a]lways still to come, always in the past already, always present" (1981: 113).

10 Molly's assertion "shes as much a nun as Im not" (*U* 18.22) may have as much to do with vows of silence as it does with vows of chastity.

11 I have discussed related problems of punctuation and pronunciation in Joyce in Conley (2014).

12 Joyce called his last chapter "the clou of the book" (*Letters I* 170), but he might just as well have called it "the clue of the book" since "the word *clue* derives from the Anglo-Saxon *cliwen*, originally meaning "ball of yarn." There are many stories in which a ball of yarn has been used to help one find one's way out of a forest or maze, thus any help given to solving riddles became known as "clues" (Kruger 2001: 30).

References

Bergren, A. (2008), *Weaving Truth: Essays on Language and the Female in Greek Thought*, Washington, DC: Center for Hellenic Studies.

Blanchot, M. (1981), "Song of the Sirens: Encountering the Imaginary," in *The Gaze of Orpheus, and Other Literary Essays*, trans. L. Davis, 105–13, New York: Barrytown/Station Hill Press.

Boyle, Fr. R. (1974), "Penelope," in C. Hart and D. Hayman (eds), *James Joyce's* Ulysses : *Critical Essays*, 407–33, Berkeley: University of California Press.

Butcher, S. H. and Lang, A. (trans.) (1906), *The Odyssey of Homer, Done into English Prose*, New York: Macmillan Company.

Conley, T. (2014), "'Tuck in your blank!': Antiaposiopetic Joyce," in E. M. Bonapfel and T. Conley (eds), *Doubtful Points: Joyce and Punctuation*, 193–210, Amsterdam: Rodopi.

Cunliffe, R. J. (1963), *A Lexicon of the Homeric Dialect*, Norman: University of Oklahoma Press.

Derrida, J. (2013), "Ulysses Gramophone: Hear Say Yes in Joyce," trans. F. Raffoul, in A. J. Mitchell and S. Slote (eds), *Derrida and Joyce: Texts and Contexts*, 41–86, Albany: State University of New York Press.

Fagles, R. (trans.) (1996), *The Odyssey*, New York: Penguin.

Fitzgerald, R. (trans.) (1990), *The Odyssey*, New York: Vintage.

Franko, G. F. (2005–6), "The Trojan Horse at the Close of the 'Iliad'," *Classical Journal*, 101, no. 2: 121–3.

Gogan, R. (ed.) (2012), *Ulysses* by James Joyce, Sraheens: Music Ireland Publications.

Kenner, H. (1955), *Dublin's Joyce*, London: Chatto and Windus.

Kruger, K. S. (2001), *Weaving the Word: The Metaphorics of Weaving and Female Textual Production*, Selinsgrove, PA: Susquehanna University Press.

Lattimore, R. (trans.) (1975), *The Odyssey of Homer*, New York: HarperCollins.

Rose, D. (ed.) (1997), *Ulysses: A Reader's Edition*, London: Picador.

Senn, F. (1984), *Joyce's Dislocutions: Essays on Reading as Translation*, ed. J. P. Riquleme, Baltimore, MD: Johns Hopkins University Press.

Skeat, W. W. (2005), *An Etymological Dictionary of the English Language*, Mineola, NY: Dover Publications.

Stein, C. (trans.) (2008), *The Odyssey*, Berkeley, CA: North Atlantic Books.

Stevens, B. E. (2013), *Silence in Catullus*, Madison: University of Wisconsin Press.

van Boheemen, C. (1999), "Molly's Heavenly Body and the Economy of the Sign: The Invention of Gender in 'Penelope,'" in K. J. Devlin and M. Reizbaum (eds), *Ulysses: En-Gendered Perspectives*, 267–81, Columbia: University of South Carolina Press.

Wawrzycka, J. (2014), "Memory and Marital Dynamics in *Ulysses*," in R. M. Bollettieri Bosinelli and I. Torresi (eds), *Joycean Memories II*, 1–20, *mediAzioni* 16, http://mediazioni.sitlec.unibo.it (accessed March 17, 2017).

Williams, K. (2010), "Odysseys of Sound and Image: 'Cinematicity' and the *Ulysses* Adaptations," in J. McCourt (ed.), *Roll Away the Reel World: James Joyce and Cinema*, 158–73, Cork: Cork University Press.

Part Four

Translating Silence

12

Silent Translation in Joyce

Serenella Zanotti

Joyce as a translator

Translation was, as suggested by Stephen Yao, "an integral part of the Modernist program of cultural renewal, a crucially important mode of writing distinct from, yet fundamentally interconnected with, the more traditionally esteemed modes of poetry and prose fiction" (2002: 6). Joyce did not practice translation as intensely as did other modernists. Nevertheless, as Maria Jolas aptly remarked, even though "Joyce did very few translations," the fact itself that he discovered an interest in translation at "an early age" and committed himself to translating Gerhardt Hauptmann's *Before Sunrise* and *Michael Kramer* does reveal "an interesting facet of his mind" (cited in Perkins 1978: 13). Equally interesting is the fact that, while in Pola, in 1904, Joyce set out to work on the translation of "Mildred Lawson," the first story in George Moore's *Celibates* (1895) (Zanotti 2013: 24–31).[1] As Wawrzycka (2009: 130) observes, these early attempts seem to indicate that "Joyce was already establishing a 'translation context' for his future works." A few years later, in 1909, he collaborated with Niccolò Vidacovich on the translation of Synge's *Riders to the Sea*, eventually published in 1929 in the Italian journal *Solaria* (see Bigazzi 1990 and Fitzgerald 1988), while in 1912 he sponsored and supervised Vidacovich's Italian translation of the first version of W. B. Yeats's *Countess Cathleen* (see Marengo Vaglio 1988). Eric Bulson has convincingly shown that Joyce used translations strategically as part of a well-orchestrated campaign of self-promotion (2001a). As his career progressed, translation occupied a more liminal position even though it continued to provide fertile ground for experimentation. In 1927 Joyce translated two lines from Ibsen's *Peer Gynt* and sent them to Harriet Weaver (*Letters I* 252), and in 1932 he translated a poem by James Stephen into five languages including Latin (*JJII* 655–6). More importantly, perhaps, he was involved—and in some cases also had an active role—in the translation of his works in different languages (see Risset 1979, Brown 1983, Bollettieri Bosinelli 1996 and 1998, Slote 2004). In all such cases, Joyce experimented with the creative potential of translation by elaborating "on what are possibilities only in the original" (Tysdahl 1967: 241).

The role translation plays in Joyce's writing was masterfully illustrated decades ago by Fritz Senn (1967, 1971, 1984) and Hugh Kenner (1971), but only recently has it started to attract significant scholarly attention (see among others Wawrzycka 2009, Baron 2010, and Conley, this volume). Focusing on the inherently translational nature of Joyce's radically intertextual writing method, as suggested by Scarlett Baron (2010 and 2012), this chapter aims to explore *silent translation*, a process that I define as an unacknowledged incorporation of textual material from other sources by means of translation into one's writing. Such process encapsulates operations carried out by authors who appropriate (more or less covertly) the words of others by means of translation. The specificity of "silent translation" lies in the fact that assimilation is obtained through a process of interlinguistic transfer which remains deliberately covert. Below I illustrate the extent to which such operations inform Joyce's writing.[2]

Deliberate deviations: Joyce's early critical writings

As is well known, Joyce wrote extensively in the Italian language both as a journalist for the Trieste paper *Il Piccolo della Sera* and as an invited lecturer at the Università Popolare. His critical production during the years he spent in the Austro-Hungarian city had an almost exclusive focus on Irish history and literature. According to Hans Gabler, Joyce's "main impulse" was "interpretative," as these texts were written "with a desire to bring things Irish—history and politics, myth and religion, culture and lore—to the knowledge and appreciation of his fellow Triestines" (2004). As Giorgio Melchiori (1995) has demonstrated, Joyce attempted to publish his articles in book form, and since the publisher eventually declined to go ahead, he made plans to publish the collection in English.[3] An aspect of Joyce's critical writing that has gone largely overlooked, however, is that it heavily relies on translation.

Since he was writing in another language, Joyce frequently resorted to instrumental translation to quote passages in English. For instance, in the text of his 1912 lecture on Daniel Defoe, he offered his own translation of a passage from *The Life and Adventures of Mrs. Christian Davies commonly Called Mother Ross* (1740). In his lecture on James Clarence Mangan (1907), he also translated two four-line stanzas from "O'Hussey's Ode to the Maguire." The manuscript bears second-thought signs of revision, which point to a nonlinear textual gestation (Bulson 2001b: 437–8). In the article *Oscar Wilde: il poeta di Salomè* (1909), Joyce offered his own translation of a passage from a letter by Oscar Wilde to Robert Sherard in which he allowed himself some creative deviations, as he did in the case of Mangan's *Ode*, aiming to emphasize the lyrical element of Wilde's prose:

> **I think of you often wandering** in violet valleys with your honey-coloured hair.
>
> Sherard 1908: 83

> **Amo vederti errare** per le vallate violacee, **fulgido** colla tua chioma color di miele.
>
> Joyce 2000: 551

> [I love to see you wandering through the purple valleys, with your shining honey-coloured hair.]
>
> JJA I, 671[4]

In a similar fashion, Joyce resorted to archaic diction (*talamo* for "bed") as he translated a line from Blake's *Book of Thel* ("Why **a little curtain of flesh** on the **bed of our desire?**") as "**La fragile tenda della carne** . . . che giace **sul talamo del nostro desiderio**" (Joyce 1992: 622) ["The fragile curtain of flesh that lies on the marriage bed of our desire" (Joyce 2000: 176)].

In his 1907 lecture on James Clarence Mangan, Joyce offered an expanded and revised version of his 1902 Mangan essay (see Bulson 2001b, MacCarthy 2001/2002, McCourt 2014). In translating his juvenile piece of criticism, he made a number of changes to the original English text which cannot be explained solely as an attempt to adapt it for a different target audience. An interesting case in point is the passage where he refers to the reception of Ibsen's work, clearly modelled on a similar passage in his 1900 piece *Ibsen's New Drama*, where he stated that

> [Ibsen] has been rigorously denounced as a meddlesome intruder, a defective artist, an incomprehensible mystic, and, **in the eloquent words of a certain English critic, "a muck-ferreting dog".**
>
> Joyce 2000: 30; my emphasis[5]

In the text of his Trieste lecture, Joyce expanded on the original passage and transmuted the original image of the "muck-ferreting dog" into that of "a dirty dog sticking his snout in the mire," thus further emphasizing the abusive label that had been used against the Norwegian playwright.

Per essempio chiunque abbia capito la tendenza distruggitrice e fieramente egoarca di tutta l'opera di Enrico Ibsen non si stupirà all'udire i più influenti critici di Londra alla dimane della prima serata ibseniana inveire contro il drammaturgo, chiamandolo (**cito le parole esatte del defunto** critico del *Daily Telegraph*) **un cane immondo che ficca il ceffo nel loto**.

Mangan 1907, in Joyce 1992: 596

[For instance, anyone who understands the destructive and proudly self-centred tendencies of all Henrik Ibsen's works will not be astonished to hear the most influential critics in London, the morning after an Ibsen first night, railing against the playwright, calling him (**I quote the precise words of the now deceased *Daily Telegraph* critic**) "a dirty dog sticking his snout in the mire".]

Joyce 2000: 131

The source from which the quote derives has been recognized as George Bernard Shaw's *The Quintessence of Ibsenism* (1891: 92), where press extracts containing descriptions of both Ibsen and his admirers were reported to illustrate the context of the reception of Ibsen's plays, "the temper" in which he worked. Joyce erroneously (or perhaps consciously) reported the words as being directed against Ibsen himself rather than against the playwright's supporters, who were described as "Educated and muck-ferreting dogs" in an article published anonymously in a journal called *Truth*.[6] In moving from English into Italian, the vague allusion to "a certain English critic" contained in the 1900 article was replaced by a more specific reference to a "now deceased *Daily Telegraph* critic," whose words Joyce claimed to quote verbatim. In rewording the passage into another language, Joyce thus used strategic alterations in the service of the intended rhetorical effect. It is through similar shifts in translation that Joyce imposed his stylistic and interpretative signature on the quoted material.[7]

Joyce relied extensively on silent translation as he was preparing his lectures. This procedure enabled him to silently incorporate whole passages from his sources, often leaving them unacknowledged thanks to the concealing effect of translation. As Theo Hermans posits, "all translation implies a degree of manipulation of the source text for a certain purpose" (1985: 11). In Joyce's case, textual manipulation realized through reformulations, additions, and all sorts of strategic alterations aim at creating epiphanic effects both in the narrative and in the overall linguistic texture, resulting in what we may label "authorial appropriation." A comparison between Joyce's portrait of James Clarence Mangan and the portrait sketched by John Mitchel in his famous introduction to Mangan's *Poems* immediately reveals the extent to which Joyce's "deliberate deviations" (Baron 2010: 525) result in an appropriation of the source text:

The first time the present biographer saw Clarence Mangan, it was in this wise: Being in the college library, and having occasion for a book in that gloomy apartment of the institution called the "Fagel Library," which is the innermost recess of the stately building, an acquaintance pointed out to me **a man perched on the top of a ladder**, with the whispered information that the figure was Clarence Mangan. **It was an unearthly and ghostly figure, in a brown garment**; the same garment (to all appearance) which lasted till the day of his death. The **blanched hair** was totally unkempt; **the corpse-like features still as marble; a large book was in his arms, and all his soul was in the book.**

Mitchel 1859: xxxiv–xxxv[8]

In line with the mode of "emblematic story-telling" (Gabler 2004) he experimented with in his journalistic writing, Joyce relied on Mitchel to construct an emblematic narrative of the poet's life but carefully removed the gothic elements that characterized Mitchel's portrayal of Mangan (e.g. "an unearthly and ghostly figure," "the corpse-like features still as marble"):

Fu ivi che il Mitchell, il suo biografo ed amico, lo vide per la prima volta e ci descrive nella prefazione alle opere del poeta, l'impressione che gli fece **un ometto mingherlino, dal volto cereo e dai cappelli pallidi, il quale seduto in cima ad una scaletta colle gambe incrociate era intento al decifrare nella luce crepuscolare un immenso volume polveroso.**

Joyce 1992: 593–4

[It was there that Mitchell [sic], Mangan's biographer and friend, first saw him. In his preface to the poet's works, he describes the impression made upon him by this skinny little man with a waxen face and colourless hair, sitting cross-legged on the top of a step-ladder intent on deciphering a huge dusty tome in the dusky light.]

Joyce 2000: 129

Quite similarly, Joyce isolated emblematic episodes from the life of William Blake in his 1912 lecture on the English poet, largely drawing on Edwin Ellis's *The Real Blake* (1907). As pointed out by Gleckner, "virtually the whole of the lecture is taken from Ellis' book, often verbatim" (1982: 140), as illustrated by passages such as the following, "an account to which Joyce adds little more than the epithet 'lower-class'" (Barry in Joyce 2000: 332, n. 55):

Such good interest was made for him in high places that he was even offered the post of drawing-master to the Royal Family. Had he accepted this he might have become permanently prosperous. But he refused, **for he feared that his art**

would languish in the Court atmosphere, and the offer almost ruined him, for in order not to seem insulting to the Sovereign **he gave up all his pupils at once**, a very serious sacrifice.

Ellis 1907: 184

Gli fu offerto nel '99 il posto di maestro di disegno per la famiglia reale: lo rifiuto, **temendo che nell'ambiente artificioso della corte la sua arte non avesse a perire d'inanizione**, ma in pari tempo, per non offendere il sovrano, **rinunziò a tutti gli altri allievi plebei** che formavano il suo maggiore cespite di rendita.

Joyce 1992: 621

[In 1799, he was offered a position as drawing master to the royal family. He refused it, **fearing that his art would die of inanition in the artificial environment of the court**, but, at the same time, so as not to offend the sovereign, **he gave up all his other lower-class students** who formed the greater part of his income.]

Joyce 2000: 176

Even though "Joyce's phrasing is clearly recognizable as having its origin in *The Real Blake*," as pointed out by Gleckner (1982: 140), the alterations of the source text that Joyce carried out to a greater or lesser extent clearly show that he did not limit himself to the silent incorporation of textual material from his primary source. In the passage below, the narrative of the death of Blake's younger brother, while still recognizably derived from Ellis, stands out as a partial rewriting performed "with a consummate mastery of register and style" (Gabler 2004):

He did not leave the nursing to his wife. He threw himself into the desperate struggle with death, as though he could force the enemy out by his own strength. During the last fortnight he **watched day and night by his brother's bed without sleeping**. He had his reward. He **saw the soul spring from the suddenly still, blind** body, and ascend upwards, clapping its hands for joy. Then **taking this sight with him** Blake went to bed and **slept continuously for three days and nights**.

Ellis 1907: 100

Vegliò al suo capezzale ininterrottamente per molti giorni prima della sua morte e, **al momento supremo, vide l'anima amata sprigionarsi dal corpo inerte** e salire verso cielo battendo le mani dalla gioja. Poi, **spossato e tranquillo**, si coricò e **dormì di un sonno letargico per settantadue ore consecutive**.

Joyce 1992: 622

[Blake took him in, maintained him, loved him, and looked after him during his long illness; he would speak to him of the eternal world and give him comfort. He stayed up constantly by his bedside for days on end before his death and, at the last moment, he saw the soul he loved free itself from the lifeless body and rise towards heaven clapping its hands in joy. Then, exhausted and at peace, he lay down in a deep sleep that lasted for seventy-two consecutive hours.]

Joyce 2000: 176

As Richard Ellmann remarks, Joyce's method of composition consisted of "the imaginative absorption of stray material. The method did not please Joyce very much because he considered it not imaginative enough, but it was the only way he could work" (*JJ* 250). The "imaginative absorption" of material from the most diverse sources is precisely the method that we see at work in his critical writings, a method that, I would like to suggest, relies entirely on silent translation. This type of covert assimilation is only made possible by the translation medium, in that the manipulation inherent in the translatorial act allows for the blurring of boundaries between quotation and original writing. Thanks to its concealing effect, translation has become quite a productive tool in the making of narratives in Joyce's critical writings, while at the same time allowing for an appropriative reframing of the original source. Joyce incorporated material from the most diverse sources and manipulated them to some extent so as to have them serve his own purposes. In the context of Joyce's critical writing, silent translation thus qualifies as both an appropriation of and a comment on the original.

"There was something in his mind": silent translation in *Ulysses*

As Fritz Senn points out in *Joyce's Dislocutions*, translation was for Joyce not so much a genre as an approach, a distinct feature of his writing method. In Senn's words, "Joyce's works consist of translation and glorify all cognate processes" (1984: 38). The radically translational approach that characterizes *Ulysses* becomes manifest, at the macro level, in the title itself—a hybrid Latin version of the name of a Greek hero, Odysseus, which "intimates that the work so named is also a transmutation of Homer's epic" (Senn 1984: 38). At the micro level, instances of what Senn terms "the transformative dynamisms of *Ulysses*" are found throughout the novel, for example in the discourse that takes shape in the silence of Stephen's mind as he investigates the ever-fluctuating nature of reality in "Proteus." Stephen tries out a series of synonymous verbs based on equivalents from various languages of the verb *trudge*: "She trudges, schlepps, trains, drags, trascines her load" (*U* 3.393–4). As suggested by Fritz Senn, this passage can be taken to represent, by synecdoche, Joyce's method in that translation functions here as a principle governing the mechanics of Stephen's mind and Joyce's writing more generally.

Quite remarkably, the interior monologue first makes its appearance in *Ulysses* by way of a translatorial act that silently disrupts the novel's narrative flow.

> —For this, O dearly beloved, is the genuine christine: body and soul and blood and ouns. Slow music, please. Shut your eyes, gents. One moment. A little trouble about those white corpuscles. **Silence, all**.
>
> He peered sideways up and gave a long slow whistle of call, then **paused awhile** in rapt attention, his even white **teeth** glistening here and there with **gold** points. **Chrysostomos**. Two strong shrill whistles answered through the calm.
>
> *U* 3.26

As Senn argues, the word "Chrysostomos" appears unitalicized and "in tacit juxtaposition" to the previous and the subsequent line, marking "the first metaphorical departure from the realist framework of the opening" (1984: 141). Senn points out that "both its foreignness and its syntax come as a surprise for the reader" (139). The word *chrysostomos* entails an act of translation since—as is well known—it is not only the name of both a Greek orator and a Father of the early Church, but, in this specific context, a verbal translation of a visual input: that is, how Mulligan appears to Stephen (see Gifford 1989: 14). In the context of this episode, the word *chrysostomos*, a Greek compound meaning 'golden-mouthed', clearly refers back to Mulligan's golden teeth. As readers, we wonder who does the translating. Joyce critics take the translator to be Stephen, who is describing Mulligan in Hellenic terms in the silence of his mind. Interestingly, as Fritz Senn remarks, "[t]he word fills a gap, the first acoustic pause" that occurs after Mulligan's imperative "Silence, all" (*U* 3.23), as he pretends to wait for the transubstantiation to take place.

> Paradoxically enough, at the moment when silence prevails, when words are neither spoken nor told, when the prominent mouth ceases to be phonetically active, a golden *mouth* and a renowned *orator* are invoked. Silence is proverbially golden; a new oratorical device is signaled, a different sort of rhetoric is introduced.
>
> Senn 1984: 140

The fact that Stephen's silent monologue begins in the very moment when, in Wakean terms, "silence speaks the scene" (*FW* 13.1–3) and stops the current of the narrative with an act of silent translation, seems particularly meaningful.

Mulligan's translatorial acts are the polar opposite of Stephen's, as is apparent in the passage from "Telemachus" where an oft-cited passage from Homer is mockingly translated:

> God! he said quietly. Isn't the sea what Algy calls it: a great sweet mother? **The snotgreen sea. The scrotumtightening sea.** *Epi oinopa ponton.* Ah, Dedalus, the Greeks! I must teach you. You must read them in the original. *Thalatta! Thalatta!* She is our great sweet mother. Come and look.
>
> U 4.78

Mulligan is quoting the formulaic Greek phrase ἐπὶ οἴνοπα πόντον, the meaning of which is "over/upon the wine-dark sea," *wine-dark* being a recurrent Homeric epithet in the *Odyssey*, most typically in the formulaic phrase *wine-dark sea* (Foley 2010: 179). Mulligan's rephrasing ("The snotgreen sea. The scrotumtightening sea") obviously casts a sarcastic light on the Homeric trope. It is no coincidence that Stephen recalls it in "Proteus," silently restoring its meaning (*"oinopa ponton*, a winedark sea"):

> Across the sands of all the world, followed by the sun's flaming sword, to the west, trekking to evening lands. She trudges, schlepps, trains, drags, trascines her load. A tide westering, moondrawn, in her wake. Tides, myriadislanded, within her, blood not mine, *oinopa ponton*, **a winedark sea.**
>
> U 3. 391–4

Stephen's English rendition seems to rely on Butcher and Lang's prose translation of Homer, which was published in 1879 and remained the standard English version up to the mid-twentieth century (Kenner 1985: 3): "And grey-eyed Athene sent them a favourable gale, a fresh West Wind, singing *over the wine-dark sea*" (Butcher and Lang 1879: 29; my emphasis).[9] The exact meaning of the Homeric compound οἴνοπα has been the subject of endless debate among scholars. As Kenner (1971: 217) recalls, Liddell and Scott's *Greek–English Lexicon* analysed the word as being composed from *oinos* meaning *wine* and *ops* for *eye* or *face*, hence the various English renditions of the trope as *wine-dark, wine-coloured, wine-faced,* and so on. For Kenner, a word "means what has been continuously understood by it" and it is tradition that "instructs us to understand that the sea, modified by this epithet, shall be understood to be 'wine-dark'" (1971: 218). Stephen's rendition is thus probably indebted to Butcher and Lang, and what matters here is not so much the accuracy of this translation as its functioning as a trope universally recognized as Homeric and, in broader sense, as Joyce's silent translation of that trope.

Silently translating Dante: translation, allusion, and quotation in *Ulysses*

The sense of a simultaneous order of past and present is the driving force of Joyce's *Ulysses* and one of the main reasons why Joyce uses "translation and quotation (and quotation in translation or translation as quotation)" (Baron 2010: 521). In what follows, I will look briefly into Joyce's translatorial approach to Dante in *Ulysses* to highlight an aspect of his understanding of translation in relation to intertextuality and tradition.

As Mary Reynolds (1981) has shown, echoes of Dante's *Divine Comedy* abound in the novel, particularly in connection with Stephen, who "laces both his thoughts and his conversation with snippets of Dante" (Weir 2015: 146), both in Italian and in translation. It is no coincidence that the first Dantean allusion occurs during one of Stephen's interior monologues in the first chapter, in the passage about the key to the tower, as pointed out by Reynolds (1981: 223):

> He walked on, waiting to be spoken to, trailing his ashplant by his side. Its ferrule followed lightly on the path, squealing at his heels. My familiar, after me, calling, Steeeeeeeeeeeeephen! A wavering line along the path. They will walk on it tonight, coming here in the dark. He wants that key. It is mine. I paid the rent. **Now I eat his salt bread**. Give him the key too. All. He will ask for it. That was in his eyes.
>
> U 1.627–32

Stephen's response to Mulligan's words ("It is mine. I paid the rent"), reported "between invisible quotation marks" according to Kenner (1987: 55), contains an obvious allusion to *Paradiso* xvii, 58–9. "Now I eat his salt bread" is in fact an echo of Cacciaguida's words predicting Dante's imminent exile ("Tu proverai sì come sa di sale lo pane altrui"; "You are to know the saltiness of others' bread"), a textual cue that unambiguously hints at Stephen's identification with Dante (Gifford 1989: 24).

Reynolds also observes (1981: 224) that "Joyce may construct his allusion either in the original Italian, or *in a freely adapted English equivalent*" (my emphasis). The place in the novel where Dantean echoes accumulate and intertwine is in the section RHYMES AND REASONS of the "Aeolus" chapter.

RHYMES AND REASONS

Mouth, south. Is the mouth south someway? Or the south a mouth? Must be some. South, pout, out, shout, drouth. Rhymes: **two men dressed the same, looking the same, two by two.**

...........................*la tua pace*

.....................*che parlar ti piace*

Mentre che il vento, come fa, si tace.

He saw them three by three, approaching girls, in green, in rose, **in russet, entwining,** *per l'aer perso,* in mauve, **in purple,** *quella pacifica oriafiamma,* gold of oriflamme, *di rimirar fè più ardenti.* But I **old men, penitent, leadenfooted,** underdarkneath the night: mouth south: tomb womb.

U 7.714-24

Stephen is trying out rhymes and he quotes fragments of three lines from Dante in Italian (*Inf.* v) to illustrate the perfection of *terza rima.* These fragments are preceded by an allusion to *Purg.* xxix, 134–5, where Dante sees "two old men, unlike in dress but alike in bearing, venerable and grave" ("vidi due vecchi in abito dispari, / ma pari in atto ed onesto e sodo"),[10] which is turned by Joyce into "two men dressed the same, looking the same, two by two." The translation of Dante's lines continues in the following paragraph: "He saw them three by three, approaching girls, in green, in rose, in russet, entwining." The girls that Stephen sees approaching, "three by three," are an anthropomorphic representation of Dante's *terza rima*: Dante's lines rhyme three by three and each group of rhymes is composed of three lines that are arranged and entwine in a continuous sequence, like rings in a chain—which is the reason why Dante's *terza rima* is also called *rima incatenata* (enchained rhyme).

The interest of this passage lies in the complex intertextual web that Joyce creates, as the translated echoes from *Purgatorio* xxix connect this passage to the lyrical variation that Stephen constructs in "Telemachus," in the passage where he broods on "the twining stresses, two by two" of Yeats's song "Who Goes With Fergus?":

His head vanished but the drone of his descending voice boomed out of the stairhead:

—And no more turn aside and brood
Upon love's bitter mystery
For Fergus rules the brazen cars.

> **Woodshadows** floated silently by through the morning peace from the stairhead seaward where he gazed. Inshore and farther out the mirror of water whitened, spurned by lightshod hurrying feet. **White breast** of the **dim sea**. The **twining** stresses, **two by two**. A hand plucking the harpstrings, merging **their twining chords**. Wavewhite wedded words shimmering on **the dim** tide.
>
> U 1.237–47

The word *twining*, which is repeated twice in the "Telemachus" passage, is echoed by the word "entwining" in the "Aeolus" passage. Furthermore, the word "russet" in the "RHYMES AND REASONS" section in "Aeolus" silently links it back to Yeats's poem (the connection remains implicit as Yeats's song is quoted only in part and the line containing the word "russet" is never mentioned directly in *Ulysses*):

> Who Goes With Fergus?
> Who will go drive with Fergus now,
> And pierce the deep **wood's woven shade**,
> And **dance** upon the level shore?
> Young man, lift up your **russet** brow,
> And lift your tender eyelids, maid,
> And brood on hopes and fear no more.
>
> And no more turn aside and brood
> Upon love's bitter mystery;
> For Fergus rules the brazen cars,
> And rules **the shadows of the wood**,
> And **the white breast of the dim sea**
> And all dishevelled wandering stars.
>
> Yeats 1956: 43

The "woodshadows" that Stephen sees floating silently by as he gazes the horizon from the Martello tower are thus a verbal link to Yeats's song ("Fergus ... rules the shadows of the wood" mingled with "the deep wood's wooden shade").

Towards the end of the "Circe" episode we see Bloom standing over Stephen, who lies still unconscious, while he murmurs the words from Yeats's song that have been in his mind all day.

BLOOM

(communes with the night) Face reminds me of his poor mother. **In the shady wood**. The deep white breast. Ferguson, I think I caught. A girl. Some girl. Best thing could happen him.

U 15.4949–51

Bloom evidently misunderstands Stephen's words and it is extremely revealing to note that, in his attempt to decode Stephen's murmur, Bloom drops in an unmistakable Dantean allusion: "In the shady wood." The connection between Dante and Yeats already established by Stephen in the previous episodes is reinforced here, although Bloom's translation of Stephen's murmuring sounds—a close rendition of Dante's well-known passage "per una selva oscura" ("in a dark wood") (see Reynolds 1981: 189)—verges on the comic as Bloom's deciphering continues ("The deep white breast. Ferguson, I think I caught. A girl. Some girl").

That "Circe" was to be read as Joyce's recreation of Dante's Descent into Hell is an aspect that was immediately apparent to readers such as Ezra Pound and T. S. Eliot (see Rainey 2007: 19), who both had access to the manuscript before it went into print. As Joyce scholars have noticed (Gozzi 1972, Reynolds 1981, Weir 2015: 146), the connection with Dante's first *cantica* is evidenced by numerous textual hints. From the translation angle, there is one passage that is particularly revealing of Joyce's intertextual strategies and of his use of translation:

BLOOM

Keep to the right, right, right. If there is a signpost planted by the Touring Club at Stepaside who procured that public boon? **I who lost my way** and contributed to the columns of the Irish Cyclist the letter headed **In darkest Stepaside. Keep, keep, keep to the right**. Rags and bones at midnight. A fence more likely. First place murderer makes for. **Wash off his sins of the world.**

U 15.231–6

Bloom is walking through Nighttown in search of Stephen. Like the protagonist of Dante's poem, Bloom has "lost" his "way" "in darkest Stepaside" ("for the straight way was lost" = "ché la diritta via era smarrita," *Inf.* I, 3) and, again drawn to the left, admonishes himself to "keep to the right" (see Gozzi 1972: 217–18). A cursory glance at the translations available at the time when *Ulysses* was written reveals that Joyce's rendition of Dante's lines cannot be identified with any of them, as lexical deviations can be spotted easily.

In the midway of this our mortal life,
I found me **in a gloomy wood**, astray,
Gone **from the path direct** . . .

Cary 1871: 1

In the middle of the journey of our life, I found myself **in a dark wood**; for **the straight way** was **lost**.

Carlyle 1849: 14

Midway upon the journey of our life
I found myself within **a forest dark,**
For **the straightforward pathway** had been **lost.**

Longfellow 1867: 25

Midway upon the road of our life I found myself within **a dark wood,** for **the right way** had been **missed.**

Norton 1892: 1

Evidence that Joyce "read Dante seriously" (*SH* 169) in the original, as did Stephen, can be found in a manuscript located among the papers acquired by the National Library of Ireland in 2002, which contains notes on Dante in Joyce's handwriting (see van Hulle 2004, Zanotti 2013: 18–24). It is therefore not unlikely that the allusions that Joyce incorporated in the text of *Ulysses* were not drawn from any particular translation, but came directly from Joyce's pen. As Weir argues, Joyce "worked in certain phrases in English that are easy to interpret as references to Dante" (2015: 146). What becomes apparent in comparing Joyce's versions with those of his predecessors is that, in transposing some of the most recited lines in Western literature into his text, Joyce was "appropriating (thieving) and transforming (metamorphosing) them for his own purposes" (Boldrini 2001: 2). In weaving allusions to Dante's *Commedia* into his writing, Joyce strategically opted for translatorial solutions that allowed him to further entwine an already complex web of intertextual relations, always converting them to his own purposes.

"sonorous silence"

Previous studies have shown that not only was Joyce "intensely concerned with translation" (Wawrzycka 2009: 134), but translation as both a principle and a method represented a core aspect of his writing. And while Fritz Senn's groundbreaking work, starting in the 1960s, paved the way for conceptualizing translation as an approach to reading Joyce's *oeuvre*, as Wawrzycka observes, "Joyce's brand of translational writing" (2009: 131) is still to be fully understood in detail, "and we have yet adequately to situate *Finnegans Wake* in the context of translation" (134).

The above discussion has aimed at illustrating the ways in which Joyce explored the potential of translation in relation to intertextuality, "which is concerned with the ways in which authors translate, transpose, and adapt the words and structures of other works into their own creations" (Baron 2010: 527).

Silent translation, a process entailing textual operations such as transfer, absorption, and appropriation, stands out as a prominent feature of *Ulysses* and of Joyce's working method more generally.

As shown by Scarlett Baron (2010), Stephen's silent translation of Flaubert's letter to Mlle Leroyer de Chantepie in *A Portrait of the Artist as a Young Man*, in the passages in which he spells out his theory of impersonality, reveals a fundamental aspect of both the character and the novel, for "Joyce's elected mode of writing in these passages—translation—enhances the texts' ironic significance" (Baron 2010: 532). Stephen, as Baron suggests, is deliberately concealing his source, and yet traces of the source text impinge on the surface of his speech, most prominently when he coins the unusual reflexive verb "impersonalises itself" (*P* 215), which "makes for a noticeably awkward, conspicuously French-sounding phrase" (Baron 2010: 526) that denounces itself as a translation.

According to Jacques Derrida (1979: 118), all translation "leaves something out, an untranslated remnant." As Lori Chamberlain (2004: 325) observes, the point of Derrida's argument is that "there is ... always something left over which blurs the distinctions between original and translation. *There is no 'silent' translation*" (my emphasis), which is due to the inherent resistance to translation that resides within all literary writing. This has important implications for the arguments offered in this chapter, in that Joyce's use of silent translation in his writings does in fact expose the translatorial act, although in various manners and for different purposes. While epitomizing the impossibility of "the dream of translation without remnants" put forward by Derrida (1979: 119), Stephen's silent translation of Flaubert in *A Portrait* is an act of appropriation which Joyce seems to expose. As Baron (2010: 532) suggests, he "uses a moment of translation—that most intrinsically intertextual of processes—to undercut Stephen's aspirations to originality."

In *Ulysses*, silent translation serves a multiplicity of functions. Typically associated with mental processes, it plays a crucial role in Joyce's attempt "to transpose the myth *sub specie temporis nostri*" (*Letters I* 146), which is enacted textually through an intricate web of intertextual allusions. An instance of Joyce's extreme intertextuality—perhaps the most striking example of silent translation in *Ulysses*—can be found at the very end of the novel. Molly's last words compose, as Hugh Kenner has masterfully argued, a Homeric hexameter with one more stressed syllable appended—the final "Yes" (1980: 147):

Yés ănd hĭs | heárt wás | góĭng lĭke | mád ánd || yés Ĭ săid | yés Ĭ wĭll || Yés

Here Joyce's use of silent translation comes to perfection, since the intertextual relation is established by means of rhythmic patterning, silently absorbing and appropriating the Homeric rhythm into his prose. This is silent translation brought to perfection, a beautiful instance of Joyce's "sonorous silence."

Notes

1   On December 15, 1904, Joyce informed Stanislaus that he was "setting about (with the aid of the Director, Francini) the translation into Italian of 'Celibates' for a big publisher in Florence" (*Letters II* 74). The manuscript, now at Cornell, is reproduced in *JJA* I, 534–90.

2   While my understanding of "silent translation" emphasizes interlinguistc appropriations of what Joyce translated and what he read in other languages, in discussing the presence of Yeatsian elements in Joyce's *Chamber Music*, Wawrzycka (2015: 105) has since proposed the notion of "silent translexion" that stresses "deliberate but covert intralingual assimilation of lexis and imagery" from another author.

3   The typescripts of these translations are reproduced in *JJA* I, 653–703.

4   This is how Wilde's line was rendered in the unpublished English translation of this article available in transcript in the *James Joyce Archive*.

5   Henceforth, unless otherwise stated, bold print is my emphasis.

6   See Kevin Barry's annotations in Joyce 2000: 294, n. 1.

7   It must be noted, however, that at least in the case of the two Mangan essays, "Joyce was working from memory and did not have the texts open before him when composing the essays" (MacCarthy 2001/2002: 7).

8   According to McCarthy (2001/2002: 8), "Joyce had read Meehan's The Poets and Poetry of Munster before writing the 1902 and the 1907 essays and had definitely been familiar with Mitchel's introduction to his Poems by James Clarence Mangan for his 1907 treatise on the earlier writer."

9   See Ames (2005) for a discussion of the Homeric translations that Joyce might have read.

10 Unless otherwise stated, all translations from Dante's *Comedy* follow Charles Singleton's prose translation, while references to Dante's Italian text follow the Petrocchi edition.

References

Alighieri, D. (1966), *La Commedia secondo l'antica vulgata*, ed. G. Petrocchi, Milan: Mondadori.

Alighieri, D. (1989), *The Divine Comedy*, trans. C. S. Singleton, Princeton, NJ: Princeton University Press.

Ames, Keri Elizabeth (2005), "Joyce's Aesthetic of the Double Negative and His Encounters with Homer's *Odyssey*," in C. Jaurretche (ed.), *European Joyce Studies 16: Beckett, Joyce and the Art of the Negative*, 15–48, New York: Rodopi.

Baron, S. (2010), "'Will you be as gods?' (U 3.38): Joyce Translating Flaubert," *James Joyce Quarterly* 47, no. 4: 521–35.

Baron, S. (2012), *"Strandentwining Cable": Joyce, Flaubert, and Intertextuality*, Oxford: Oxford University Press.

Bigazzi, C. (1990), "*Riders to the Sea*: problemi di traduzione," in *Joyce. I luoghi, i momenti*, 6–20, Rome: Astrea.

Boldrini, L. (2001), *Joyce, Dante, and the Poetics of Literary Relations: Language and Meaning in* Finnegans Wake, Cambridge: Cambridge University Press.

Bollettieri Bosinelli, R. M. (1996), "A proposito di *Anna Livia Plurabelle*," in J. Joyce, *Anna Livia Plurabelle*, 33–86, Turin: Einaudi.

Bollettieri Bosinelli, R. M. (1998), "Anna Livia's Italian Sister," in K. Lawrence (ed.), *Transcultural Joyce*, 193–8, Cambridge: Cambridge University Press.

Brown, J. (1983), "*Ulysses* into French," in D. Oliphant and T. Zigal (eds), *Joyce at Texas: Essays on the James Joyce Materials at the Humanities Research Center*, 29–60, Austin: Humanities Research Center, University of Texas at Austin.

Bulson, E. (2001a), "Getting Noticed: James Joyce's Italian Translations," *Joyce Studies Annual* I: 10–37.

Bulson, E. (2001b), "On Joyce's Figura," *James Joyce Quarterly* 38, no. 3–4: 431–52.

Butcher, S. H. and Lang, A. (trans.) (1879), *The Odyssey of Homer Done into Prose*, London: MacMillan.

Carlyle, J. (trans.) (1849), *Dante's Divine Comedy: The Inferno: A Literal Prose Translation*, London: Chapman and Hill.

Cary, H. F. (trans.) (1871), *The Vision; or, Hell, Purgatory, and Paradise of Dante Alighieri*, London: F. Warne & Co.

Chamberlain, L. (2004), "Gender and the Metaphorics of Translation," in L. Venuti (ed.), *The Translation Studies Reader*, 306–21, London and New York: Routledge.

Derrida, J. (1979), "Living On: Border Lines," trans. J. Hulbert, in H. Bloom et al., *Deconstruction and Criticism*, 75–176, London: Routledge and Kegan Paul.

Ellis, E. (1907), *The Real Blake: A Portrait Biography*, London: Chatto & Windus.

Fitzgerald, J. (1998), "James Joyce's Translation of *Riders to the Sea*," *Joyce Studies in Italy* 2: 149–60.

Foley, J. M. (2010), *Homer's Traditional Art*, University Park: Pennsylvania State University Press.

Gabler, H. W. (2004), "James Joyce *Interpreneur*," *Genetic Joyce Studies* 4, http://www.geneticjoycestudies.org/articles/GJS4/GJS4_Gabler (accessed August 28, 2017).

Gifford, D. (1989), *Ulysses Annotated: Notes for James Joyce's Ulysses*, rev. and expand. edn, Berkeley, Los Angeles, and London: University of California Press.

Gleckner, R. (1982), "Joyce's Blake: Paths of Influence," in R. Bertholf and A. Levitt (eds), *William Blake and the Moderns*, 135–63, Albany: State University of New York Press.

Gozzi, F. (1972), "Dante nell'Inferno di Joyce," *English Miscellany* 23: 195–229.

Hermans, T. (1985), "Introduction. Translation Studies and a New Paradigm," in T. Hermans (ed.), *The Manipulation of Literature: Studies in Literary Translation*, 7–15, London and Sydney: Croom Helm.

Joyce, J. (1992), *Poesie e Prose*, ed. F. Ruggieri, Milan: Mondadori.

Joyce, J. (2000), *Occasional, Critical, and Political Writings*, ed. Kevin Barry, Oxford: Oxford University Press.

Kenner, H. (1971), *The Pound Era*, Berkeley and Los Angeles: University of California Press.

Kenner, H. (1980), *Ulysses*, Baltimore, MD, and London: Johns Hopkins University Press.

Kenner, H. (1985), "Pound and Homer," in G. Bornstein (ed.), *Ezra Pound Among the Poets*, 1–12, Chicago: University of Chicago Press.

Longfellow, H. W. (trans.) (1867), *The Divine Comedy of Dante Alighieri*, Vol. I, *Inferno*, Boston and New York: Houghton Mifflin.

MacCarthy, A. (2001–2), "A Study of the Sources for James Joyce's Essays on James Clarence Mangan," *Papers on Joyce* 7/8: 1–12.

Marengo, C. (1988), "Yeats' *The Countess Cathleen* in Vidacovich and Joyce's Translation," *Joyce Studies in Italy* 2: 197–211.

McCourt, J. (2000), *The Years of Bloom: James Joyce in Trieste 1904–1920*, Dublin: Lilliput Press.

McCourt, J. (2014), "'The Last of The Bardic Poets': Joyce's Multiple Mangans," in S. Sturgeon (ed.), *Essays on James Clarence Mangan: The Man in the Cloak*, 124–39, Basingstoke: Palgrave Macmillan.

Melchiori, G. (1995), "Joyce and Formiggini," in F. Ruggieri (ed.), *Joyce's Feast of Languages: Seven Essays and Ten Notes, Joyce Studies in Italy* 4: 117–21.

Mitchel, J. (1859), "Biographical Introduction," in J. Clarence Mangan, *Poems*, 7–31, New York: P.M. Haverty.

Norton, C. E. (trans.) (1892), *The Divine Comedy of Dante Alighieri*, Vol. I, *Hell*, Boston and New York: Houghton, Mifflin and Company.

Perkins, J. (1978), *Joyce and Hauptmann*, San Marino, CA: Huntington Library.

Rainey, L. (2007), *Revisiting "The Waste Land,"* New Haven, CT: Yale University Press.

Reynolds, M. (1981), *Joyce and Dante: The Shaping Imagination*, Princeton, NJ: Princeton University Press.

Risset, J. (1979), "Joyce traduce Joyce," in James Joyce, *Scritti italiani*, 197–214, Milan: Mondadori.

Senn, F. (1967), "The Issue is Translation," *James Joyce Quarterly* 4, no. 3: 163–4.

Senn, F. (1971), "Joycean Translatitudes: Aspects of Translation," in R. Bates and H. Pollock (eds), *Litters from Aloft: Papers. Delivered at the Second Canadian James Joyce Seminar*, 26–49, Tulsa, OK: University of Tulsa.

Senn, F. (1984), *Joyce's Dislocutions: Essays on Reading as Translation*, ed. P. Riquelme, Baltimore, MD, and London: Johns Hopkins University Press.

Shaw, G. B. (1891), *The Quintessence of Ibsenism*, London: Walter Scott.

Sherard, R. (1908), *Oscar Wilde, the Story of an Unhappy Friendship: With Portraits and Facsimile Letters*, n.p.: Hermes Press.

Slote, S. (2004), "'Apres mot, le deluge': Critical Response to Joyce in France," in G. Lernout and W. van Mierlo (eds), *The Reception of James Joyce in Europe*, 382–410, London: Continuum.

Tysdahl, B. J. (1967), "Two Translations by Joyce," *James Joyce Quarterly* 4, no. 3: 240–1.

Van Hulle, D. (2004), "Joyce and Beckett Discovering Dante," *Joyce Studies* 7, ed. Luca Crispi and Catherine Fahy, Dublin: National Library of Ireland.

Wawrzycka, J. (2009), "Translation," in J. McCourt (ed.), *James Joyce in Context*, 125–36, Cambridge: Cambridge University Press.

Wawrzycka, J. (2015), "'Ghosting Hour': Young Joyce Channeling Early Yeats," in J. McCourt (ed.), *Joyce, Yeats and the Revival*, 103–18, *Joyce Studies in Italy* 4 (New Series), Rome: Edizioni Q.

Weir, D. (2015), *Ulysses Explained: How Homer, Dante, and Shakespeare Inform Joyce's Modernist Vision*, New York: Palgrave Macmillan.

Yao, S. (2002), *Translation and the Languages of Modernism*, Basingstoke: Palgrave.

Yeats, W. B. (1956), *The Collected Poems*, London: Macmillan.

Zanotti, S. (2013), *Italian Joyce: A Journey through Language and Translation*, Bologna: Bononia University Press.

13

"Mute chime and mute peal": Notes on Translating Silences in *Chamber Music*

Jolanta Wawrzycka

. . . the joint of Finnegans Wake, *"A way a lone a last a loved **a long the** . . . **riverrun**", echoes the first line of the second stanza in* Chamber Music *I: ". . . music along the river". Closing a circle.*

Fritz Senn[1]

In one of the telling passages of *Stephen Hero*, we observe Stephen walking "through the ways of the city" from Amiens Street station to College Green, "ever prompt to receive impressions" of sounds and sights, as he collects "words for his treasure-house": he finds them "in the shops, on advertisements, [and] in the mouths of the plodding public" (*SH* 30). He also finds them in Skeat's *Etymological Dictionary* that he reads "by the hour" with great "sense of wonder," and in William Morris's prose from which he makes "a garner of words," reading it "as one would read a thesaurus" (26). Easily "hypnotised by the most commonplace conversation" and equally easily dismayed at the "ignobility" of language and people's ignorance "of the value of words," Stephen resolves to uphold higher standards of "the ancient terms" (26). He is "hammering noisily" as he constructs his "house of silence" (30), a complex and evocative metaphor that conjures up a "house of silence" built of the "silent" pages of words that result from Stephen's leafing "noisily" through Skeat and Morris (and many other writers mentioned in the passage), and from the overheard conversations he recorded. As scholars, we know the former as Joyce's notebooks, and the latter as his epiphanies. We also recognize that Stephen's habit of repeating the words to himself, "till they lost all instantaneous *meaning* for him and became wonderful *vocables*" (30; my emphasis), is an early indication of Joyce's expanding sense of language whose mere semantic utility and "market-place—a debased value" (*SH* 27) Joyce will soon transcend.[2] Thus, Stephen of *Ulysses* will listen to "a fourworded wavespeech:

seesoo, hrss, rsseeiss, ooos" of the sea (*U* 3. 546–7) and engage in a moment of creation: "His lips lipped and mouthed fleshless lip of air: mouth to her moomb. Oomb, allwombing tomb. His mouth moulded issuing breadth, unspeeched: ooeeehah ... wayawayawayawayaway" (*U* 3.401). In *Finnegans Wake*, full of "changeably meaning vocable scriptsigns" (*FW* 118.27) and "alphybettyformed verbage" (*FW* 183.13), Joyce will bring language to the near limit of "imeffible tries at speech unasyllabled" (*FW* 183. 15). But already in *Stephen Hero*, Joyce has Stephen exalt sounds of words over their meaning in a contrarian attitude that is paralleled by his trading of one kind of silence for another: once "'chary of speech' in obedience to a commandment of silence" of Jesuit doctrine, Stephen begins instead to "[school] himself to silence" on his own terms, "lest words should return him his discourtesy" (30). We are presented with an image of a budding poet (Stephen, but also Joyce) devoted, in self-imposed silence, to "piecing together meaningless words and phrases with *deliberate, unflagging seriousness*" (31; my emphasis).

I'm tempted to read these words as first glimpses of what Kenner (1963) calls "ironic distance" that enabled Joyce very early on to cast a cold eye on his poetic output, produced contemporaneously with the epiphanies that generated some of the poems in *Chamber Music* (S. Joyce 1962: 28, 62–3). Recent rereadings of the poems (essays in Conner 2012: Garnier, Campbell; Wawrzycka 2015), recontextualize *Chamber Music* through the lens of, for instance, Joyce's modernism and Irish and continental influences.[3] My interest here is to consider the poems in terms of "silence" that Joyce problematizes in *Stephen Hero*, though less in terms of the "scornful silence" of a young artist who forges ahead alone,[4] and more in terms of *language effects* that invoke silence. The insights presented below come from my translatorial focus on Joyce's "wonderful vocables."

It may appear that probing *Chamber Music* for silence is counterproductive, given that the poems resonate with titular music (playing of strings, harp, and piano), with sounds of nature, or with the clatter of the army of charioteers.[5] However, the process of translating the poems into Polish revealed that many poems also convey measured silences of stylized pauses and near-stillness amidst the imagery of feebly stirring breezes, subdued muffled sighs, faint, sometimes distant music, and the air of quietude and repose. In his presentation of the Lover's musings and utterances, Joyce's poetic language frequently conjures up the Lover's *aporia* that matches the reader's. The language does so through syntactic and rhetorical strategies that produce consternation and whose cumulative effect creates what I would call "the poetics of the ineffable." We see these strategies embedded in a number of rhetorical questions[6] that express the Lover's trepidation articulated though *erotema*, a type of rhetorical question that confirms its own point.[7] The result of such circuitousness is discursive silence. It is pervasive in, for instance, poem XXIX, where the answer to the poem's opening question, "Dear heart, why will you use me so?," cannot be forthcoming; the poem's last line repeats the question in a chiasmic (non-)closure that renders the very asking somewhat bathetic. This dynamic is reinforced by the silence of what is withheld and only signaled tacitly by "dear eyes that" "upbraid" the Lover. Like silences generated through elisions or through semantic constructs, the Lover's aporetic moments add to the poems' tenuousness; they are akin to the silences and ellipses in the soon-to-be composed *Dubliners* (analysed elsewhere in this volume by, among others, Laura Pelaschiar). Lexically, the poems suggest "silence" through such markers as the ambiguous "still" ("And still she's combing her long hair," XXIV; and "Still are you beautiful," XXIX); through the promissory and equally ambiguous end-of-the-poem's "rest" ("Shall have rest," XVIII); or through adverbial presentation of (non-)action ("Silently," XXIV; "secretly," XV). A trace of silence/quietude is antonymously denoted by a Yeatsian "unquiet heart" (XXXIV)—Yeatsian, because Joyce would have encountered the word "unquiet" in Yeats's early poems.[8]

My reading of silence in *Chamber Music* considers silences in terms of poetic concretizations embedded in the phonemic layer of words, "where the *soft long vowels* hurtl[e] *noiselessly* . . . in *mute* chime and *mute* peal and *soft low swooning cry*," that in *A Portrait* summon in Stephen a sensation of "soft liquid joy" (*P* 226; emphasis added). It is that mute flow of long vowels that interests me here, because, in my reading, the *phonemic* stratum of *Chamber Music* is the predominant carrier of repose, a mood generated and sustained through reduplications and diphthongal permutations of vowels' sound-sense.[9] Similarly, many of the subtly rustling sibilants, while not exactly "silent," gesture towards the hushed and the muted. In the process of translating *Chamber Music* into Polish, I treated these phonemic repetitions as clusters of alerting devices,[10] and labored to chisel out similar effects in Polish. My goal was to recreate the effects of Joyce's lexical and prosodic formations, particularly those that signal or connote—but shy away from naming and denoting—silences. I was also hyper-attentive to the poems' remarkable lexical economy and I tended to both the number and the length of words in order to preserve Joyce's visual layer. Furthermore, I strove to retain what Matthew Campbell calls Joyce's "metrical delicacy" (2012: 60) and to recreate Joyce's metrical and rhyme scheme without compromising the poems' semantic layer (to the extent that that layer is clear, which it frequently is *not*). Below are some of the solutions to my efforts at relanguaging Joyce's poems and refostering his poetic apparatus; they are set against the Polish translations by Maciej Słomczyński. Additional context is provided by Marina Capodilista's and Alfredo Giuliani's Italian translations[11] reproduced in the Addendum.

I start with poem XX as one of the poems where stillness and silence is a predominant ambiance and where the presumed hum of nature suggested by the pine forest (not made inaudible in the poem) is stirred only by lovers' kisses. The poem's tranquility is embedded in a series of signifiers whose diphthongs and reduplicative vowels ("oo" in "wood," "cool," "noon"; "ee" in "deep," "sweet") sustain the implied lull of the forest. Sibilants in "shadow," "forest," "sweet," and "descending" join sibilants in "kiss" and "soft" tumult of falling hair, to disturb the poem's silence, but only on the phonetic level. My translatorial challenge here was to tend to all these elements while also minding Joyce's iambs and dactyls. Thus, where Joyce's first stanza resonates with elongated vowels in "-wood," "would," "we," "deep," "cool," and "noon" and diphthongs in "lay," "shadow," and "day," my translation reproduces these sounds through elongation, diphthongs, and triphthongs:[12]

XX	XX
In the dark pinewood	Wśród ciemnych sosen [ó pron. as oo]
I would we lay,	Położyć się, [oło pron. as owo]
In deep cool shadow	W głębi chłodnej cienia
At noon of day.	W południe.

To Joyce's one sibilant in this stanza, "shadow," Polish has five and they do play into the mollifying ambiance carried by the stanza's phonemic stratum.

The second stanza evens out the ratio of sibilants: to Joyce's "sweet," "sweet to kiss," "pineforest," and "is," Polish has "słodko," "całować się," "sosnowy," and "jest":

How sweet to lie there,	Słodko tam leżeć,
Sweet to kiss,	Całować się,
Where the great pineforest.	Gdzie bór sosnowy
Enaisled is!	Unawiony jest!

If there are six sibilants in Polish to Joyce's five, a case could be made for the sixth visual sibilant buried in Joyce's "enisled," all underscoring onomatopoeically the lovers' intimate preoccupations. To recreate the neologism, "enisled," one of Joyce's nonce words, I resorted to a calque formation, "unawiony," a neologism whose peculiarity in Polish matches that of Joyce's word in English and yet is readily understood by readers in both languages.[13] In my intent to make the second stanza's vowels in Joyce correspond to those in Polish, I relied on the lucky coincidence of "-**ow** in "**how**" mirrored by "-**ło-**" [wo] in "**sł**odko" (sweet) which is, in turn, echoed in "-**ało-**" [awo] in "c**ało**wać" (to kiss), with the added bonus of the semantic and phonetic closeness of the initial sounds in "**sł**odko" [swo-] and "**sweet.**"

Another lucky coincidence played into preserving Joyce's lexes sound-sense in stanza three, thanks to the phonetic similarity in line one of "**thy**" and "t**wój**" [-**ooy**] also echoed in –**ału** [–**awoo**] (and where Joyce's sibilants "-**ss**" and "**sc-**" in "ki**ss**" and "de**sc**ending" are approximated in **c-** and -**ć s-** in "**c**ałowa**ć s**ię"). Vowels and liquids in "**Swee-**" and "**were**" in the second line of stanza three appear as "**sło-** [swo-] and "-**ył-**" [-**iw-**] while they also preserve the sibilant **s**. I rendered Joyce's somewhat paradoxical "soft tumult" of hair as "soft cascades" of hair and, whereas I managed to keep the rustling effect of the phonetic resonance between "**with** a **soft**" and "**wśród**" ("among"), my "kaskad" (plural genitive) is phonetically a bit noisier that Joyce's "tumult." Rhetorically, however, courtesy of the subjunctive, *irrealis* mood, the actual sound of the "tumult," or cascading, is absent from the poem: no other sound accompanies the "noise"—suggested by the sibilants—of kissing.[14]

The vowel pattern in stanza four is in near-chiasmic relation to that in stanza one. Once again, to approximate in Polish the sounds of Joyce's quasi-homonyms and vowel-driven words in "**O,**"[15] "**unto**," "**wood**," "**noon**," "**come**," "**with**," "**me**," "**now**," "**sweet**," "**love**," "**away**," I used elongated vowels, diphthongs, and triphthongs.[16] Joyce's "**me now**" is echoed in "**mną**" and his visual repetition of a's in the final "**away**" is recreated in the closing "-**ana ma.**"[17] Setting those lines side by side shows the degree to which Joyce's sound layer is approximated in this translation (note that the Polish **ch** is pronounced as **h** in "hear"):

vowels, diphthongs	vowels, diphthongs	sibilants	sibilants
Thy kiss descending	Twój pocałunek	Thy kiss descending	Twój pocałunek
Sweeter were	Słodszy byłby	Sweeter were	Słodszy byłby
With a soft	Wśród miękkich	With a soft	Wśród miękkich
tumult	kaskad	tumult	kaskad
Of thy hair.	Włosów twych.	Of thy hair.	Włosów twych.
O, unto the pinewood	O, w bór sosnowy	O, unto the pinewood	O, w bór **sosnowy**
At noon of day	W południe dnia	At noon of day	W południe dnia
Come with me now,	Pójdź ze mną teraz,	Come with me now,	Pój**dź*** ze mną teraz,*
Sweet love, away.	Kochana ma.	Sweet love, away.	Kochana ma.

*-**dź** and **z** are voiced in Polish, but their final position devoices them; they become, respectively, a -**tch** sound (technically, a voiceless palato-alveolar affricate) and a sibilant **s**.

Like the rhyme scheme in stanza four, rhymes in the whole poem in translation stay close to Joyce's scheme, thanks to the fact that, in each quatrain, only the second and fourth lines rhyme. In the first stanza, "**lay/day**" is recreated as a quasi-half rhyme ("**się/-nie**"), a strategy repeated in stanza two to render the rhyme of "**kiss/is**" ("**się/jest**").

This rather pedantic (if not off-putting) description of features I labored to retain in Polish is partly prompted by my translatorial philosophy of *literary relanguaging* that proposes, after Ingarden, to preserve all layers of a work of art ("sound, rhythm, semantic coloration of lexes, phrases, and syntactical units of the original"; Wawrzycka 2007: 44) by refostering them in the target language, a challenging and often insurmountable task. As illustrated in the Addendum, Maciej Słomczyński translated poem XX beautifully, preserving its visual layout and successfully recreating Joyce's rhyme scheme. And if the line-by-line back-translation reveals minute sacrifices to Joyce's semantic layer, the translation still offers Polish readers a fulfilling aesthetic experience, on a par with the original poem and with the Italian translations.

Some of Joyce's rhyme schemes are more challenging than the one in poem XX. The scheme in poem III is a variant on the English quintain (A B A B B). In Joyce's treatment, it is thoroughly remade, with additional, radical variants in stanzas two and three:

A B B A B
C D D C C
E F F E F

This intricate scheme is made additionally complex by the poem's rhetorical modalities: the quintain's two complex questions and the closing command present a cognitive impasse. The questions are posed to the sky watcher by an undetermined voice[18] and, if the question in stanza one is rather straightforward—does the watcher of the sky *hear* the winds and sighs of harps that play until sunrise?—stanza two complicates it: is it the watcher *alone* who *awakes* to hear the harps play, in antiphon with winds, "Till night is overgone?" *Awake* suggests that the watcher has just emerged from a state of slumber, which problematizes the ontological status of sounds to be heard, as they might have been but a reverie that befell him. Whether the term "overgone" extends or annihilates time,[19] the word's lexical uniqueness plays into the semantic indeterminacy of the poem. The invocation in stanza three, bidding that the unseen harps "play ... to Love," corroborates the sound's illusory nature: like Love itself, the sound—Dantean heavenly music—appears to be a part of the speaker's inner landscape full of "soft light" and "soft sweet music." In a similar poetic reverie, Stephen also experiences "in his heart the *soft peace of silent spaces* of fading tenuous sky" as the "verses [croon] in the ear of his memory" full of joy, flowing "through the words where the *soft long vowels* hurtl[e] *noiselessly* . . . in soft low swooning cry" (*P* 225–6; my emphasis).[20] A glance at the first five lines reveals the presence of such vowels and diphthongs: "hour/ all/ repose"; "O/ lonely/ skies"; "o/ you/ hear/ night/ wind/sighs"; "harps/ play- Love/ -close"; "pale/ gates/ -rise."[21] Similar strings of vowel sounds drive all lines in this poem and the feminine rhyme scheme, traditionally undervalued in mainstream English prosody, is particularly successful here in enhancing the haunting and lulling effect of the slow flow of cadences: "repose/ unclose" interwoven with eye rhymes in "skies/ sighs/ sunrise" in stanza one; "alone/ antiphon/ overgone" with an enclosed rhyme "play/ way" in stanza two; and "Love/ above" knit in near-rhymes with "aglow/ go/ below" in stanza three.[22]

Translatorial challenges in this poem included rendering the elements highlighted above without rewriting the poem in the target language. While preserving Joyce's feminine rhymes in Polish poses no problems (they are a salient feature of Polish prosody), the challenge was to preserve, in addition to Joyce's meaning, also Joyce's quintain. The result is as follows:

ABBAB is reflected in word endings –ło/-cy/-ca/-ła/-ca.
CDDCC is matched by –nie/-ać/-ać/-nie/-nie.
EFFEF is approximated in –ane/-osa/-asa/-ami/-esach (again, in Polish, ch=h).

Stanza three contains a forced rhyme "Uchow**ane**/ponad **nami**" carried by the –**a**– sound, whose open and frequently elongated value joins other vowels and diphthongs in preserving Joyce's vowel sounds.[23]

In poem VII, the metrical foot and the rhyme scheme ABAB/CDCD/EFEF are deceptively simple. It is difficult to replicate in Polish Joyce's largely iambic rhythm because, with a few exceptions, the stress in Polish words falls on the penultimate syllable, resulting in the predominance of trochees and amphibrachs. The precedence in English of monosyllabic words adds to the difficulty: all but two rhymes in poem VII ("attire/desire" in stanza one) are masculine. My attempt to approximate the masculine rhyme is imperfect to say the least: "-**ieść/się**" in stanza two is a slant-rhyme carried by the phonetic closeness of –**ść** (masculine ending) and **się** whose prosodic value is feminine. Stanza three also contains a mixed rhyme, "nieb**iosa**/un**osząc**," though other rhymes are closer to Joyce's pattern.[24] In addition, Joyce's poetic syntax in stanzas two and three—"My love goes slowly / My love goes lightly"—are matched to read in back-translation as "Slowly goes my love / Lightly goes my love." In both cases, the participial phrases "bend**ing**/hold**ing**" are preserved in "chyl**ąc** si**ę**" and "unosz**ąc**." These intricacies may not always concern translators and they tend to be particularly difficult to retain in poetry if, for instance, rhyme/rhythm are to be preserved as well. Thus, Słomczyński's version of this poem forgoes the said participial phrases; they are recreated, respectively, through an adverb—"schylona" ("bent")—and a present continuous verb—"unosi" ("carries")—none of which detracts from the grace of this translation and from the excellence of the harmonious feminine rhyming scheme (highlighted in the Addendum).

Philological pedantry aside, I want to close by coming back to young Joyce's language to reflect on his awesomely acute linguistic—translatorial—sensibility and his predisposition to use English less as "familiar" and more as "so foreign" (*P* 189). This sensibility allowed Joyce to render at the age of about fifteen Horace's Ode III, 13, with a masterful "linguistic introspection" (Wawrzycka 2009: 127). Soon after, he composed his first collection of poems, *Moods*, and throughout the early 1900s, the time of the composition of *Chamber Music*, Joyce's evolving sensibilities would move him away from, for instance, Yeatsian "moods" as "metaphysical realities to be transfixed by the artist" (*JJII* 50) and closer to the rhythm and timbre of language marching in "acatalectic tetrameter[s] of iambs" (*U* 3.23). As I hope to have illustrated here, the poetic tonality of *Chamber Music* is driven as much by the abstract and non-representational sound-sense of language as it is by its referentiality, which is why I focused here on those few instances where silences in the poems are *connoted* through the "alphybettyformed" (*FW* 183.13) formations of vowels, rather than through words that *denote* silences. Translating *Chamber Music* meant, for me, tending to the "vocable scriptsigns" (*FW* 118.27–8) and to the "ooeeehah" (*U* 3.403) of language; it also meant reproducing, as closely as the Polish language allows, refigurations of those "soft long vowels" as they hurtle "noiselessly" *on their way* to signification.

Addendum

Reproduced below are side by side translations of Joyce's poems III, VII, and XX in Słomczyński's and Wawrzycka's Polish renditions; bold and underlined font highlight the translators' efforts to preserve a uniform rhyme scheme; back-translations show observance of Joyce's semantic layer. Italian translations close the Addendum.

III

At that hour when all things have rep**ose**,
O lonely watcher of the sk<u>ies</u>,
Do you hear the night wind and the s<u>ighs</u>
Of harps playing unto Love to uncl**ose**
The pale gates of sunr<u>ise</u>?

When all things repose do you al**one**
Awake to hear the sweet harps pl<u>ay</u>
To Love before him on his <u>way</u>,
And the night wind answering in antiph**on**
Till night is overg**one**?

Play on, invisible harps, unto **Love**,
Whose way in heaven is agl<u>ow</u>
At that hour when soft lights come and g<u>o</u>,
Soft sweet music in the air ab**ove**
And in the earth bel<u>ow</u>.

III (Słomczyński)	III *(back-translation)*:
W tej godzinie, gdy spoczywa rzecz ka**żda**,	*At this hour then each thing is resting*
O samotny, śl**ą**cy w niebo spojrz<u>enia</u>,	*O lonely-one, sending glances to the sky,*
Czy słyszysz wiatr nocny i westchni<u>enia</u>	*Do you heat the night wind and the sighs*
Harf prosz**ą**cych Miłość, by otwar**ła**	*Of harps asking Love to open*
Blade wrota słonecznego prom<u>ienia</u>?	*Pale gates of the sunbeam?*
Gdy spoczywa rzecz każda w tej godz**inie**,	*When each thing is resting in this hour,*
Czy ty jeden słyszysz w samotn<u>ości</u>	*Are you the [only] one who hears in loneliness*
Słodkie harfy gdy graj**ą** Mi<u>ło</u>ści;	*Sweet harps when they play onto Love;*
Antyfon**ę** wiatru, która pł**ynie**	*Antiphon of the wind, that flows*
Noc**ą**, póki noc ta nie przem**inie**?	*Through the night, until that night does not end?*
Grajcie harfy niewidzialne, Mi**łości**,	*Play, harps unseen, to Love,*
Która pójdzie przez niebiosa w jasn**ości**,	*That will go through the heavens in brightness,*
W tej godzinie, gdy blask bł**ą**dzi mi<u>ękki</u>,	*In that hour, when soft radiance wanders,*
Słodk**ą** muzykę w napowietrznej wysok**ości**	*Sweet music in airy height*
I w dole, na ziem<u>i</u>.	*And below, on earth.*

III (Wawrzycka)	III *(back-translation)*:
W tej godzinie gdy wszystko już zam**arło**	*At this hour when all came to a standstill*
O samotniku w niebo wpatrz**ony**,	*O lonely one gazing into the sky*
Czy słyszysz wiatr nocny i westchnień t**ony**	*Can you hear the night's wind and the sighs*
Harf co błagają by Miłość otw**arła**	*Of harps that plea that Love open*
Blade wschodu słońca br**amy**?	*The pale gates of sunrise?*
Gdy wszystko zamiera, czy ty jed**ynie**	*When all is at a standstill, is it you only*
Czuwasz by słodkiej gry harfy słuch**ać**	*That keeps watch to hear sweet play of harp*
Gdy Miłość ma w drogę wyrusz**ać**,	*Before Love sets out on a journey,*
I nocny wiatr odpowie w anty**fonie**	*And the night wind will answer in antiphon*
Aż noc zaprzem**inie**?	*Until the night will be overgone?*
Harfy utajone, grajcie dla Mi**łości**,	*Hidden/invisible harps, play to Love,*
Której szlak rozświetlają niebi**osa**	*Whose path [is] illumined by the heavens*
W tej godzinie gdy światło przyg**asa**,	*In that hour when lights are dimming*
Cicha słodka muzyka w powietrza wysok**ości**	*Quiet sweet music in the air above*
I poniżej na ziemi kr**esach**.	*And below on the earth's ends.*

VII

My love is in a light att**ire**
Among the apple tr**ees**,
Where the gay winds do most des**ire**
To run in compan**ies**.

There, where the gay winds stay to w**oo**
The young leaves as they p**ass**,
My love goes slowly, bending **to**
Her shadow on the gr**ass**;

And where the sky's a pale blue c**up**
Over the laughing l**and**,
My love goes lightly, holding **up**
Her dress with dainty h**and**.

VII (Słomczyński)	VII *(back-translation)*:
Jest miła moja w zwiewnej suk**ience**	*My love is in a light dress*
Pośród jabł**oni**,	*Among apple trees*
Tam gdzie podmuchów lekkich najwi**ęcej**	*There where [there are] the most of light breezes*
Śmieszny wiatr g**oni**.	*Funny wind chases.*
Gdzie wiatr ów śmieszny w listkach swa**woli**,	*Where that funny wind among little leaves plays*
Błądząc ciek**awie**,	*[being] lost curiously*
Schylona idzie miła po**woli**	*Bent goes my love slowly*
I cień jej w tr**awie**;	*And her shadow [is] in the grass.*

VII (Słomczyński)	VII *(back-translation)*:
Lecz tam, gdzie kielich niebios się w**znosi**	*But there, where the chalice of heaven arises*
Nad jasna **łączką,**	*Over the bright little meadow,*
Miła mknie lekko, a mknąc u**nosi**	*My love runs lightly, and running, [she] lifts*
Kraj sukni **rączką.**	*Dress-hem in her little hand.*

VII (Wawrzycka)	VII *(back-translation):*
Miła ma jest w sukni lekk**iej**	*My love is in a light dress*
Pośród jabłonek w **sadzie,**	*Among apple trees in orchard,*
Gdzie wiatry wesołe pragną najchętn**iej**	*Where merry winds desire the most*
Wiać złączone w grom**adzie.**	*To blow united in company.*
Tam, gdzie wesołe wiatry chcą zw**ieść**	*There, where merry winds want to woo*
Listki wśród których się b**awią,**	*Little leaves among which they play,*
Wolno idzie ma miła, chyląc **się**	*Slowly goes my love, bending*
Do swego cienia na tr**awie;**	*To her shadow on the grass.*
Gdzie są kielichem błękitnym nieb**iosa**	*Where the sky is a blue chalice*
Nad roześmianą **łąką,**	*Over the laughing meadow,*
Lekko idzie ma miła, un**osząc**	*Lightly goes my love, carrying*
Suknię subtelną swą **ręką.**	*Her dress in her dainty hand.*

XX

In the dark pinewood
I would we l**ay,**
In deep cool shadow
At noon of d**ay.**

How sweet to lie there,
Sweet to k**iss,**
Where the great pineforest.
Enaisled **is!**

Thy kiss descending
Sweeter w**ere**
With a soft tumult.
Of thy h**air.**

O, unto the pinewood
At noon of d**ay**
Come with me now,
Sweet love, aw**ay.**

XX (Wawrzycka)	(back-translation of W):	XX (Słomczyński)	(back-translation of S):
Wśród ciemnych sosen	*Among dark pine trees*	Byśmy leżeli	*[That] we [would] lay*
Położyć **się**,	*To lie down,*	W sosnowym b**orze**,	*In the pine forest,*
W głębi chłodnej cienia	*In deep cool shadow*	W cieniu głębokim,	*In a deep shadow,*
W połud**nie**.	*At noon.*	W południa **porze**.	*At noon time.*
Słodko tam leżeć,	*[It's] sweet to lay there*	Słodko był**oby**	*It would be sweet*
Całować **się**,	*to kiss*	Leżeć, cał**ować**,	*To lay, to kiss,*
Gdzie bór sosnowy	*where the pineforest*	W bór się sos**nowy**	*In the pine forest*
Unawiony **jest**!	*enisled is!*	Jak w kościół s**chować**	*As in church to hide.*
Twój pocałunek	*Your kiss*	Twój pocałunek	*Your kiss*
Słodszy był**by**	*Would be sweeter*	Też byłby s**łodszy**	*Also would be sweeter*
Wśród miękkich kaskad	*Among the soft cascades*	A miękka burza	*And the soft storm*
Włosów t**wych**.	*Of thy hair.*	To twoje w**łosy**.	*That is your hair.*
O, w bór sosnowy	*O, into the pine forest*	Ach, odejdź ze mną	*O, come away with me*
W południe d**nia**	*At noon*	W południa **porze**,	*At noon time,*
Pójdź ze mną teraz,	*Come with me now*	Pójdźmy, by skryć się	*Let's go to hide*
Kochana **ma**.	*My beloved.*	W sosnowym b**orze**.	*In the pine forest.*

III (Giuliani)	III (Capodilista)
In quell'ora che ogni cosa ha quiete,	In quell'ora quando tutto ha riposo,
O solitario custode dei cieli,	o solitario che osservi i cieli,
Non senti il vento notturno	non odi il vento notturno e i sospiri
E le arpe sospiranti Amore che schiuda	di arpe invitare Amore a schiudere
I pallidi cancelli dell'alba?	le pallide porte dell'alba?
Tu solo desto, quando la vita riposa,	Quando tutto riposta tu solo
Ascolti le dolci arpe sonare,	vegli per udire le arpe soavi
Nunzie di Amore, e il vento	precedere Amore nel suo cammino,
Notturno che in antifona risponde	e il vento notturno rispondere in antifona
Finché la notte è svanita?	finché la notte è sparita?
Sonate, arpe invisibili, per Amore	Suonate, arpe invisibili, per Amore
Il cui cammino arde nel cielo	il cui cammino in cielo splene
In quell'ora di luci tremanti,	in quell'ora quando lievi luci tremano,
In aria lassù lieve musica soave	lieve musica soave su nell'aria
E quaggiù sulla terra.	e giù sulla terra.

VII (Giuliani)	VII (Capodilista)
L'amor mio è vestita di luce	L'amore mio è in abiti leggeri
In mezzo ai meli	fra gli alberi di melo,
Dove i lieti vènti più bramano	dove dei venti gai è desiderio
Di correre insieme.	correre in compagnia.

VII (Giuliani)	VII (Capodilista)
Là dove i vènti lieti restano un poco	Là, dove i venti gai sostano a corteggiare
A corteggiare le giovani foglie,	le giovani foglie passando,
L'amor mio va lentamente, china	l'amore mio va lenta, chinandosi
Alla propria ombra sull'erba.	alla sua ombra nell'erba;
Là dove il cielo è una coppa azzurrina	e dove il cielo è una coppa azzurrina
Rovescia sulla terra ridente,	sopra la terra ridente,
Va l'amor mio luminoso, sostenendo	l'amore mio va leggera, tenendo
Con garbo la veste.	la veste con mano aggraziata.

XX (Giuliani)	XX (Capodilista)
Nella buia pineta	Nella pineta scura
Vorrei con te giacere,	vorrei giacere,
Nella frescura dell'ombra densa	nell'ombra cupa e fresca
A mezzogiorno.	a mezzogiorno.
Là com'è dolce distendersi,	Come è dolce giacere,
Soave baciarsi,	dolce baciare,
Della vasta pineta	dove la grande foresta
Sotto le navate!	sale in navate!
Più dolce scenderebbe	Il tuo bacio scendendo
Il tuo bacio	sarà più dolce
Nel soffice tumulto	con un tumulto soffice
Dei capelli	di capelli.
Oh, vieni con me, ora	Verso la pineta
A mezzogiorno	a mezzogiorno
Verso la buia pineta,	vieni con me ora,
Vieni, dolce amore.	dolce amore, vieni.

Notes

1 Private email correspondence, May 15, 2015.
2 Elsewhere I argued that Joyce will do so, among others, through translation, "an interesting facet of his mind" according to Maria Jolas (2009: 130).
3 For a useful roster of earlier criticism on *Chamber Music*, see Mahaffey (1990). For recent discussions of *Chamber Music*, see essays in Conner (2012) and his comprehensive Introduction. See also R. Spoo (1989). For Yeats's influence on Joyce's early poetry, see Wawrzycka (2015).

4 The stance of a lonely poet silenced by the hostile environment is stipulated in poem XXI and echoed in "Of dark life" ("The curse of loneliness broods silent on thee still") and in "The Holy Office."

5 In *Joyce's Music and Noise*, Jack Weaver (1998) posits that *Chamber Music* "is largely content to suggest music by allusion to winds and the naming of musical instruments" and by the use of such musical terminology as "antiphon" and "chant—to give the impression of the score" (8). He also sees two instruments "punningly submerged" in "unconsortable one" (XXI) and in "virginal" (VIII); see his discussion of the poems, esp. pp. 8–11.

6 They are integral to poems III, IV, VIII, XVI, XIX, XXIII, XXVI, XXIX and XXXVI; my discussion will address the questions in poem III.

7 See also Wawrzycka (2018), esp. p. 95.

8 The word "unquiet" appears in the following early poems by Yeats: "The Stolen Child"—"unquiet dreams"; in "Memory of Alfred Pollexfen"—"unquiet seas"; in "The Old Age of Queen Maeve"—"unquiet heart"; in "To a Shade"—"unquiet wanderer"; and in "The Indian to His Love"—"unquiet lands."

9 This feature will be exploded decades later in *Finnegans Wake*, chock full of "whispering" of words "keen again [to] begin again to make soundsense and sensesound kin again" (121.13–16).

10 "Alerting-device" is a term used by Adam Piette (1996) in his discussion of rhythmical sound effects, phonemic reduplications or repetitions of words in prose passages that create a particular effect; see especially pp. 12–20.

11 In her discussion of Giuliani's translation of the poems, Sara Sullam (2014) comments that they are successful "in catching the overall rhythmical quality of Joyce's poems" (192), and that Giuliani's "rhythmical interpretations" rely on *versi accentuativi*, where "the rhythmical effect actually [takes] over the strict rule of syllable count" (193). That both Giuliani and De Angelis understood the importance of rhythm "not in terms of prosody but as a motif" can be credited to their familiarity with Eliot's "The Music in Poetry," according to Sullam. While translations by Słomczyński are also successful in this respect, it is difficult to assess whether he was familiar with, or had access to, Eliot's text in English before November 1969 (the date that marks Słomczyński's "Introduction" to *Utwory poetyckie—Poetical Works*). The Polish translation of Eliot's piece appeared in 1972 in *Szkice krytyczne*, translated and edited by Maria Niemojowska (Warszawa: PIW).

12 Elongation in "Wśród" [ó = oo]; diphthongs in "ie," "ię," and "iu"; triphthongs in położyć [oło = owo], południe [ołu = owoo] and głębokim [łę = weh], with nasal *eh* as in the French –*vin*.

13 Słomczyński rendered the phrase interpretatively. In back-translation, it reads as follows: "in the pine forest to hide as in the church" ['W bór sosnowy jak w kościół się schować," 23]. Another Polish translator, Ewa Tomaszewska (not otherwise

included in this study) preserves "-aisle-" in "nawy" (genitive of "nawa")—thus the
kissing happens "among the pinetrees as huge as the pillars of the nave" ['miedzy
sosnami wielkimi jak filarami nawy," 43]. The Italian translators render the lines as
"vasta pineta sotto le navate" (Giuliani 43) and "la grande foresta sale in navate"
(Capodilista 68). The French translation, excluded from this study for copyright
reasons, offers "la grande forêt de pins lève sa nef" (Borel 54).

    Nonce words, incidentally, dwell in a peculiar sort of silence as lexical units: they
are absent from everyday usage and, frequently, from dictionaries. James Murray
uses this term in the *New English Dictionary*. See also Campbell (2012: 76, n. 2).

14 In addition, diphthongal vocalizations of Joyce's **"thy hair"** are approximated in
    Polish by "włosów twych:" -ło- [**wo**] and -y- [-ih-], with an intruding sibilant **s**.
    Joyce's quasi-homophonic rhyme **"were/hair"** is reflected in "-yłby/-ych" [-iwby/-ih],
    an approximate visual and phonetic rhyme.

15 Easily overlooked here, the occurrences of "O" in Joyce's successive works become
    increasingly semantically charged. Elsewhere in this volume, Fritz Senn suggests that
    the "O"s and "Ah"s in *Ulysses* warrant critical attention.

16 In: "**O**," "bór" [-**oo**-], "południe" [-**owoo**-], "dnia" [-**ya**], "pójdź" [-**ooy**-], "ma" [-**ah**].

17 In the two Italian translations at my disposal, the poems' successful, slightly varied
    vocabulary reproduces the *sound* of Joyce's w**oo**d, w**ou**ld, c**oo**l, n**oo**n in the first
    stanza through the sounds in b**u**ia, -s**cu**ra, **o**mbra, mezz**o**giorno (Giuliani), and
    through s**cu**ra, **o**mbra, c**u**pa, mezz**o**giorno (Capodilista), with a higher incidence of
    sibilants to Joyce's just one, the unavoidable reality of the target language. The lexes
    of Joyce's first stanza in French translation by Jacques Borel include d**ans**, b**ois**, p**ins,**
    somber—**onsons**-**nous**, l'**o**mbre, prof**on**de—where the frequency of nasals echo
    Joyce's elongated sounds; there are three sibilants in Borel to Joyce's one (though
    many more "visual" sibilants add to the play in Borel). See Addendum for full Italian
    translations.

18 In "Joyce's Poetics of Knowledge," Marc Conner (2012) remarks on the speaker's
    isolation, stating that "it is unclear if this watcher refers to an imagined beloved or to
    himself" (150). While one can assume the presence of two subjects in the poem, such
    reading seems to collapse in stanza three. In broader terms, Marie-Dominique Garnier
    (2012) wonders about the stability of the subject of the lover's affection ("is the 'gentle
    lady' of XXVIII the same as 'Goldenhair' in V and the 'yellow hair' in XI?") and
    concludes that "the poems circulate a series of disorganized, partial characters . . . who
    shuffle about as semi-detached, co-erring rather than cohering voices" where "the
    lyrical subject is "curbed," made to occupy a strange, liminal status between subject and
    object" and where characters "operate as dissolved selves, partial beings . . ." (80–1). See
    her "Verse After Verlaine, Rime after Rimbaud" (in Conner 2012: 78–104).

19 The *OED* lists the meanings as: "far gone"; "obsolete"; "gone beyond bounds"; "gone
    out of use."

20 Of note is the complex rhetoricity of Joyce's phrasing—oxymoronic "hurtle noiselessly ... in soft ... cry"—that points to Joyce's wrestling with language in a challenge to express (or reconcile) the *noiselessness* of vowels as "scriptsigns" that cannot but *sound* as "vocables."

21 The lines' rhythm is slowed by three spondees in this stanza: "all things," "night wind," and "pale gates." Stanza two repeats "all things" and "night wind," and adds "sweet harps"; in stanza three, we have "soft lights" and "soft sweet."

22 A version of this passage also appears in Wawrzycka (2018: 91–2).

23 Translation of this poem by Słomczyński successfully retains Joyce's rhyme scheme, even though the quintain in stanza one appears as a monorhyme A A A A A (the pattern could be described more precisely as A A$_1$A$_1$A A$_1$): the rhyming word endings are -da/-nia/-nia/-ła/-nia; stanza two follows the pattern BCCBB: -nie/-ści/-ści/-/-nie/-nie; in stanza three the pattern CCDCD is created by interlocking the second stanza's C rhyme with a new, oblique D rhyme: -ści/-ści/-ki/-ści/-mi. The French translator plays with a series of interlocking but not consistently patterned rhymes and with numerous internal rhymes; the whole sound layer is resplendent with permutations of vowel and nasal sounds that play into the poem's unique aura of quietude and repose that interests me here. While vowels and diphthongs in the Italian translations create a similar effect, no rhyme is preserved in Giuliani's and Capodilista's versions. About Giuliani, however, see n. 11.

24 In "niebi**osa**/un**osząc**," the first component, feminine collective noun for "skies" signals a feminine rhyme that is "upset" by the second component, a present (adverbial) participle where the final –**c** marks a masculine rhyme (with an ameliorating effect of the near-eye-rhyme of "-**osa/-oszą**"). The other rhymes in the translation are more successful. In stanza one, the rhyme "lekk**iej**/-chetn**iej**" corresponds to Joyce's oblique rhyme "**trees**/-n**ies**" (with "sa**dzie**/groma**dzie**" matched with "att**ire**/des**ire**"). In the second stanza, "-**wią** /-**wie**" corresponds to Joyce's perfect rhyme "**pass/grass**," and "**łąką/ręką**" matches very closely Joyce's perfect rhyme "**land/hand**" in stanza three.

References

Attridge, D. (1990) (ed.), *The Cambridge Companion to James Joyce*, Cambridge: Cambridge University Press.

Campbell, M. (2012), "The Unconsortable Joyce: *Chamber Music*," in M. Conner (ed.), *The Poetry of James Joyce Reconsidered*, 51–77, Gainesville: University Press of Florida.

Conner, M. (2012), *The Poetry of James Joyce Reconsidered*, Gainesville: University Press of Florida.

Garnier, M. -D. (2012), "Verse After Verlaine, Rime after Rimbaud," in M. Conner (ed.), *The Poetry of James Joyce Reconsidered*, 78–104, Gainesville: University Press of Florida.

Joyce, J. (1967), *Poèmes*, trans. J. Borel, Paris: Gallimard.

Joyce, J. (1969), *Muzyka kameralna*. In *Utwory poetyckie*, trans. M. Słomczyński, Kraków: Wydawnictwo Literackie.

Joyce, J. (1978), *Poesie*, trans. M. Capodilista, Rome: Newton Compton.

Joyce, J. (1990), *Muzyka kameralna*, trans. E. Tomaszewska, Kraków: Wydawnictwo Miniatura.

Joyce, J. (1991), *Chamber Music*, in Richard Ellmann et al. (eds), *James Joyce: Poems and Shorter Writings*, London: Faber and Faber.

Joyce, J. (1992), *Musica da camera*, trans. A. Giuliani, in Franca Ruggieri (ed.), *James Joyce: Poesie e Prose*, Milan: Mondadori.

Joyce, S. (1962), *The Dublin Diary of Stanislaus Joyce*, London: Faber and Faber.

Kenner, H. (1963), "The *Portrait* in Perspective," in S. Givens (ed.), *James Joyce: Two Decades of Criticism*, 132–74, New York: Vanguard Press.

Mahaffey, V. (1990), "Joyce's Shorter Works," in D. Attridge (ed.), *The Cambridge Companion to James Joyce*, 185– 211, Cambridge: Cambridge University Press.

Piette, A. (1996), *Remembering and the Sound of Words: Mallarmé, Proust, Joyce, Beckett*, Oxford: Clarendon Press.

Spoo, R. (1989), "Rival Confessors in *Chamber Music*: Meaning and Narrative in Joyce's Lyric Mode," *James Joyce Quarterly* 26, no. 4: 483–98.

Sullam, S. (2014), "The Translation of Joyce's Poetry in Post-war Italy," in M. Canani and S. Sullam (eds), *Parallaxes: Virginia Woolf Meets James Joyce*, 178–96, Newcastle upon Tyne: Cambridge Scholars Publishing.

Wawrzycka, J. (2007), "*'Tell us in plain words'*: Textual Implications of Re-Languaging Joyce," in R. M. Bollettieri Bosinelli and I. Torresi (eds), *Joyce and/in Translation*, *Joyce Studies in Italy* 10, 39–52, Rome: Bulzoni Editore.

Wawrzycka, J. (2009), "Translation," in J. McCourt (ed.), *Joyce in Context*, 125–36, Cambridge: Cambridge University Press.

Wawrzycka, J. (2015), "'Ghosting Hour': Young Joyce Channeling Early Yeats," in J. McCourt, (ed.), *Joyce, Yeats, and the Revival*, 103–18, *Joyce Studies in Italy* 4, New Series, Rome: Edizioni Q.

Wawrzycka, J. (2018), "'If thou but scan it well': Markers of Time in *Chamber Music*," in J. Wawrzycka (ed.), *Reading Joycean Temporalities*, 85–100, Amsterdam: Brill/Rodopi.

Weaver, J. W. (1998), *Joyce's Music and Noise*, Gainesville: University Press of Florida.

Yeats, W. B. (1983), *The Poems of W. B. Yeats*, ed. R. J. Finneran, New York: Macmillan.

14

"Music hath jaws": Translating Music and Silence in *Ulysses*

Erika Mihálycsa

"Words? Music? No: it's what's behind" (*U* 11.703) Bloom muses on what appears to be at once music heard and unheard, the aria from Flotow's opera *Martha* sung by a singer who remains unseen to him, and the unheard rhythms of the "language of flow" deployed in the interior monologues. The latter are born from the contingencies of the tunes present through textual allusion and the sound effects—lexical and non-lexical onomatopoeia—brought to life by silent or voiced reading. The "Sirens" passage, and the episode in general, thematizes, with an intensity unparalleled in English prose fiction, the permeable boundaries of sound/noise/music on the one hand, and silence/pause on the other hand, creating a dense texture of nonce constellations that turns syntax and the larger textual structures into systems organized on a musical basis.

Reading "Sirens" one is prompted to ask, "What is it behind language that elicits the sensation of music, of immersion in the sound-world and in its extension, silence; and how can such a sensation be translated, carried over into another language?" In what follows I will try to map linguistic sound effects and allusiveness in translation, focusing on the recent retranslations of *Ulysses* into Italian—by Enrico Terrinoni (2012) and Gianni Celati (2013)—and Hungarian, a partial retranslation and thorough re-editing carried out by scholars András Kappanyos, Marianna Gula, Gábor Zoltán Kiss, and Dávid Szolláth (2012), succeeding canonical translations with an agenda of addressing translation problems left unsolved, or downright silenced, in the previous versions.[1]

Preliminaries

The key conceit of "Sirens" is making language appear as though it were music, privileging the aural effects of the signifier over the semantics of the signified. Yet the fundamental irony of this experiment is precisely that it brings out the ways in which language simultaneously is and *is not* music since, being text, it cannot but be silent, even if it emulates a language-based system of musical and noise notation. In Karen Lawrence's words, the episode at once lives up to, and debunks, the Paterian ethos that "all art constantly aspires to the status of music" (Lawrence 2010: 35). Jean-Michel Rabaté was the first to point out that in the Joycean text "the real song of the Sirens is a song of silence,"[2] and that the central trope of the episode is the reciprocal transformation of the aural into the visual (an imaginary song) and of vision into music (hallucination): "the ear becomes a shell which conjures up an imaginary sound, a sound which exists without actual presence" (Rabaté 1986: 86). The constant exchange between the sonorous and the visual (or imaginary) ultimately turns the writing (and, one might add, reading) mode of "Sirens" into a "deaf-eared transcribing" that shares the predicament of the episode's deaf listener, Pat the waiter, who "seehears lipspeech" (Lawrence 2010: 38), where the event of voicing the text's silent music is transferred to the reading.

As a musical analogy of sorts to the silent music "seeheard" in "Sirens," one could cite contemporary composer György Kurtág's "found object" from the series of minimalist pieces for the piano, *Games (Játékok)*: a C note, the basis of the musical scale, is held for an extended time, and then finished with a brief H-C-D flourish. To add to the dialectic tension between tonic and the cluster of sounds around it, the score stipulates a crescendo and decrescendo on C after it is sounded. However, since no pianist can tamper with the volume of a chord already sounded, or with its length of reverberations, the score in fact demands that the performer achieve an intellectual illusion of hearing a nonexistent dynamics and make it heard solely by his/her power of concentration (Halász 2006: 117). Thus the crescendo–decrescendo dynamics is transposed into the player's (and, virtually, the listener's) act of concentrated, participatory listening where this silent potentiality can become auditory.

The event of reading, which ultimately displaces the aural with the visual to conjure up the imaginary sound of "Sirens," establishes the relational nature of listening in/to the text. According to Jean-Luc Nancy, the aural or sonorous is "tendentially methexic (that is, having to do with participation, sharing or contagion)"—in contradistinction to the visual which is always "tendentially mimetic" (Nancy: 2007: 10). Therefore the aural is characterized by an ability to invite and induce participation, of crucial importance to the reciprocal mode of exchange of music and musicality. This relationality can be traced to the ability of listening to establish resonances between self and subject: "one in the echo of the other, and this echo is like the very sound of its sense" (Nancy 2007: 10). For Nancy, to be listening means "to be straining toward or in an approach to the self (we should say, in a pathological manner, *a fit of self*: isn't [sonorous] sense first of all, every time, a crisis of self?" (2007: 9).

Translating silence

In a masterly essay on translation, "Variations on the Right to Remain Silent," Anne Carson differentiates between two kinds of silence translators have to face: physical and metaphysical. The first is produced by an absence of text—(un)intended lacunae, for instance due to a missing manuscript fragment; the latter is a silence that resides in the words themselves. She gives a surprising array of texts and images as examples for the second type of silence: a passage from the *Odyssey* where the god Hermes uproots a healing plant and pronounces its name, yet the name, *molu*, inexistent in Greek, is left untranslated as an instance of the gods' language (*Odyssey* 10.302–6); foreign words absorbed into a language unchanged—as in, for instance, *cliché*, originally a printing term meaning to make a stereotype from a relief printing surface, having onomatopoeic origins on which the borrowing language falls silent; and instances of Francis Bacon's painting where what is painted is not the object but direct sensation that resists narrativity—a direct "jar on the nerves" (Woolf 1981: 193)—a rupture in mimesis, sometimes achieved through a violent gesture on the canvas, such as throwing white paint on the nearly-finished painting. By analogy, in literature most disruptive stylistic features would be conducive to this second type of silence.

Still, Carson's most surprising example is Joan of Arc's refusal to speak in the terms demanded by her judges who were simultaneously translating her eloquent testimony into the official language of the law and into Latin. When pressed to give details, to flesh out her "voices," she throws white paint on her testimony, closing doors of silence on her inquisitors—as in the puzzling sentence, "The light comes in the name of the voice," translated into the Latin of the legal protocol as *in nomine vocis venit claritas* (Carson 2010: 10).

In other words, this second, metaphysical silence, is born from the original text's, or agent's, refusal to translate something inherently foreign into its own medium or language; a deliberate stopping short of representation, a refusal of narrativity, of normativity, of succumbing to conceptual language, conveyed by a gesture of withdrawal or violent paint-throwing that at once solicits and resists translation. One such gesture is, in Carson's essay and demonstrative practice, the *catastrophizing* of translation, a procedure similar to Hölderlin's wringing of the Greek syntax of Sophocles into his native German.

It is seductive to take Joan of Arc's sentence as a motto for a discussion of how a text apparently as remote as "Sirens" uses disruptive eloquence, going against narrative normativity and even against the communicative function of language, to achieve *claritas*—the Joycean, epiphanic *radiance*—in the name and language of the voice(s), of sound and music, of onomatopoeia. This radiance, far removed from the metaphysical sense implied in the original sentence of the *Vierge d'Orléans*, will here be seen as the repository of the literary work's inventive singularity. Such inventive singularity is, according to Derek Attridge (2004: 136), "what provokes translation (in all senses) as a creative response, rather than a mechanical rewording." The singular literary work is singular—that is, unaccountable for based on the repertory of a culture, and involving "the irruption of alterity into the cultural field"—"only by virtue of its translatability and its imitability (as well as its capacity to provoke new and singular responses)" (Attridge 2004: 74–5).

When Simon Dedalus starts singing *M'appari* in the bar of the Ormond Hotel, unseen by Bloom who is in the dining-room, the latter listens to the voice that gradually metamorphoses into the voice of love itself: "Love that is singing" (*U* 11.681). This peculiar language, made up almost entirely of lexical and non-lexical onomatopoeia, turns words into the flesh of sound/music; narrative seems to issue from an instance that Susan Mooney calls the *aurteur*—an aural *auteur*, "the creative (often unconscious) organizer or mediator of acoustic fragments (instances of memories of voices, music, noise, sounds)," the result of creative transference between writer and reader, author and work (Mooney 1999: 239). In this unbound flow of language, the effect of music, the direct "jar on the nerves," is translated into visual images:

> Through the hush of air a voice sang to them, low, not rain, not leaves in murmur, like no voice of strings or reeds or *whatdoyoucallthem* dulcimers touching their still ears with words, still hearts of their each his remembered lives. Good, good to hear: sorrow from them each seemed to from both depart when first they heard.
>
> *U* 11.674–7; my emphasis

The singing human voice is likened to all manner of instruments: strings or winds (the reed metonymically standing for winds); the words that reach the ear lobe—a resonance box, thus itself an instrument—invoke a range of unvoiced sounds in an instance of sonorous material creating a pocket of silence that emits its own music. Within this pocket of radiant silence the word *dulcimer* pops up from memory, appearing on account of its melodious, outlandish name, an echo of Bloom's first journey in the mind earlier in the day: "High wall: below strings twanged . . . Strings. Listen. A girl playing one of those instruments what do you call them: dulcimers. I pass" (*U* 4.97–9). The mental image of a girl playing the dulcimer is an unselfconscious echo of *Kubla Khan*, "a damsel with a dulcimer / In a vision once I saw"; Bloom's oriental reverie in "Calypso" even replicates the topos of Coleridge's classic, of imaginary music recreating the oneiric edifice in a mutual displacement of sonorous and visual: "Could I revive within me / Her symphony and song, / To such a deep delight 'twould win me, / That with music loud and long, / I would build that dome in air, / That sunny dome! those caves of ice!"

Here, translation faces a twofold dilemma: to address the silent translation, or (mis)quotation, of a classic in the original[3]—which presupposes the echoing of a canonical translation text that would be inevitably far less embedded into target-language cultural memory; and to recreate the effect of the instrument's strange name, which remains silent in the fragment. The name *dulcimer* evokes music both etymologically and due to its unique phonesthetic configuration: it is a borrowing from Norman French whose etymology combines Greek (*melos: melody*) and Latin (*dulce*). While not originating in an imitative root, it is nevertheless able to etymologically connote a musical quality of mellifluousness, balancing on the threshold of lexical onomatopoeia. As such, its evocative power relies on our reading-as-translation: on the fact that it behaves like a pocket of silence in English, that at once invites and resists translation. It is this very effect that translation has to tackle:

> Attraverso il silenzio d'aria una voce cantava per loro, bassa, non pioggia, non foglie murmuri, come nessuna voce di arco o di fiato o *di comesichiamano ribeche* accarezzando con parole le loro quiete orecchie … (I/DA[4] 252; my emphasis) [Through the silence of air a voice sang for them, low, not rain, not murmuring leaves, like no voice of strings or of winds or of whataretheycalled cither caressing with words their calm ears …]
>
> Attraverso la calma dell'aria una voce cantava per loro, bassa, non pioggia, non foglie a mormorare, come la non voce degli strumenti a corda dei fiati *o comesichiamano i dulcimer*, a sfiorar le loro orecchie inerti con parole … (I/T 281; my emphasis) [Through the quiet of the air a voice sang for them, low, not rain, not leaves (that are) murmuring, like the non-voice of string instruments of winds or whataretheycalled of dulcimers, ever so slightly touching their inert ears with words …]
>
> Attraverso la quiete dell'aria una voce veniva a loro, bassa, non suon di pioggia, non murmure di foglie, neppur suono di accordate corde o *come-si-chiama*

di ribeca, lambendo con parole le loro quiete orecchie . . . (I/C 377; my emphasis)
[Through the stillness of the air a voice came to them, low, not sound of rain, not murmuring of leaves, nor sound of well-tuned strings or what-is-the-word-for cither, lapping against their still ears with words . . .]

The canonical Italian translation *La Ballata di Kubla Khan* features *dolcemele*.[5] De Angelis' canonical translation, and, in its wake, Celati's, opt for the domestic *ribeca*, a santoor-like medieval instrument of Arab origins belonging to the dulcimer family, with two to five strings, but held and played with a bow like a violin. Terrinoni alone enhances the word's foreignness by adopting the English form rather than the Italianized *dulcimero, dulcimelo*, or *dolcemele*, so his translation, while maintaining the link to Coleridge's verse in Italian, empowers the word's etymological allusiveness and harnesses its effect of strangeness, to explain Bloom's momentary hesitation in calling it to mind. This effect is all the more striking since his translation generally employs colloquial vocabulary and turns-of-phrase, whereas De Angelis's and Celati's translations make recourse to a heightened sense of literariness, frequently using obsolete word forms. Terrinoni's translation also curiously displaces the negation "like no voice," to the absence of voice or sound, in the instruments themselves ("come la *non voce*"), highlighting the passage's literal silence:

> Az álló levegő csöndjében egy hang dalolt, nem eső, nem suttogó levelek, nem nádasok zizegése, nem *hogyismondjákok, cimbalmok* zöngéi, hanem szavakkal érintette a hallgató fülüket . . . (H/Sz 339; my emphasis) [In the motionless air's silence a voice sang, not rain, not whispering leaves, not rustle of reeds, not the whatsits', cimbaloms' rings, but with words (it) touched their listening ears . . .]
>
> Az álló levegő csöndjében egy hang dalolt nekik, mélyen, nem eső, nem suttogó levelek, nem vonósok vagy fúvósok hangja, nem *hogyishívják cimbalmok* zöngéi. Szavakkal érintete hallgató fülüket . . . (H/"R" 266; my emphasis) [In the motionless air's silence a voice sang to them, low (adv.), not rain, not whispering leaves, not sound of strings or winds, not whatsit cimbaloms' rings. With words (it) touched their listening ears . . .]

In the Hungarian versions, faithfulness to the canonical translation of *Kubla Khan*[6] results in an irreconcilable conundrum. Although belonging to the dulcimer family, *cimbalom* (whose name derives from the Latin *cymbalum*, and ultimately from the Greek *kymbalon/kymbe*—originally a tambourine-like percussion instrument that gave the name to a family of instruments, including the Italian *cembalo*) is a typical Hungarian folk instrument, its etymology and distant, foreign onomatopoeic roots obliterated by familiarity. Moreover, the

Irish Bloom imagining *cimbalom* in the context of daydreaming about the Orient is maladroit, and the momentary lapse seems hardly motivated. Where the English original exploits foreignness and a word's phonestetic properties to the fullest, the Hungarian versions, sticking to philological accuracy, lose sight precisely of the effect the original elicits.

A similar case of a silent translation, or (mis)quotation, occurs a few pages later when Bloom muses on the origin of sounds, noises, and music, on objects easily turned into sound-making instruments:

> Shah of Persia liked that best. Remind him of home sweet home. Wiped his nose in curtain too. Custom his country perhaps. That's music too. Not as bad as it sounds. Tootling. Brasses braying asses through uptrunks. Doublebasses helpless, gashes in their sides. Woodwinds mooing cows. *Semigrand open crocodile music hath jaws.* Woodwind like Goodwin's name.
>
> U 11.1050; my emphasis

The highlighted phrase throws white paint on the canvas of communicability in its intentional miswriting of a verse well embedded in the host language cultural memory, from Congreve's play *The Mourning Bride* (1697): "Music hath charms to sooth a savage breast" (Act I, Sc. I). The morphed literary echo appears in a process-sentence that dramatizes a concatenation of associations from the visual association to an open crocodile's mouth, to the aural association to the (near) homophonous "charms" of the Congreve verse. The musical instrument, so far the source of seductive music standing, synechdochically, for the disembodied voice of love, is turned into a potentially threatening body, revealing the deathly side of siren song, in a context where in Bloom's interior monologue musical sounds turn to wounds issued by a variety of instruments appearing as wounded or, potentially, *wounding* bodies, crossing the boundary between inanimate and animate. The sequence is closed off by an aural association to the name of the Blooms' piano teacher, Goodwin.

How can a translation text empower, and not erase, these silences in the original—especially when the literary allusion is unavailable, not given in canonic form, in the receiving language?

> De hát ez is zene. Nem is olyan rossz, mint ahogy hangzik. *Futamtutam.* Rézfúvósok ordítása, feltartott ormányok. *Nagydögbőgők, f-luk sebek az oldalán.* Fafúvósok, birkabú. Kereszthúros zongora nyitva krokodil szája van. *Fagott és fuvola mintha falliteráció.* (H/Sz 353; my emphasis) [But this is music too. Not as bad as it sounds. *Futamtutam: futam*, musical run + onom. *ra-run. Nagydögbőgők* (pl., portmanteau *nagybőgő*: double bass + *nagy dög*: big carcass/big whore of

sg.), f-key wounds in their sides. Woodwinds, sheep-woe. Semigrand piano open
crocodile's mouth is. Bassoon and flute as if f-alliteration.]

Szentkuthy's portmanteau-studded passage bypasses the silent quote altogether;
it underscores the visual association between the open piano and the crocodile's
jaws by a conspicuously gauche distribution of the phrase "is open" [*nyitva van*]
between the two objects, making an original attempt at rendering Bloom's mental
shorthand. The translator visibly concentrates on the crux that combines the
name Goodwin (abandoned in translation) and the sound of woodwinds in a
wilful attempt at shock-effect, cutting through the Gordian knot of the English
homophony with much aplomb: "*Fagott és fuvola mintha falliteráció*" [Bassoon
and flute, as if *f*alliteration]. The Hungarian sentence f-alliterates on two musical
instruments in a word amalgam with a recognizably phallic touch, from whose
casual encounter with the sexually charged flute the cultivated readers could also
spell out a hint at fellatio.[7]

> De hát az is zene. Nem is olyan rossz, mint ahogy hangzik. Tülkölés. Fatörzsnyi
> rézfúvósok szamárbőgése, tehetetlen nagybőgődögök, oldalukon tátongó seb.
> Fafúvók, búgó-bőgő marhák. Goodwin zongorájának nyitott fogsora,
> krokodilszájban zene. *Fagott fogért*. (H/"R" 276; my emphasis) [But this is music
> too. Not as bad as it sounds either. Tooting. Treetrunk-size brasses' ass-braying,
> helpless double bass-carcasses, on their sides gaping wound(s). Woodwinds, crying-
> braying cattle. Open denture of Goodwin's piano, music in crocodile's mouth.
> Bassoon for tooth (*fagott*: bassoon, playing on idiom *fogat fogért*: "tooth for tooth").]

The "Revised" translation's compound on double basses disambiguates
Szentkuthy's portmanteau; the name of Goodwin is salvaged, but mainly as a
visual memory connected to the piano, not as an aural one; similarly, there is no
attempt to "fake" a quote on the charms of music, with a contiguous bodily term
substituted. However, we get a play on the name of a musical instrument and
teeth, derived from the image of crocodile-like piano denture: the chance
language effect offered by Hungarian, "*fagott fogért*" ("bassoon for tooth"), has
the advantage of being a slightly gauche pun on "tooth for tooth," that Bloom
might be credited with.

Translating Joyce's onomatopoeic language

What is it exactly in such language that creates the effect of music? Relying on
the Jakobsonian definition of the quality of literariness in (mainly poetic)

language—an excess or addition supplementing functions of 'normal' language—Derek Attridge in *Peculiar Language* focuses on onomatopoeia (especially lexical), and shows how all the factors of imitativeness through "phonestetic constellations" (Attridge 1988: 149) on the one hand, and semantic valences on the other hand, are in themselves inadequate to account for the distinctive quality of Joyce's language in "Sirens." The semantic context of lexical onomatopoeia is inalienably present in these words. The readers' experience is not of immediacy of the sound-world (as conveyed by non-lexical onomatopoeia), nor is it of speech-sounds as pure sounds; on the contrary, it is of "the momentary and surprising reciprocal relationship established between phonetic and semantic properties, a mutual reinforcement that intensifies *both* aspects of language," and which accounts for the pleasure experienced by the reader (Attridge 1988: 151; emphasis in original). Rather than a simple relationship of resemblance or imitation, what such language makes readers experience is a heightened sense of "language *as language*," that is, "of language in the act of *producing meaning* and thereby momentarily fusing the abstractness of *langue* and the concreteness of *parole*" (Attridge 1988: 152; emphasis in original). The nonce "phonoesthetic constellations" of Joyce's "Sirens" sensitize the mind to the physical properties of speech, so that attention is diverted to "the materiality of language *as it does its work of bringing meaning into being*" (Attridge 1988: 154; emphasis in original). So lexical onomatopoeia can indeed be considered a "model for all literary language" (Attridge 1988: 154).

Accordingly, music, musicality, and silence are constituted in language by the specific, non-normative treatment of linguistic material, by structuring speech into certain patterns of rhythmicity, by repetition (mainly in the form of echoes and rhymes), and by highlighting its sound valences (onomatopoeia) that Bloom collectively calls "musemathematics" (*U* 11.834). Reflecting on the nature of poetic language in an earlier episode, he naively intuits something about these structuring principles—namely, that the etymologically cognate *rhythm* and *rhyme*, principally responsible for the musical qualities of (poetic) language, are derived from the Greek verb *rhein*, to flow:

The hungry famished gull
Flaps o'er the waters dull.
That is how poets write, the similar sounds. But then Shakespeare has no
    rhymes: blank verse. The flow of the language it is. The thoughts. Solemn.
Hamlet, I am thy father's spirit
Doomed for a certain time to walk the earth.

                                                            U 8.62

"Sirens" is underpinned by a recurring network of correspondences between music (song /singing standing, synechdochically, for love /the act of love-making) in its linguistic valences of rhythmic/rhyming repetition or imitative sound ("It's only on account of the sound it is"; *U* 11.836), flow, flower, and love. This network of motifs mostly appears in recurrent, synaesthetic constellations of these elements, and where some sort of gap—erasure, clipping of a word, silence—brings out the fact that the first syllables of these words can be mutually inscribed into each other:

> Are you not happy in your home? *Flower* to console me and a pin cuts *lo*. Means something, *language of flow*. Was it a daisy?
>
> > *U* 11.296; my emphasis

> Shebronze, dealing from her oblique jar thick syrupy liquor for his lips, looked as it *flowed* (*flower* in his coat: who gave him?) and syrupped with her voice: Fine goods in small parcels.
>
> > *U* 11. 365; my emphasis

> Bloom dipped, Bloo mur: dear sir. Dear Henry wrote: dear Mady. *Got your lett and flow*. Hell did I put? Some pock or oth. It is utterl imposs. Underline imposs. To write today.
>
> > *U* 11.860; my emphasis

Due to the unique homophonic and homographic properties of English, these concatenating words connote each other when clipped: physical erasures highlight their semantic, motivic interrelatedness, while rendering them lexical onomatopoeia. Unlike many of the episode's other clippings, these erasures may be filled in more than one way, generating lateral proliferation of meaning:

> Fiore per consolarmi e uno spillo *porta male*. Vuol dire qualcosa, linguaggio dei *fio*./ Ellabronzo, versando dall'orciolo obliquo spesso liquido sciropposo per le sue labbra, lo guardava *fluire* (*fiore* all'occhiello: chi gliel'ha dato?), e sciroppava con la voce ... (I/DA 243, 245; my emphasis) [Flower to console me and a pin brings bad (luck). Means something, language of flo(wers). / Shebronze, pouring from the oblique jar dense syrupy liquid for his lips, looked at it flowing (flower at the buttonhole: who gave it to him?), and syrupped with the voice ...]
>
> Fiore per consolarmi e spillo allontana *l'am*. Significa qualcosa, linguaggio dei *fio*./ Ellabronzo, versando dalla caraffa denso liquore sciropposo per le labbra di lui, lo guardò *fluire* (*fiore* nel cappotto: chi gliel'ha dato?), e con la voce sciroppò ... (I/T 271, 273; my emphasis) [Flower to console me and pin drives away lo(ve). Means something, language of flo(wers). / Shebronze, pouring from the caraffe

thick syrupy liquor for the lips of him, looked at it flowing (flower in his coat: who gave it to him?), and syrupped with the voice ...]

Fiore per consolarmi e una puntura di spillo *porta male.* Vuol dire qualcosa, linguaggio dei *fiori.*/ Essabronzo, versando dall'orciolo denso liquor sciropposo, destinato alle labbra di lui, guardava mentre il liquore *fluiva* (*fiore* all'occhiello: chi gliel'ha dato?) e gli sciroppò con la propria voce ... (I/C 362, 365; my emphasis) [Flower to console me and a prick of a pin brings bad (luck). Means something, language of flowers. / Shebronze, pouring from the jar thick syrupy liquor meant for his lips, was looking while the liquor was flowing (flower at the buttonhole: who gave it to him?), and syrupped to him in her own voice ...]

The Italian translations can harness the near-homophony of the fricative-liquid clusters *flui, fio,* similarly expressive of a fluent passage of breath. De Angelis's and Terrinoni's versions underline the homophony by using the infinite of the verb *fluire* to echo *fiore*; only Terrinoni's translation reproduces the clipped "*l'am/lo*," the others explicitating it to *porta male* (*brings bad luck*). De Angelis's version supplements musicality with extra alliteration; he and Celati occasionally opt for obsolete wording (for example *orciolo,* used mostly in Florentine Italian, for "jar"). In Hungarian, since there is no similitude between flow (*foly-ik*) and flower (*virág*), Szentkuthy's translation and the "Revised" version clip a different set of words:

A virág vigasztalás nekem, és a tű megöli a *szerel. Virágnyelv valamit jel.* [Standard Hungarian: ... a tű megöli a *szerelmet.* Virágnyelv valamint *jelent*] (H/Sz 325; H/"R" 256; my emphasis) [Flower is consolation to me, and the needle kills *lo* (*szerelem:* love). Flower language something *sign* (*jel = sign; jelent = signify*).]

Bronzalány, töltögetve-öntögetve a ragadós, szirupos folyadékot a flaskóból a férfi szájának szánva, nézte ahogy *folyik* (*foly*vást a virág a mellén: kitől? kitől?) és szirup-szirénkedve ... (H/Sz 327; with minor changes; H/"R" 257; my emphasis) [Bronzegirl, pouring-gushing the gluey, syrupy fluid from the flask to the man's mouth destined, watched as it *flowed* (*continuously* that flower on his chest: from whom? from whom?) and syrup-sireningly ...]

Szentkuthy's translation capitalizes on strong alliterative sound-effects, using for bottle the slightly archaic *flaskó* (flask). The original's fricative-liquid *fl*-cluster is approximated in the aural association *folyik* (flows)—*folyvást* (continuously; the root of the word being "*foly*," *flow*), so the whole phrase is transformed into a (lexically) onomatopoeic "language of flow" organized on the basis of "the similar sounds"—rhyme, rhythmicity, (temporal, spatial) repetition. Disrupting the verbal surface, such echoes, rhymes, and homophonies contribute to a disseminative language poetics, a prioritizing of lateral proliferation of meaning. In "Sirens," these effects of language are poignantly linked with word clippings and gaps to be filled—(physical) silences created in the text that provoke translation while resisting it.

The episode's most orgasmic example of the language of flow that encapsulates the syllable of *love*, open, unended, comes at the culmination point of *M'appari*:

> Words? Music? No: it's what's behind.
> Bloom looped, unlooped, noded, disnoded.
> Bloom. Flood of warm jamjam lickitup secretness flowed to flow in music out, in desire, dark to lick flow invading. *Tipping her tepping her tapping her topping her. Tup.* Pores to dilate dilating. *Tup.* The joy the feel the warm the. *Tup.* To pour o'er sluices pouring gushes. Flood, gush, flow, joygush, *tupthrob.* Now! Language of love.

> U 11.703; my emphasis

The passage seems a textbook example of poetic language in which the physical world "seems to come closer than is usually possible in language" (Attridge 1988: 149), and where the artful patterning of phonetic content—the descending scale of vowels in rhythmically repetitive monosyllabic verbs—enhances semantic content, fluidifying and eroticizing speech:

> *Tapintani, tapogatni, tépegetni, tiporgatni. Tipp.* Táguló pórus tágassága. *Topp.* Milyen jól érezni a melegét. *Tapp.* Ömlengő ömlő nedvet önteni. Áradás, ömlés, folyás, ráalélás. Ez az! Szerelem nyelve. (H/G I/221; my emphasis) [To (keep) feel(ing), finger(ing), tear(ing), stomp(ing) (suffix *-gat/get*: repetitive act). Tip. Widening pore's width. Top. How well you can feel its warmth. Tapp. Overflowing pouring juice to pour. Flooding, pouring, flowing, swooning-on-it. That's it! Language of love.]
>
> *Hímjajoddal bimbaját, kéjecsengő csiklaját, most, most nyomd a nászod jászolát.* Nyomd. Táguló szövet tágulatot követ. Nyomd. Melegérzésörömea. Nyomd. Tágul, tömítsd, ondó te omló. Áradás, szatírszökőkút, folyik, kéjpatak—most! *Hormonheréd hímharmatát!* Szerelem *szókincse.* (H/Sz 340; my emphasis) [(*With your) male-woe (her) bud, (her) pleasure-ringing clitoris, now, push now your nuptial's manger.* Push. Dilating tissue follows dilation. Push. Warm-feel's-joy-the. Push. (It) dilates, fill it, sperm thou streaming. Flooding, satyr-artesian-well, (it) flows, bliss-brook—now! (Acc.) Your hormone-testicles' male-dew! Vocabulary of love.]

In examining how the successive Hungarian translations deal with this passage, it is worth citing a 1947 essay by novelist Miklós Szentkuthy, the translator-to-be of *Ulysses,* on the first Hungarian translation by Endre Gáspár that came out in 1947. What makes this early critique especially interesting are its powerful statements against a domesticating translation practice that tends to normalize unruliness, to disambiguate, homogenize, discursify, and its declarations of faith by Joyce's anomalies and disruptive musical language effects. Szentkuthy almost programmatically selects examples where Joyce prioritizes sound effects over syntax, and claims that such ungrammaticalities should not be ironed out in translation either; on the other hand, he praises his predecessor for his occasional bold, inventive departures from literariness, where strong sound effects are created—again, tellingly for his own later practice.

Here Szentkuthy objects to Gáspár's rendering, in the Overture, of "Full tup. Full throb" (*U* 11.25) with the longer and less erotic "Teli fekvés. Teli lüktetés" (Full lying. Full vibration [H/G I/205]), and to Gáspár's failure to recognize that in the sequence of monosyllabic verbs referring to animal copulation organized along a descending scale of "light" to "dark" vowels, Joyce repeats the same verb "tup" three times, whereas in Hungarian three different words are used (Szentkuthy 2014: 138–9). Gáspár's word choices, similarly on a descending scale of vowels (*Tipp–Topp–Tapp*) may be termed lexical onomatopoeia: whereas *tipp* means *tip* (e.g. a horse race tip), and *tipp-topp*, "tip-top, ship-shape," *topp* associates the verb *(be)toppan*: "to step in, enter (suddenly)"; *tapp* would associate the verb *tapint* ("feel, palpate")—thus with no or very weak sexual connotations, seemingly assembled on the basis of their closeness to Joyce's originals. To enhance the sense of foreignizing, almost literalist translation, we have the nonce compound "*meleg jimjam*" for Joyce's "warm jamjam," suggestive mostly of an *English* onomatopoeia: *yum-yum*, since the Hungarian equivalent would have been (*nyim/nyam-*)*nyam*.[8]

In Szentkuthy's translation, the original's alliterating plosives are supplanted by soft bilabial *m*-s and palatal *ny*-s; even the recurring verb for copulation, "tup," is rendered with a soft *nyomd* ("push": low coll., "copulate"). The sequence of monosyllables is liberally traded in for a rhythmic and internally rhyming line with a strong trochaic lilt; the intense musical effect comes from the alliterating nonce compounds, with pervasive erotic overtones and explicit sexual content that yields an intensely erotic language of flow.

As against Szentkuthy's flights of fancy, the "Revised" text returns on many points to Gáspár's solutions of more than half a century earlier:

> *Tapogasd, tiporgasd, tépegesd, teperd magad alá. Döfd.* Táguló nyílások tágulnak. *Döfd. Melegérzésörömea. Döfd.* Gáttörő, áttörő, zúduló ömlések. Áradás, ömlés, áramlás, örömömlés, dobbanó döfés. Most! Szerelem szókincse. (H/"R" 267; my emphasis) [(Imper.) (Keep) finger(ing), stomp(ing), tear(ing), press (her) under you. Thrust. Dilating openings dilate. Thrust. Warm-feel's-joy-the. Thrust.

Dam-breaking, through-breaking, cascading pourings. Flooding, outpouring, streaming, joy-streaming, throbbing thrust. Now! Vocabulary of love.]

The verb "tup" becomes *döfd* (imperative "thrust"), while the list of alliterating, eroticized verbs share a violent quality; the participial sequences have a somewhat more subdued pattern of internal rhymes but even so, an almost full word repetition ("Gáttörő, áttörő": "dam-breaking, through-breaking") adds playfulness.

> *Tastarla, tenerla, titillarla, toccarla. Tup.* Pori dilatati che si dilatano. *Tup.* Il piacere il tocco il calore il. *Tup.* Scrosciare delle cateratte di scrosci scroscianti. Fiotto, scroscio, flusso, scroscio di piacere, *tuppalpito.* Ora! Linguaggio d'amore. (I/DA 253; my emphasis) [Feeling (her), holding (her), tickling (her), touching (her). Tup. Dilated pores that are dilating. Tup. The pleasure the touch the warmth the. Cascading (*onom.*) of waterfalls of cascading outpours. Gush, outpour, flux, outpour of pleasure, tupthrob. Now! Language of love.]
>
> *Toccala, coccola, tappala, coprila. Copula.* Pori dilatanti dilatandosi. *Copula.* La gioia il tatto il caldo il. *Copula.* Trabocca sulle cateratte traboccanti fiotti. Fiume, fiotto, getto di gioia, *palpitacopula.* Ora! Lingua dell'amore. (I/T 281–2; my emphasis) [(Imper.) Touch her, cuddle, plug her, cover her. Copulate. Dilating (trans.) pores dilating. Copulate. The joy the touch the warmth the. Overflowing with gushes on the overflowing waterfalls. Stream, gush, jet of joy, throbcopulate. Now! Language of love.]
>
> *Nel ticchio d'un tremulo tocco alla tumida toppa. Tàppete.* Dilatansi i debili pori dolciori spandendo. *Tìppete.* Subisso dei sensi instradati nel gaudio in sopranza. *Tòppete.* Nel flusso di foia versando umidori felici. Fiotto, scroscio, flusso, sgorgo del piacere, tip-tap-palpito. Ecco! Lingua dell'amore. (I/C 378; my emphasis) [In the tic of a trembling touch on the swollen keyhole. *Tàppete.* The weak pores dilate spreading sweet(ish) odours. *Tìppete.* Overwhelming (= condition of being overwhelmed) of the derouted senses in extreme pleasure. *Tòppete.* In the flux of rut pouring happy moistness. Gush, outpour, flux, spurt of pleasure, tip-tap-throb. Behold! Language of love.]

The Italian translations also show considerable differences in emulating the original's staccato. De Angelis lists four verbs related to the tactile and to erotic fingering, and preserves Joyce's "tup" unchanged, as a quasi-onometopoeic word that throbs in the Italian "tuppalpito." Terrinoni substitutes a string of rhyming, near-homophonous verbs with a strong dactylic lilt, playing on the rhythmic variation of *to-* and *co-* syllables (*toccala, coccola, tappala, coprila*), culminating in the explicit "*copula*" for "tup." Gianni Celati's alliterative phrase, chimingly descending on the phonetic scale, "*Nel ticchio d'un tremulo tocco alla tumida toppa,*" seems to prioritize sound effects over semantics; it is euphemistic and circumlocutory ("toppa" meaning "keyole") where Joyce's original is explicit. Curiously, the repetitive Joycean "tup" is replaced by *tuppete tappete*, the onomatopoeic sound of horse's hooves or horse trap in Italian, also used in child language for the sound of objects tumbling—and the refrain of a traditional Naples song[9]—in an instance of similar phonesthetic configuration with vastly different semantic connotations from the original. In addition, Celati employs alliterative strings with a liberal amount of arcane vocabulary: the obsolete *debili* for *deboli*, "weak"; the archaic *gaudio* for "pleasure, joy," with sacred rather than erotic overtones; a north Italian dialect term, *sopranza*, also used by Dante as a verb, for "supreme, extreme," slipping in another silent Dante quote.[10]

What happens when it is translation that brings additional erasure, white paint, beyond the silences offered by the original? Such a case is at work with one of the specific translation problems of "Sirens": of passages where the closed monosyllables, transcending their semantic valences, become sound-events, lexical onomatopoeia whose reading depends on their rhythmicity. The passages describing the movements of the bald and deaf waiter Pat are perhaps the best-known candidates for this staccato technique: the rigorous eight-syllable sequences of the Overture and of the third example below suggest the musical scale's eight tones with their musical variations. The stylistic effect depends on the possibilities of syntactically ordering a series of monosyllabic words, yet what English as a nearly isolating language can achieve may prove impossible with either inflecting or agglutinating languages.

> Deaf bold Pat brought pad knife took up.
>
> U 11.30

> Bold Pat at a sign drew nigh. A pen and ink. He went. A pad. He went. A pad to blot. He heard, deaf Pat.
>
> U 11.822

> Bold deaf Pat brought quite flat pad ink. Pad set with ink pen quite flat pad. Pat took plate dish knife fork. Pat went.
>
> U 11.847

One of the stylistically most daring solutions brought by the "Revised" Hungarian *Ulysses* touches these passages. Whereas Szentkuthy's earlier translation attempted to make up for the lost staccatoing effect with enhanced rhythmicity (the first and second sentence of the example below spelling out the traditional meter of Hungarian folk poetry, with stressed first syllables: 4/4 and 6/6), and in the Overture experimented with grammatically indeterminate, anomalous verb and noun forms lacking the proper ending that would inscribe person, number, and tense, respectively the accusative, the new version operates with eight clipped, closed monosyllables that the reader has to supplement morpho-syntactically:

> A kopasz Pat intésre jön. Tollat és tintát. Elment. És itatóst a papírhoz. Hallotta a süket. (H/Sz 344) [The bald Pat comes at a wave (4/4 rhythm). (Acc.) Pen and ink. And blot for the paper. Heard the deaf (has).]
>
> Kopasz süket Pat lapos tömböt hoz. Tintával a tollat leteszi laposan. Elvitte a tányért, tálat, kést, villát. Elment. (H/Sz 345) [Bald deaf Pat flat pad brings. With ink the pen he places flatly (5/5, 6/6 rhythm). He took away the plate, knife, fork. He went.]

The "Revised" version instead presents the reader with a rigorous staccato in the overture and its variation midway through the episode:

> Kop sük Pat hoz tömb visz kés vill. (H/"R" 249) [normative Hungarian: Kop*asz* süke*t* Pat hoz tömb*öt* (Acc.) visz kés*t* vill*át* (Acc.): Bald deaf Pat bring(s) pad take(s) knife fork.]
>
> Kop sük Pat hoz toll tint lap tömb. Pat tesz tint toll Bloom lap tömb le. Pat visz tány tál kés vill. Pat megy. (H/"R" 270) [normative: Kop*asz* süke*t* Pat hoz toll*at* tint*át* lap*ot* tömb*öt* (Acc.). Pat (le)tesz tint*át* toll*at* Bloom (elé) lap*ot* tömb*öt* **le**. Pat visz tény*ért* tál*at* kés*t* vill*át*. Pat megy: Bald deaf Pat bring(s) pen ink sheet pad. Pat put(s) ink pen Bloom sheet pad down. Pat take(s) plate tray knife fork. Pat go(es).]

Arguably, the "Revised" text, with its patches of white paint, its poignant erasures, is even more defamiliarizing and disruptive than the original, and therefore the sound effect is more heightened. Not only does the Hungarian reader need to supply noun and verbal suffixes and postpositions, but even some of the root words are clipped (for instance, "kop-asz, sük-et": bald, deaf). What is particularly striking in this tiny theme and variations sequence is that even Hungarian grammar is estranged and virtually back-dated: the particle "le" (*down*) at the end of the second sentence seems to suggest either a verbal prefix (usually agglutinated to the verb, as in German) that achieved independence—presumably from the verb *tesz: le-tesz*, put down—or a quaint feature of medieval Hungarian, known from the earliest text documents in the language, where a range of suffixes or post-positions inscribing location and direction, agglutinated to the noun in modern Hungarian, were used independently, after the noun. This may well be a positive example of inventiveness in translation that withstands the domesticating pull of the receiving cultural field by affirming the multiple powers of language in a (re)creative transfer that seeks to empower the original's singularity and cultural alterity.

At the end of her essay, Anne Carson writes:

> As a classicist I was trained to strive for exactness and to believe that rigorous
> knowledge of the world without any residue is possible for us. This residue,
> which does not exist—just to think of it refreshes me. To think of its position,
> how it shares its position with drenched layers of nothing, to think of its motion,
> how it can never stop moving because I am in motion with it, to think of its
> shadow, which is cast by nothing and so has no death in it (or very little)—to
> think of these things gives me a sensation of getting free.
>
> Carson 2013: 32

Translation, by definition, makes a text understood to the foreign-language
reader. In this sense, a deliberate stopping short of mediation, of the transfer of
meaning, is a gesture that provokes translation and faces it with its limit, where
achievement, solving the crux, becomes a betrayal of the original's silence. These
instances of falling silent, or non-achieving "untranslating" (Carson 2013: 32),
are vital to the adventure of translation: in them the space between languages,
between foreignnesses, becomes audible, like the tissue of overtones and
(impossible) dynamics in the participatory listening to Kurtág's *Games*.

Notes

1   Both Terrinoni and Celati introduce their translation objectives in their prefaces.
    Terrinoni published two in-depth discussions of his essentially foreignizing poetics
    in retranslating Joyce's classic, "Beyond Mutability and Change" and "Who's Afraid
    of Translating *Ulysses*?" (2013), with particular emphasis on recreating the
    indeterminacies of Joyce's text. The most detailed comparative analysis of the Italian
    translations of *Ulysses* to date is found in Serenella Zanotti's *Italian Joyce* (2013), and
    in Michaela Marroni's essay "Silenzio, Molly parla italiano" (2012/2013). As regards
    the Hungarian translations, the members of the translator team have explained their
    methodology and objectives in a series of articles and interviews in both Hungarian
    and English; of these, the most sensitive to Joyce's disruptive stylistic features are
    Marianna Gula's "Lost a Bob but Found a Tanner" (2010) and "The Irish Dimension
    of the Canonical Hungarian Translation of *Ulysses* (1974) and Its Remake (2012)"
    (2015), whereas team coordinator András Kappanyos's outlines of the retranslation/
    re-editing process ("At the End of One's Witz," 2008 and "Fragments of a Report,"
    2010) are limited to presenting the solutions for a few translation cruxes, important
    in the novel's scaffolding of recurring motifs. To date, the most nuanced comparative
    analysis of the Hungarian translations is Dalma Véry's 2014 study; see also my "The
    Trials of Foreignization" (2016).

2 Rabaté confronts the inherent silence of language in "Sirens" with Kafka's 1917 short prose piece "The Silence of the Sirens" (1986) where the sirens are literally, and actively, silent. In his wake, Richard Brown addresses the working of synaesthesia, of "displacement and transference between the senses," mostly the aural and the visual (2012: 95) in both works, illuminating it with philosopher Michel Serres's *The Five Senses: A Philosophy of Mingled Bodies* (2008).

3 In her essay "Silent Translation in Joyce" in this volume Serenella Zanotti describes a scaffolding of covert allusions to Dante throughout Joyce's text-world as "silent translations." At the same time, such literary allusions that pepper *Ulysses*, of which the "Calypso" passage is an example, could be seen as part of Joyce's consistent aesthetic of error, "miswriting," and (mis)quotation that, as Tim Conley shows, relativizes any distinction between "correct" and "mis"quotation, rendering any quote out of context and, ultimately, a reauthoring or "metempsychosis" of the original at the hand of Joyce's characters or the novel's metaconsciousness (Conley 2013: 213–19).

4 The following abbreviations of Italian and Hungarian translations of *Ulysses* will be used throughout this chapter: Italian text by Giulio De Angelis will be referenced as I/DA; by Terrinoni, as I/T; by Celati, as I/C. Hungarian text by Gáspár will be referenced as H/G; by Szentkuthy, as H/Sz, and by Kappanyos et al., as H/"R" ("Revised").

5 "D'una dama col dolcemele/ un tempo ebbi visione," trans. Alessandro Ceni, *La Ballata del Vecchio Marinaio, Kubla Khan*, 61. A previous translation renders these lines as "Una fanciulla con salterio/ Io vidi in una visione," with *salterio*—the psaltery or cither, that can refer either to the hand-plucked or to the somewhat larger, hammered variant of the instrument family—occupying a middle stance.

6 By poet Lőrinc Szabó: "Ismertem egy lányt valaha . . ./ Abora hegyéről dalolt / s *cimbalmot* pengetett," in *Wordsworth és Coleridge versei* (1982: 262).

7 Szentkuthy's flamboyant 1974 translation studs the *Ulysses* text with portmanteaux, seemingly approaching it from the unbound semiosis of the *Wake*—packaging the experience of reading two texts in one for the Hungarian reader: see my "Horsey Women and Arse-temises" (Mihálycsa 2012). His appropriating translation reorchestrates Joyce's polyphonic language into Szentkuthy's idiosyncratic, but ultimately repetitive medley of nonce compounds, erudition terms, and at times multilingual puns. This tendency, together with Szentkuthy's carelessness in recreating the text's vital network of structural echoes, has invited criticism very similar in content to the criticism written of Celati's translation.

8 The closest connotation of "jam" in Hungarian at the time of the translation's publishing (1947) would have been the (English-derived) word *jam*, marmalade—as well as invoking a ghost of *yin-yang*, of male and female principles joined. Another contiguity is that "Sirens" is punctuated by the *tap, tap, tapping* of the blind piano tuner's stick, which is rendered both by Gáspár and in the "Revised" text as *tapp*.

9   https://musopen.org/sheetmusic/34776/teodoro-cottrau/tippete-tuppete-tappete/
(accessed March 17, 2017).

10 I am indebted to Enrico Terrinoni for his help in clarifying Celati's Italian
translation. Just like Szentkuthy, Celati is an acclaimed experimental novelist who
seems to have approached translation with evident writerly ambitions, tending to
"hypercodify" the *Ulysses* text (Marroni 2012/2013: 62). Critiques of his *Ulisse*, while
highlighting the text's linguistic inventiveness, point out that it abuses the same
layers of vocabulary (mostly archaic and northern Italian regional terms; d'Erme
2013: 127), and ends up being "more visible than the language of the translated
author," while "rather limited in comparison with the linguistic mechanisms and
polysemy of *Ulysses*" (Marroni 2012/2013: 61, 70).

References

Attridge, D. (1988), *Peculiar Language: Literature as Difference from the Renaissance to
James Joyce*, Ithaca, NY: Cornell University Press.

Attridge, D. (2004), *The Singularity of Literature*, London and New York:
Routledge.

Brown, R. (2012), "Joyce's and Kafka's 'Sirens' and the Modernity of the Senses," in
D. Vichnar, D. Spurr, and M. Groden (eds), *Praharfeast: James Joyce in Prague*,
90–103, Prague: Litteraria Pragensia.

Carson, A. (2013), "Variations on the Right to Remain Silent," in *Nay, Rather*, Cahiers
Series 21, London: Sylph Editions.

Coleridge, S. T. (1994), *La Ballata del Vecchio Marinaio, Kubla Khan*, trans. A. Ceni,
Milan: Feltrinelli.

Coleridge, S. T. (n.d.), *Kubla Khan*, http://www.poetryfoundation.org/poem/173247
(accessed March 17, 2017).

Congreve, W. (n.d.), *The Mourning Bride. A Tragedy*, http://quod.lib.umich.edu/cgi/t/
text/text-idx?c=ecco;idno=004792189.0001.000 (accessed March 17, 2017).

Conley, T. (2013), "Misquoting Joyce," in R. B. Kershner and T. Mecsnóber (eds), *Joycean
Unions: Post-Millenial Essays from East to West*, 209–24, European Joyce Studies 22,
Amsterdam: Rodopi.

d'Erme, E. (2013), "James Joyce, *Ulisse*. Gianni Celati," in F. Ruggieri and E. Terrinoni
(eds), *Joyce in/and Italy*, 127–34, *Joyce Studies in Italy* 14, Rome: Edizioni Q.

Gula, M. (2010), "Lost a Bob but Found a Tanner: from a Translator's Workshop,"
Scientia Traductionis 8: 122–33, http://www.periodicos.ufsc.br/index.php/scientia/
article/view/17629/18129 (accessed March 17, 2017).

Gula, M. (2015), "'The spirt has been well caught': The Irish Dimension of the Canonical
Hungarian Translation of *Ulysses* (1974) and Its Remake (2012)," *Hungarian Journal
of English and American Studies* 21, no. 1: 123–50.

Halász, P. (2006), "Kurtág-töredékek" [Kurtág fragments], in D. Moldován (ed.), *Tisztelet Kurtág Györgynek* [Hommage à György Kurtág], 83–141, Budapest: Rózsavölgyi.

Joyce, J. (1947), *Ulysses*, trans. E. Gáspár, Vols. I–II, Budapest: Franklin.

Joyce, J. (1973), *Ulisse*, trans. G. De Angelis, with G. Cambon, C. Izzo, and G. Melchiori, intro. G. Melchiori, 1st edn 1960, Milan: Mondadori.

Joyce, J. (1974), *Ulysses*, trans. M. Szentkuthy, ed. T. Bartos, Budapest: Európa.

Joyce, J., *Ulysses* (1993), ed. H. W. Gabler, with W. Steppe and C. Melchior, afterword M. Groden, 2nd edn, New York: Vintage.

Joyce, J. (2012), *Ulisse*, ed. and trans. E. Terrinoni with C. Bigazzi, Rome: Newton Compton.

Joyce, J. *Ulysses* (2012), trans. and ed. A. Kappanyos, M. Gula, G. Z. Kiss, and D. Szolláth, based on the trans. of M. Szentkuthy, Budapest: Európa.

Joyce, J. (2013), *Ulisse*, trans. G. Celati, Turin: Einaudi.

Kappanyos, A. (2008), "At the End of One's Witz (Translation Theory – and Some Practice)," *Papers on Joyce* 14: 38–49.

Kappanyos, A. (2010), "Fragments of a Report: Ulysses Translation in Progress," *James Joyce Quarterly* 47, no. 4: 553–66.

Lawrence, K. (2010), *Who's Afraid of James Joyce?*, Gainesville: University Press of Florida.

Marroni, M. (2012/2013), "Silenzio, Molly parla italiano. Perché tradurre *Ulysses*," *Traduttologia. Rivista di Interpretazione e Traduzione* 7–8 (July–January): 57–80.

Mihálycsa, E. (2012), "Horsey Women and Arse-temises: Wake-ing *Ulysses* in Translation," in F. Ruggieri and E. Terrinoni (eds), *Why Read Joyce in the 21st Century?*, *Joyce Studies in Italy* 13, 79–91, Rome: Edizioni Q.

Mihálycsa, E. (2016), "The Trials of Foreignization: Transposing Joyce's 'Farraginous Chronicle'," in P. Paparunas, F. Ilmberger, and M. Heusser (eds), *Parallaxing Joyce*, 247–74, Tübingen: Günter Narr.

Mooney, S. (1999), "Bronze by Gold by Bloom: Echo, the Invocatory Drive, and the 'Aurteur' in Sirens," in Sebastian Knowles (ed.), *Bronze by Gold: The Music of Joyce*, 229–44, New York and London: Garland.

Nancy, J.-L. (2007), *Listening*, trans. Charlotte Mandell, New York: Fordham University Press.

Rabaté, J.-M. (1986) "The Silence of the Sirens," in M. Beja, M. Harmon, P. Herring, and D. Norris (eds), *James Joyce: The Centennial Symposium*, 82–8, Urbana and Chicago: University of Illinois Press.

Szentkuthy, M. (2014), "James Joyce," trans. E. Mihálycsa, *Hyperion* VIII, no. 1: 119–45, http://contramundum.net/wp-content/uploads/2012/05/10.0%E2%80%94SzM-JJ_Summa_Atheo%E2%80%93H-8.1.14.pdf (accessed March 17, 2017).

Terrinoni, E. (2012), "Beyond Mutability and Change. Translating Joyce's *Ulysses*: A Study in Ambiguity," *Scientia Traductionis* 12, no. 2: 45–56, https://periodicos.ufsc.br/index.php/scientia/article/view/1980-4237.2012n12p45/23805 (accessed March 17, 2017).

Terrinoni, E. (2013), "Who's Afraid of Translating *Ulysses?*," *Translation and Literature* 22, no. 2: 240–8.

Véry, D. (2014), "Az *Ulysses*t olvasva" [Reading *Ulysses*], *Nagyvilág* 59, no. 5: 541–96.

Wordsworth és Coleridge Versei [The Poems of Wordsworth and Coleridge] (1982), Budapest: Európa.

Woolf, V. (1981), *To the Lighthouse*, New York: Harcourt Brace Jovanovich.

Zanotti, S. (2013), *Italian Joyce: A Journey through Language and Translation*, Bologna: Bononia University Press.

Zanotti S. (2018), "Silent Translation in Joyce's Writing," this volume.

Coda: Modernism/Silence

15

Forms of Silence in Literary Writing: James Joyce and Modernism

Franca Ruggieri

The use of the term *silence* is not limited to suggest a void of articulate or inarticulate sounds. In colloquial as well as in literary language, both the notion and the term *silence* suggest multifarious associations of ideas, metaphors, and oxymora. "The rest is silence," Hamlet's last, incisive, apodeictic words (Act V, Sc. 2, 395) announce his immediate death and the end of his narration, but also stigmatize the inanity of the tragic tangle of passions and words that has been unfolding through the five acts of the play.

A "speaking silence" is part of everyday communication. And around us, in nature, as well as in fiction, there is also a special silence that is a metaphor for the unspeakable made audible: a silence that seems to interpret all the sounds of the universe. It is this form of supreme silence that features in any musical composition and performance, and which Riccardo Chailly, present operatic conductor at La Scala, seems to hint at when, in discussing the function of the musical pause in the context of any musical text, he defines *the sound of silence* as the *most intense music* (2015: 9).

Edvard Munch's *The Scream* (1893) is perhaps the most expressive image of the anguished silence that the individual felt condemned to during the *fin de siècle*. A specific medical condition, the description of a precise autobiographical event meticulously described in Munch's diary, seems to preannounce a more general sense of the unease and impotence of an entire generation, a generation sorely tested by the inadequacy of words and thus drawn to silence. The silent scream in all four versions of the work, all dramatic in their different ways, is rendered by the curving contorted lines of the body, consumed by, and unformed against, an inflamed, red-streaked fragmented sky above a green and blue landscape. This seems an eloquent metaphor of the silence that anticipates the alienation and crisis of "The Short Twentieth Century," as the subtitle of Eric Hobsbawm's book, *The Age of Extremes*, describes it.

Silence in literary texts is a vast, and inevitably elusive, topic, which is much discussed in aesthetics and psychoanalysis. Indeed, such a subject immediately suggests an analysis which ideally should prod much deeper than the interpretation offered here. Rather than highly structured, the present reading is impressionistic and rhapsodic, albeit furnished with some specific examples. Considering the deep philosophical, aesthetic, and psychoanalytic aspects of this issue, Franco Rella's essay, *Il silenzio e le parole* (1984), might be still extremely revealing, since his investigation follows the complex development of his topic from Friederich Nietzsche to Gianni Vattimo, and is occasionally supported by literary texts, mostly by French and German writers.

*   *   *

Our age is strongly conditioned by a deep, ongoing crisis at every level, including that of everyday speech. It started with the great *fin de siécle*, and it continued throughout the twentieth century and into the present one. The long experience of "weak thought"[1] was blindly followed by other forms of thought, often centralized and populist. Indeed, the discourse of crisis regarding the value of culture and tradition, and the sense of the fragmentariness and lack of identity, are themes that convey a common sense of confusion and fragility. There is still a loss of a center that can hold things together; the distance between the falcon and the falconer increases and "things fall apart," as Yeats says in "The Second Coming" (1920). T. S. Eliot echoes this in *The Waste Land* (1922): we have little but the "fragments I have shored against my ruins." It is a century-long "work in progress," as our reflections on the crisis continually evolve. These reflections, depending on the context, trigger different responses to the crisis itself: criticism, rejection, acceptance, opportunism, exploitation, resignation, silence. And meanwhile, the general lessening of any promise of progress in culture and literature, as well as of an ethical vision and enlightened politics, is reflected in the stale chatter of the media, the din of advertising, the music of commerce, the obsession with celebrity and visibility, and even in the tired but relentless consumerism of literary production. For these very reasons, our times display a fascination with, and even the need for, silence. This, however, often seems unachievable or impossible in a culture that increasingly rewards the appearance of things rather than asking what their true meaning really is. On the other hand, the forms, functions and languages of silence have marked, and continue to mark, history and communication in its development from an oral to a written tradition, and its complicated, subsequent evolution.

In the early twentieth century, modernist culture was the most intense expression of disquiet with its complete renewal of form, its modes, genres, and languages, as well as with the challenges posed by new codes and new registers. There was curiosity and experimentation, new techniques, the acceptance of fragmentation and the everyday routine as proper subjects, the revisitation of myths, the search for a new "total art." At the same time, there was also a persistent attempt at giving prose the quality of poetry—lyricism and rhythm—with an exploration of different hybrid forms of literary expression, which, as Giorgio Melchiori announced in *The Tightrope Walkers* (1956), was eventually fully achieved in *Finnegans Wake*. These were just some of the varied and various challenges that the culture and the writing of modernism proposed. In this shifting, fertile terrain, allusive silence played an essential role in its interaction with the speech spoken aloud. It was a fruitful contest, ranging from the silence of the empty space of an absence of story within the text, to the expression of the solitary voice of the stream of consciousness, which, when the voice falls silent, suggests—with limitless hyper-realism—its own reproduction and representation, which is also part of the real. And this form of silence was also a close, and not coincidental, rendering of the necessary correspondence between form and matter that Joyce announced in that letter to Carlo Linati dated September 21, 1920, in which he anticipated that each adventure should not only condition but even create its own technique (*SL* 270–1).

*   *   *

The experience of eternal return had concluded, for Zarathustra, in profound silence, since he could not find the words to express the thoughts of others:

> ... but Zarathustra did not hear that they [the animals that had called him "the master of eternal return"] were silent. On the contrary, he lay quietly with closed eyes like a person sleeping, although he did not sleep; for he communed just then with his soul. The serpent, however, and the eagle, when they found him silent in such wise, respected the great stillness around him, and prudently retired.
>
> Nietzsche 1974: 240

The idea of eternal return ended in total silence. Zarathustra "made the first great act of accusation against the dominant rationalist order, although he did not have the words to formulate an alternative philosophy" (Rella 1984: 113).

It was in 1902 that Hugo von Hofmannsthal made the choice of silence in order to express his frustration with the inadequacy of language and to communicate his decision to give up writing. Resorting to a traditional literary ploy, he took the pseudonym of Lord Chandos, the youngest son of the "Lord of Bath," and he wrote an imaginary letter to Francis Bacon which he dated August 22, 1603. This was not a random date: in the same year the reign of James I began and, a few months earlier, Bacon was knighted. In the letter, von Hofmannsthal announced his definitive and irrevocable abandonment of literary life because of the failure of language, the collapse of the "natural" relationship between signifier and signified. Critical attention was drawn to the points that Hofmannsthal made in *The Lord Chandos Letter* when, many years later, the Bollingen Foundation asked Hermann Broch to write an introduction to Hofmannstahl's work. This resulted in *Hugo von Hofmannsthal and His Time: The European Imagination 1860–1920*,[2] which, to all intents and purposes, is an "intellectual history of Europe," as Broch himself defined it in a letter to a publisher friend. Indeed, it was a highly significant commentary on the state of culture and European literature, and on the roots and nature of Hofmannsthal's times. Broch believed in the need for a relationship between art and ethics, and that art is a form of knowledge, the total knowledge of man, society, and history. Some years earlier, these principles had been the inspiration for Broch's excellent and still topical essay, "James Joyce and the Present Age," published in 1936.[3] Here Joyce is hailed as representative of a new age, the creator of the new novel of simultaneity and epic totality:

> But it is also as though Joyce . . . had intended to adopt a definite position with regard to the possibility of imitating the world and to poetic creation in general. Through the complexity of his representational apparatus, through the . . . esoteric nature of his conceptual and linguistic process . . . through the gigantic superstructure he has erected over the poetic immediacy that lies hidden beneath, it is as though Joyce wanted to furnish proof . . . that it is precisely the success of this sort of enormous undertaking . . . precisely the hypertrophic power of expression to which the writer is driven, which makes it possible to express the *inarticulateness of a world that is condemned to remain mute*.
>
> Broch 1949: 74–5; my emphasis

From the time when Broch wrote this to the present, there has been an increased sense of loss of completeness, accompanied by a growth of specialist areas and the compartmentalization and fragmentation of knowledge. The echoes of such polyphonous dissonance continue to be heard: despite the excess of information, any chance for real communication is reduced, thus confirming the condemnation to silence in a world of fragmented, marginalized individuals who are neither represented nor representable, isolated, and, ultimately, increasingly *condemned to silence*.

In 1918, when Ludwig Wittgenstein was writing a short foreword to his *Tractatus Logico-Philosophicus*, he said the following: "The book deals with the problems of philosophy, and shows, I believe, that the reason why these problems are posed is that the logic of our language is misunderstood. The whole sense of the book might be summed up in the following words: *what can be said at all can be said clearly, and what we cannot talk about we must pass over in silence*" (2001: 3; my emphasis). He specified that the aim of the book was to draw a limit to the expression of thoughts. That sentence—"what can be said at all can be said clearly, and what we cannot talk about we must pass over in silence"— remains a prime theoretical reference point with regard to the reading of literary texts, and, of course, those on the philosophy of language.

For Wittgenstein, silence is pregnant with meaning, and its importance regarding various and diverse choices, reflections, and analyses is as crucial as language is, to the extent that he considered his own aphoristic propositions meaningless. The non-said, the ineffable, is also part of the potential of expressivity; it works its way into language to circumvent its limits, placing itself beyond and conveying—without uttering a *word*—the unsayable. If thought, for Wittgenstein, coincides with language, then the analysis of thought is the analysis of its sayability. What is more, over and beyond what can be said is the *choice* of silence, without the imposition of either writing method or technique. It is a suggestion of the ineffable—whether it be an actual or a referential lack of speech, either mysterious or calculated aphasia—that can become part of what is sayable. The impossibility for language to overcome its limits is sublimated in the evocation of the absolute through silence. Silence accompanies what is ineffable in meditation, which also implies a "mystical" tension. We entrust to silence that which is, without it being able to be, the subject of the discourse; that which is superior to the world of experience is written in silence. Wittgenstein, however, goes further. In fact, it is here that a battle with language begins: beyond the experience of silence it is necessary to fight against the limits of language, change its rules and its laws. If the language of classical reasoning is broken and the fragments become mere "chatter," then the road that must be taken is that which passes through these very remains. It is necessary to go through "the time of words," of ordinary speech and chatter, in order to find a new divergence to reality. And this is possible only by overturning language as a whole, that is, mining the language and the mythologies that have been deposited in it. This was at the heart of the proposal made by Wittgenstein in "Remarks on Frazer's

Golden Bough": "over and beyond the discipline of silence there is a conflict with
language that has to be described," and again, according to Franco Rella, "the
difference lies in the contradictory plurality of the real" (Rella 1984: 21; my
translation). The conclusion for Wittgenstein is negative as regards the demands
of metaphysical "discourse," but it urges a form of thought that is clear, aware of
"limitations," and, as such, "subjectively" elects, beyond any expressive strategies,
what its position is with respect to the real.

*   *   *

For James Joyce, this challenge lasted his whole life. A starting point to introduce
this form of ineffable silence is the passage in *A Portrait of the Artist as a Young
Man* where Shelley's image of the "fading coal," "the luminous, silent stasis" of
aesthetic pleasure is evoked: "a spiritual state very like to that cardiac condition
which the Italian physiologist Luigi Galvani, using a phrase almost as beautiful
as Shelley's, called the enchantment of the heart" (*P* 179).[4] The silence of stasis is
the stasis of silence before the word; for Joyce, this is the very condition for a
fleeting, total vision of the instant of poetic creation.

   In this context, another statement from Joyce that deserves attention is the
often quoted phrase "silence, exile, and cunning" (*P* 208). Stephen Dedalus has
just decided to become an artist, "a priest of eternal imagination" (*P* 186), and
these are the only three weapons he allows himself to use in his fight against the
conditioning and the abuse of family, country, and the Church. Much has been
said about the theme of *exile*, clearly of prime importance to the author of *Exiles*,
while much less has been said about *silence* and *cunning*. Jean Michel Rabaté
(1982: 47) suggested a "chronological" interpretation, writing that, in working
towards intellectual freedom, Stephen's "initial silence defines his refusal to take
part in the political and linguistic" debates in Dublin to the extent of choosing
exile in Paris, as it is stated explicitly in the last lines of the "Journal" that
concludes *A Portrait*. But what role has *cunning*, the third element in this process?
Rabaté proposes associating "silence" with the family, "exile" with nationalism,
and "cunning" with the perverse refusal of religion, concluding that all three
weapons are generally used simultaneously (48). According to Ellmann (*JJII*
354), the source of Stephen's motto is to be found in Honoré de Balzac where the
motto of the hero is "*Fuge . . . Late . . . Tace*" (which translates as "escape, deceit,
silence"). As so often happens with Joyce, however, there is more than one key to
interpret this triple line of action connected to the prophetic vision of the artist.
What comes to mind is the *Ratio Studiorum* and the educational ideals of the
Jesuits which were realized as "strength," "courage," and "cunning." The wise man

should keep silent while meditating the nature of truth. Similarly, *cunning* alludes to the vision when considered from a distance. More than the two other weapons, it encapsulates what is said in the Gospel of St. Matthew (10.16): "So be as cunning as serpents and as innocent as doves." Give everything, but without forgetting the ideals of purity nor losing the soul in any way: the dove must always temper the serpent and vice versa—as another maxim from Catholic Jesuit education would have it. Then again, as Pope Francis, the most popular Jesuit of our times, has recently said, "Do not be satisfied with a mediocre life but [like the Magi] safeguard the faith with holy cunning." What also comes to mind is the role of the pairing of silence and deceit in the bitter science of dissimulation in the Baroque age. This was expressed by Torquato Accetto in 1641 in *Della dissimulazione onesta*, a short treatise that, rather than incite people to tell lies, recommends meditation and caution. Similarly, there was the notorious case of the London trial of the Jesuit Father Garnet, an "equivocator," who lied under oath for a noble cause, that of Guy Fawkes' Gunpowder Plot of 1605. Finally, there is a brief reference to the Jesuit figure of the "equivocator" in the list of stereotypes that the Porter comes out with in *Macbeth* (Act 2, Sc. 3).

In Catholic culture, there is thus a recurring motif of these three qualities to be used by Joyce; they can also be traced back to Joyce's early years and his youthful essays. In "Drama and Life" and "The Day of the Rabblement," there is the difficulty of reconciling pride, detaching oneself in "silence" from the "rabble," and refusing to give up one's beliefs, with the need to interpret life without mediation: "Life we must accept as we see it before our eyes, men and women as we meet them in the real world, not as we apprehend them in the world of faery" (Joyce 2000: 28).

Other forms follow: the experience of silence, the use of silence as a strategy for absence, the fight against it, and the challenging of its limits. We then arrive at the rhetoric of the silence of the author: solitary, distanced from his own work, filing his nails like the God of All Creation, to use the image Joyce borrowed from Flaubert.[5] Then come the "silent words" of the stream of consciousness; the silent words of the reflections and self-analysis of Stephen, Bloom, and Molly. The inner word is a silent soundtrack of their external acts and their interaction with the external reality in which they find themselves. A few examples will suffice: from the passage at the beginning of "Nestor," "Fabled by the daughters of memory" (*U* 2.7) all through that episode, from the "ineluctable modality" (*U* 3.1) in "Proteus," all through the whole novel down to Molly's final monologue: "Yes because he never did a thing like that before as ask to get his breakfast in bed" (*U* 18.1). Finally, there is the oneiric atmosphere of *Finnegans*

Wake, that mad utopia of silence and "total" language which outdoes Babel through its re-enactment of another Babel, all-inclusive, all-modern.

The absolute of silence is also the absolute of the infinite, and similarly infinite are its presences and its modalities. They differ in form and in intensity in real experience, just as they do in literary writing.

*   *   *

As already noted, a profound process of renewal in fiction and poetry was set in motion by modernism in the English-speaking world. In its early years, at the very beginning of the twentieth century, silence became a central and explicit theme in Joseph Conrad's *Heart of Darkness*, published in 1902. Marlow himself, character and narrator, criticizes the limitations of language and the limited communicative potential of the story: "No, it is impossible, it is impossible to convey the sensation of any given epoch of one's existence—that which makes its truth, its meaning—its subtle and penetrating essence. It is impossible. We live, as we dream—alone" (Conrad 1989: 86). And the words of Giuseppe Sertoli are still relevant in respect of the important role of silence in *Heart of Darkness*. Sertoli writes in his 1974 introduction to this complex and fascinating short novel:

> It is not the forest or the savages who are *formless* ... What is *formless* is the silence *of the* language *in the* language itself: this is the true, other side to language, born of the same place and with the same action that brings forth language. Silence is not a deceit of nature ... but the "other side" of spoken words, of the voice that recounts.
>
> Sertoli 1974: xxxviii

It is certainly no coincidence that Sertoli's comment is a reworking Bataille's "La vérité que seul le silence ne trahit pas"/ "The truth that only silence does not betray" (Sertoli 1974: vi). The last part of the novel takes the reader back to the *Nellie*, again anchored in the upper reaches of the Thames, just as it was at the beginning of the tale. We are left with an image of Marlow sitting apart from the others: "Marlow ceased, and sat apart, indistinct and silent, in the pose of a meditating Buddha" (Conrad 1989: 221). The tale thus closes on itself with an image that also provides an internal reference to the narrative frame which has been in place from the very beginning: there is the intense stare of the first narrator, looking out on the silent landscape at sunset, the sky, sea, and land bathed in the changing light, in different shades of colors in the calm and silent, "benign immensity of unstained light" (23). This "serenity of still and exquisite brilliance" (23) evokes for the narrator, as it does for Marlow a few lines later, the vicissitudes of history which the Thames has witnessed. The *Nellie*, "a cruising yawl" (23), is at anchor waiting for the tide to turn; the crew on board is made up of five people, nameless ex-sailors and includes the first narrator. All of them are silent: "we felt meditative," "fit for nothing but placid staring" (23). But Marlow's silent meditative pose sets him apart; his absorbed stare, the feeling that he is removed from the real world, lend him an Oriental air with an ancient timeless wisdom, his silence conjuring up profound images, while the mention of him being like an "idol" seems to suggest an identification with Buddha (24, 220). Then eventually the final silence of Marlow, who has narrated the "darkness" and the terrible story of Kurtz, explicitly echoes Buddha's choice of silence. It is the only conceivable response to fundamental questions which are beyond the domain of the possible. The same is true for that final absolute silence, in the absence of narrative, which pervades the "black bank of clouds, and the tranquil waterway leading to the uttermost ends of the earth ... into the heart of an immense darkness" (220). Into the very heart of the ineffable: that crucial nucleus, that mix of silence, mystery, and darkness that represents that mutable *discordia concors*, and the profound sense and non-sense of human experience.

And here, in this context, it is necessary to refer, at least briefly, to that complex founder of modernism, T. S. Eliot, who appreciated the work of Conrad very much, as some of the most direct allusions and references to Conrad in his poetry show. One of them is in the epigraph to "The Hollow Men": "Mistah Kurtz—he dead" (Eliot 1963: 87). Another is to the passage in *The Heart of Darkness* that relates the end of Kurtz: "The horror! The horror!" Eliot, in fact, had wanted this to be the epigraph to *The Waste Land*, but the idea was abandoned on the advice of Ezra Pound, "il miglior fabbro," who roundly opposed the choice. For Eliot, the quotation from *Heart of Darkness* must have seemed a perfect synthesis of his thoughts: a tragic epiphany, an awareness of the desolation and the crisis of humanity, which is the frustrated, mournful focus of his entire poem. In both quotations, in the announcement of the native boy as well as in the final cries of Kurtz, what is said breaks the silence of expectation and is offered as the object of a continued meditation and reflection for the listener, for the teller, and for the reader in both *Heart of Darkness* and *The Waste Land*. Perhaps it is also possible that during the creative pause at Margate, where Eliot had gone to work on his ambitious poem, he found himself influenced by Conrad's use of the Buddha image, in the solemn meditative pose of Oriental prayer, that is associated with Marlow at the start and the end of the tale. Indeed, this image may well have suggested the presence of Buddha in the third section of *The Waste Land*, "The

Fire Sermon." The fourfold repetition of "Burning" (line 308) in "The Fire Sermon" and the invocation of the *Upanishads* in "Shantih shantih shantih" ("the Peace which passeth understanding") in the final line, all share a suggestion of something that words cannot convey. That peace beyond human comprehension is absolute silence, the final and ineffable mystery of being that only silence can convey. The voice of the speaker in *The Waste Land*, "neither living nor dead," is a voice that "knew nothing, / Looking into the heart of light, the silence" (lines 39–41) and it ends up uttering the word of ineffable peace of the Hindu East.

And in Franz Kafka's short parable, *The Silence of the Sirens*, written on October 23, 1917, silence, as the oxymoron in the title suggests, is the central element. In the space of a single page, one of the most popular classical myths becomes the object of a paradox and is overturned, just as in those same years Homer's hero, Ulysses, is becoming an Irish bourgeois character. The paradox in Kafka's fable is that the Sirens do not sing at all and thus wield a still more fatal weapon than their song, namely their silence: someone might possibly have escaped from their singing, but never from their silence. It is a much more lethal weapon because the will of the divine must run its course and Ulysses' cunning challenge to divinity is the sin of human pride. Kafka frequently read Kierkegaard, Augustine, St. Paul, and Martin Luther during this period, one of the happiest in his brief life. If the central theme of his readings was the chance for man to save himself, by focusing on silence, Kafka distanced himself completely from that tradition. His Ulysses knows of the silence of the Sirens and the knowing fiction of his deception is only a means to act against divine wishes. However, it is this opposition to the divine that causes its potentially destructive force to be unleashed.

*   *   *

In "Silence in *Dubliners*," Jean-Michel Rabaté considers the silence of interpretation, saying that it is created and announced in the context of a deceptive game of interaction with the reader. The silence of interpretation in the relationship with the reader is the prime function of textual silence. It is the mirror of the text, the silence that makes the text resonate, because, without silence, discourse becomes noise, a frenzy of words. There are also the silences of characters that can be seen as the necessary markers of emptiness, conveying dislocation and therefore circularity. The final form of silence to which Rabaté refers in the brief preface to his stimulating, wide-ranging commentary on *Dubliners* and Joyce's output is that which is "the end, the limit, the death of speech, its paralysis" (Rabaté 1982: 45). In this case, silence brings together both the symptoms of silence (such as Eveline's aphasia at the end of the story) and the work of Thanatos that, in Rabaté's opinion, always accompanies the written act (45-6). Laurence Sterne/Tristram Shandy was of a different opinion: he believed that writing was the only weapon able to defeat Death (Sterne 1984: 459-61).

On the other hand, the meaning of words, lost through overuse and leading to silence, is a theme which is common to literary writing throughout the ages: from François Rabelais's metaphor of the "frozen words" (*Quart Livre*: 55-6); to Cordelia's "Nothing" in *King Lear* (Act I, Sc. 1, 86)—the metaphor for her choice to be silent; from Giacomo Leopardi's endless spaces ("interminati spazi") and superhuman silences ("sovrumani silenzi") of his poem "The Infinite" ("L'infinito," 1819) to the "Chandos experience" invoked earlier, with which Hermann Broch in "James Joyce and the Present Age" identified Joyce's hatred of cliché, as expressed by Hofmannsthal himself in *The Lord Chandos Letter*. Silence is therefore not only the absence of acoustic phenomena; it can be the expression of a mind that has put aside all attempts at interfering in events and that sees things in their essentially transitory nature. Banal simplicities of everyday life—the bird song, the babbling brook, the rustling leaves—instill the mind with the lightness of silence. Such simple identification with nature occurs beyond language—it inspired a brief conversation between Joyce and Ettore Settanni dating from 1939. Joyce claimed to have taken his lead from the "technique of deformation" of Dante himself. Having just quoted from Pluto's lines in *Inferno*: "Pape Satan Pape Satan aleppe" (*Inf.* VII: 9), Joyce explained that this technique was "to achieve a harmony that overcomes our intelligence, as music does." Then he asked Settanni, "Have you ever stopped near a flowing river? Could you give its musical worth or identify the precise notes in that flowing water that fills the ears and lulls you to sleep with happiness?" (Risset 1992: 719-20).

Silence in the writings of James Joyce often indicates the unsayable potential and mystery of the "not-said." It also indicates the cultural fragmentation and social unease of the individual whose silence is expressed in stream of consciousness. A consideration of the function of silence in Joyce thus enables us to identify a progressive movement in an exemplary way. This ranges from silence as a metaphor for the "not-said" in *Dubliners*, to the use of silence as a rhetorical device at work in the silent isolation and "dramatic" disappearance, upon which Joyce theorized in *A Portrait of the Artist as a Young Man*. There is then the form of external silence that increasingly isolates individuals from the context of their actual surroundings. This is the silence of Gabriel Conroy in the closing paragraph of "The Dead," as well as the silence of those characters in

Ulysses who, in the midst of a bustling city of Dublin, are immersed in *monologue interieur*. And in the end, there is the silence of interruption and return that, in *Finnegans Wake*, joins "riverrun" with the final "the," a materialization of what Giorgio Melchiori called "a single, gigantic epiphany: the epiphany of the human language. Rather, the epiphany of languages" (1994: 16).

Notes

1 Editors' note: The term "week thought"—*il pensiero debole*—was defined by Gianni Vattimo in his 1983 paper "Dialectics, Difference, Weak Thought," presented at the NYU conference on Hermeneutics in Contemporary Italian Thought. It first appeared in *Graduate Faculty Philosophy Journal* 10, no. 1 (1984): 99–176, in Peter Carravetta's and Thomas Harrison's translation. It has been retranslated and reprinted as an opening essay in *Weak Thought* (2012), edited by Gianni Vattimo and Pier Aldo Rovatti, trans. Peter Carravetta.

2 Hermann Broch had begun to write the Introduction to the work of Hofmannsthal in German in 1947; it was eventually published in 1955. See also the review by René Wellek (1985).

3 Originally published in German as "James Joyce und die Gegenwart" (see Broch 1936). It appeared in English as "James Joyce and the Present Age" (1949).

4 References in this chapter are to *A Portrait of the Artist as a Young Man*, ed. J. Johnson, Oxford: Oxford World Classics (2000).

5 On this point, see the thought-provoking book by Scarlett Baron (2012), esp. pp. 90–4.

References

Accetto, T. (1997), *Della Dissimulazione onesta*, con prefazione di Salvatore Silvano Nigro, Turin: Einaudi.

Alighieri, D. (1985), *La Divina Commedia*, Milan: Montadori.

Baron, S. (2012), *Strandentwiniung Cable, Flaubert and Intertextuality*, Oxford: Oxford University Press.

Broch, H. (1936), "James Joyce und die Gegenwart," Vienna: Herbert Reichner. Published in English as "James Joyce and the Present Age," in *A James Joyce Yearbook*, 68–108, Paris: Transition Press, 1949.

Broch, H. (1984), *Hugo von Hofmannstahl and His Time: The European Imagination 1860–1920*, Chicago: University of Chicago Press.

Chailly, R. (2015), *Il segreto è nelle pause. Conversazione sulla musica*, Milan: Rizzoli.

Conrad, J. (1989), *Heart of Darkness/Cuore di tenebra*, Milan: Mursia.

Eliot, T. S. (1963), *Collected Poems*, London: Faber & Faber.

Gifford, D. (1982), *Joyce Annotated: Notes for* Dubliners *and* A Portrait of the Artist as a Young Man, Berkeley: University of California Press.

Hobsbawm, E. (1994), *The Age of Extremes: The Short Twentieth Century, 1914–1991*, London: Michael Joseph.

Joyce, J. (2000), *Occasional, Critical, and Political Writing*, ed. Kevin Barry, Oxford: Oxford University Press.

Joyce, J. (2000a), *A Portrait of the Artist as a Young Man*, ed. J. Johnson, Oxford: Oxford World Classics.

Joyce, J. (2000b), *Ulysses*, intro. D. Kiberd, London: Penguin.

Joyce, J. (2008), *Dubliners*, ed. J. Johnson, Oxford: Oxford World Classics.

Kafka, F. (1931), "The Silence of the Sirens" ("Das Schweigen der Sirenen," 1917), in F. Kafka (1971), *The Complete Stories*, ed. N. N. Glatzer, intro. J. Updike, New York: Schocken Books Inc.

Melchiori, G. (1956), *The Tightropewalkers: Studies of Mannerism in Modern English Culture*, London: Routledge. Italian translation, *I funamboli, Il manierismo nella letteratura inglese da Joyce ai Giovani Arrabiati*, Turin: Einaudi, 1963, 1974; Rome: Edizioni di Storia e Letteratura, 1989.

Melchiori, G. (1994), *Joyce's Feast of Languages: Seven Essays and Ten Notes*, ed. F. Ruggieri, *Joyce Studies in Italy* 4, Rome: Bulzoni.

Munch, E. (2005), *The Private Journals of Edvard Munch: We Are Flames Which Pour Out of the Earth*, trans. and ed. J. Gill Holland, Madison: University of Wisconsin Press.

Nietzsche, F. (1974), *Thus Spoke Zarathustra*, trans. R. J. Hollingdale, London: Penguin.

Rabaté, J.-M. (1982), "Silence in *Dubliners*," in C. MacCabe (ed.), *James Joyce: New Perspectives*, 45–72, Bloomington: Indiana University Press.

Rabelais, F. (1955), *The Histories of Gargantua and Pantagruel*, London: Penguin.

Rella, F. (1984), *Il silenzio e le parole. Il pensiero nel tempo della crisi*, Milan: Feltrinelli.

Risset, J. (1992), "Joyce traduce Joyce," in F. Ruggieri (ed.), *James Joyce Poesie e Prose*, 197–214, Milan: Mondadori.

Sertoli, G. (1974), "Nota Introduttiva" to J. Conrad, *Cuore di tenebra*, Turin: Centopagine Einaudi.

Shakespeare, W. (1992), *Hamlet*, ed. B. A. Mowat and P. Werstine, New York: Simon and Schuster.

Shakespeare, W. (1997), *King Lear*, ed. R. A. Foakes, London: Routledge.

Steiner, G. (1967), *Language and Silence,* New York: Atheneum.

Sterne, L. (1984), *The Life and Opinions of Tristram Shandy, Gentleman*, London: Penguin.

Vattimo, G. (1984), "Dialectics, Difference, Weak Thought," trans. P. Carravetta and T. Harrison, *Graduate Faculty Philosophy Journal* 10, no. 1: 99–176. Reprinted in G. Vattimo and P. A. Rovatti (eds) (2012), *Weak Thought*, re-trans. Peter Carravetta, 39–52, Albany: State University of New York Press.

Wellek, R. (1985), Review of *Hugo von Hofmannsthal and His Time: The European Imagination 1860–1920, The New Criterion* (December): 75–80.

Wittgenstein, L. (2001), *Tractatus Logico-philosophicus*, trans. D. F. Pears and B. F. McGuinness, intro. Bertrand Russell, London and New York: Routledge Classics.

Index